Motor Cognition

UNIVERSITY OF
DUNDEE

University Library

OXFORD PSYCHOLOGY SERIES

Editors

Mark D'Esposito   Daniel Schacter

Jon Driver   Anne Treisman

Trevor Robbins   Lawrence Weiskrantz

Motor Cognition:
What Actions Tell the Self

MARC JEANNEROD
Emeritus Professor
Université Claude Bernard
Lyon
France

OXFORD
UNIVERSITY PRESS

OXFORD
UNIVERSITY PRESS

Great Clarendon Street, Oxford OX2 6DP

Oxford University Press is a department of the University of Oxford.
It furthers the University's objective of excellence in research, scholarship,
and education by publishing worldwide in

Oxford New York

Auckland Cape Town Dar es Salaam Hong Kong Karachi
Kuala Lumpur Madrid Melbourne Mexico City Nairobi
New Delhi Shanghai Taipei Toronto

With offices in

Argentina Austria Brazil Chile Czech Republic France Greece
Guatemala Hungary Italy Japan Poland Portugal Singapore
South Korea Switzerland Thailand Turkey Ukraine Vietnam

Oxford is a registered trade mark of Oxford University Press
in the UK and in certain other countries

Published in the United States
by Oxford University Press Inc., New York

© Oxford University Press, 2006

British Library Cataloguing in Publication Data

Data available

Library of Congress Cataloging in Publication Data

Jeannerod, Marc.
Motor cognition: what actions tell the self/Marc Jeannerod.
(oxford psychology series; no. 42)
   Includes bibliographical references and index.
   ISBN-13: 978-0-19-856964-0 (hbk.: alk. paper)
   ISBN-10: 0-19-856964-5 (hbk.: alk. paper)
   ISBN-13: 978-0-19-856965-7 (pbk.: alk. paper)
   ISBN-10: 0-19-856965-3 (pbk.: alk. paper)
  1. Brain–Physiology.   2. Motor ability.   3. Cognition.   I. Title.
II. Series.
   [DNLM: 1. Brain–Physiology.   2. Cognition–physiology.   3. Mental Processes.
4. Motor Activity.   5. Psychomotor Performance–physiology.   WL 300 J43m 2006]
   QP376.J415 2006   612.8'2–dc22   2006008852

Typeset by Newgen Imaging Systems (P) Ltd., Chennai, India
Printed in Great Britain
on acid-free paper by Biddles Ltd., King's Lynn

ISBN 0-19-856964-5 (Hbk.)   978-0-19-856964-0 (Hbk.)
ISBN 0-19-856965-3 (Pbk.)   978-0-19-856965-7 (Pbk.)

10 9 8 7 6 5 4 3 2 1

Foreword

Actions are critical steps in the interaction between the self and the external milieu. First, they are the reflection of covert processes which begin far ahead of the appearance of the muscular contractions that produce the rotation of the joints and the movements of the limbs. In that sense, actions, particularly when they are self-generated and not mere responses to external events, reveal the intentions, the desires and the goals of the acting self. Secondly, actions, when they come to execution, initiate another set of processes by which the self modifies the external milieu, by interacting with objects and with other selves. Our purpose here is to examine what actions can reveal about the self who produces them, and how they can influence the other selves who perceive them.

Studying the way actions are thought, planned, intended, organized, perceived, understood, learned, imitated, attributed or, in a word, the way they are represented, is the program of the new and rapidly expanding field of *motor cognition*. Motor cognition has its historical roots in the pragmatist school in psychology, heralded by W. James in the second half of the nineteenth century. It owes much to philosophers such as Ludwig Wittgenstein and John Searle. More recently, however, it has been the subject of intensive experimental research. First, cognitive psychology has provided experimental paradigms, based on mental chronometry, for the study of covert actions, i.e. actions liberated from the constraints of execution but devoid of their behavioral and observable counterpart. Secondly, cognitive neuroscience had introduced modern investigation techniques for functional brain mapping during these action-related mental states. Specifically, neuroimaging and brain stimulation have provided direct and quasi-instantaneous descriptions of the neural networks involved in the various modalities of action representations. Finally, cybernetics and neural modeling have provided a framework for the control of self-generated movements via an anticipation of their end result and a comparison of this end result with the desired effects. These converging efforts have led to the description of two critical properties of action representations, which could not have been disclosed without the help of this interdisciplinary experimental paradigm. One is that action representations have an identifiable structure, both in terms of their content and in terms of their neural implementation: they resemble real actions, except for the fact that they may not be executed. The other property is that action representations can originate from outside as well as from within: the observation of actions performed by other agents generates in the brain of the observer representations similar to those of the agents. This circular process, from the self to action and from action to other selves, has as a consequence that action representations can be shared by two or more people. These new findings have radically changed the traditional view of the motor system as an executive system that merely follows instructions elaborated somewhere else. Instead, the motor system now stands as a probe that explores the external world, for interacting with other people and gathering new knowledge.

The scope of motor cognition extends over several domains, with a number of implications in social psychology and psychopathology, but also in education, sport or medicine. In the following chapters, we will first discuss the theoretical implications of the notions of action representation and intention (Chapter 1). The main concern in this chapter will be to frame these rather abstract concepts into brain mechanisms. A historical survey of the early attempts at answering the question of the embodiement of action representations leads back to the early days of neuropsychology: the description of apraxia in brain-lesioned patients was the first significant account of what can happen when action representations cannot be properly formed and handled. In Chapter 2, we set the behavioral and neural background of action representations by using the paradigm of mental imagery, which has revealed a fruitful approach of a prototypical class of action representations, motor images. As for real overt actions, we will describe the kinematic properties of motor images and the brain structures involved. The fact that the motor system appears to be involved during motor images puts the action representation in a true motor format, so that it can be regarded by the motor system as the simulation of real action. This covert rehearsal of the motor system explains various forms of training (e.g. mental training) and learning of skills (e.g. observational learning) which occur as a consequence of self-representing an action. Chapter 3 addresses one of the main properties of action representations, namely their capacity to operate automatically. The questions of how and when an agent becomes aware of his own actions, and to what extent he can access the content of his representations or intentions, are raised in the context of experiments concentrating on the subjects' insight rather than on their motor performance. This strategy will reveal interesting properties of the consciousness of actions, especially in the time domain. Chapters 4 and 5 leave the descriptive aspects of motor cognition and enter into its contribution to essential cognitive functions such as self-identification and the self–other distinction. In Chapter 4, we concentrate on the role of signals arising from the execution or the representation of self-generated action in building a sense of agency, which a subject uses to self-attribute his own actions. Action appears to be the main factor in self-identification by binding together the various signals that arise from the agent's body and from its interaction with the external milieu. The self–other distinction must take into account the fact that action representations also arise from the actions of others, which raises the problem of disentangling one's representations from those of others. Pathological conditions such as schizophrenia may impair this process. Chapter 5 addresses the point of how we perceive and understand the actions of others. Body parts, faces and body motion are perceived by specific visual mechanisms, based on neuron populations specialized for encoding biological stimuli. Actions, however, cannot be solely understood by a visual description of the limb trajectories: it is also necessary to have an in-depth description of movement kinematics in order to be able to reproduce and learn the actions one observes. This is the role of another mechanism where the visual processing of body parts and objects is complemented by a motor processing, based on the simulation of the observed action by the motor system.

Finally, in Chapter 6, this idea of motor simulation will be proposed as a general framework for motor cognition, as the basic mechanism for explaining the functioning of motor representations. If one assumes that an observer can simulate in his own brain the action he observes another person performing, then the representation for that action will also be shared by the observer who will eventually become able to understand its content. This hypothesis opens new avenues in social communication: is the understanding of others' emotions and thoughts based on the same principle? Or, in other words, is motor cognition the first step to social cognition? By exploring the many attributes of motor cognition, we will discuss its contributions not only to the ability to learn, imitate and rehearse actions one performs and others perform, but also to the edification of critical social functions, such as the sense of self, the self–other distinction and the attribution of actions to their agents.

Acknowledgements

I am indebted to the many friends and colleagues who contributed to this book with their critical advice and discussions at various stages of its elaboration, and particularly Michael A. Arbib, Luciano Fadiga, Shaun Gallagher, Vittorio Gallese, Nicolas Georgieff, Sten Grillner, Patrick Haggard, Pierre Jacob, Günther Knoblich, Pierre Livet, Thomas Metzinger, Tatjana Nazir, Elisabeth Pacherie, David Perrett, Joelle Proust, Friedemann Pulvermüller, Giacomo Rizzolatti and Jean-Roger Vergnaud.

I received constant support from INSERM, CNRS and the Claude Bernard University (Lyon). International collaborations were supported by HFSPO and the European Communities.

Finally, I thank Martin Baum at Oxford University Press for his support during preparation of the publication.

Contents

Chapter 1

Representations for actions

In this introductory chapter, we try to provide a description of the elementary component of motor cognition, action representation, a concept that we will use throughout the book. In so doing, we will soon realize that this description requires the distinction between several levels. Representations for actions described by philosophers do not look like those described by neuroscientists, whereas those described by neuroscientists arguably have some resemblance to those of modelers. This is why we will use a historical approach to track the origins of this concept in the early conceptions of how actions can be self-generated, and the early models of how a self-generated action can be regulated and adapted to its goal.

1.1 Definitions

1.1.1 The prescriptive nature of action representations

Before starting, the term representation, a philosophical term with a broad meaning, requires some qualification. In the realm of perception, where this term is widely used, the representation refers to the end-product of the perceptual process. To take the example of visual perception, the representation of a visual object is built by first selecting the object from the visual array, then binding its attributes into a single visual percept, recognizing it, i.e. matching it with information and knowledge stored in semantic memory, and finally creating a belief about its nature and its use. In other words, the perceptual representation of that object is of a descriptive nature, in the sense that it represents a fact in the external world. A perceptual representation can therefore be said to have a mind to world *direction of fit*: the representation of the object in the mind fits the reality of the object in the world. The perceptual representation can also be said to have an opposite *direction of causation* (world to mind), in the sense that it is caused by the object or the external event it represents.

The same conceptual frame can be used to characterize the representation of an action. In that case, the goal of the action which is represented in the mind does not correspond to an actual state of the world, it corresponds to a possible state of the world which will arise if and when the action is effectively executed. Contrary to the perceptual representation, the action representation is of a prescriptive nature: it has a world to mind direction of fit. Because the representation will cause the state of the world that it represents, it can be said to have a mind to world direction of causation.

This philosophical analysis of the concept of representation (Searle 1983) emphasizes two major properties of action representations. First, an action representation is a state that represents future events, not present events. The notion of a mind to world direction of causation stresses the fact that action representations are anticipatory, not only with respect to the execution of the action itself, but also with respect to the state of the world that will be created by the action. As a matter of fact, insofar as action representations are the key feature of motor cognition, it follows that motor cognition in general is more looking ahead in time than looking back. It is proactive rather than reactive.

Secondly, the notion that an action representation precedes execution of the action suggests that it can actually be detached from execution and can exist on its own. This point is crucial for the rest of this book. Indeed, in several chapters, we will deal with purely represented, non-executed actions. We will develop the idea that there is a continuum between the (covert) representation of an action and the (overt) execution of that action, such that an overt action is necessarily preceded by a covert stage, whereas a covert action is not necessarily followed by an overt stage. According to this idea of a continuum, the representation is thought to be progressively and dynamically transformed into further stages of the same process. In other words, the representation is not an independent or distinctive state, the activation of which would cause the action to happen: put more simply, it is the hidden part of the action, such that, when an action representation is formed, the action is already under way. This point will become clearer when we examine the functional anatomy of action representations: we will discover that non-executed action representations involve the activation of vast areas of the motor system, including its executive parts.

1.1.2 **Action representations and intentions**

The term intention is also a philosophical term. It is tempting, because an intention refers to the execution of an action, to consider that the representation of an action and the intention to perform that action are one and the same thing. This does not seem to be the case, however. To take an absurd example, I can represent to myself (or imagine, or dream) the impossible action of flying like a bird, whereas I cannot form the intention of flying (unless I mistake myself for a bird). To take a better example, I can imagine myself performing an action (e.g. skiing or bicycling), without intending actually to perform it: this is the case of motor imagery, which will be described at length in Chapter 2. While imagining an action, I am in fact refraining from executing it.

Thus, all action representations are not intentions. Intentions, within the realm of action representations, correspond to those states that are closer from execution or, with reference to the above terminology, those that have a stronger mind to world direction of causation. Yet, there are several different types of intentions. John Searle has introduced a useful distinction between what he calls 'prior intentions' and 'intentions in action' (Searle 1983). Prior intentions are about actions with a long-term and complex goal, i.e. actions that will require a number of steps in order to be completed, or actions directed at absent or abstract goals. Take for example forming the prior intention to drink a cup of coffee while I am sitting at my desk. This will require a sequence of steps which start far ahead of the mere action of drinking coffee: collect coins, go to the coffee machine, press the appropriate buttons, etc. Each of these steps, however, requires a more local intention to perform the required movements. Those correspond to Searle's intentions in action, i.e. intentions which are directed toward immediately accessible goals. Unlike prior intentions, intentions in action are single-step intentions (putting the coin in the slot, taking the cup) which are embedded in the broader action plan of having coffee.

The complexity of the intended action (e.g. the number of steps needed to achieve the goal) may not be a sufficient criterion for distinguishing prior intentions from intentions in action. To illustrate this point, consider the following example: I am sitting at a meeting which will be concluded with a vote. While listening to the arguments, I make the prior intention of voting yes. When the time to vote comes, I accomplish my prior intention of voting yes by raising my right arm. However, the direct cause of my arm being raised at this precise moment (and not earlier or later) is the intention in action of raising my right arm. In this example, the two levels of intentions, while clearly distinct, are collapsed into a single movement: what makes the difference between these two levels is not the complexity of the subsequent action when it comes to execution, it is the conceptual content of the intention. The prior intention of voting yes is a largely conscious and explicit representation, formed according to a deliberate choice. In contrast, the intention in action to raise the arm arises from the implicit part of that representation, it is a simple consequence of the prior intention of voting yes, which accounts for the automatic execution of the arm raising. It is easy to refrain from transferring a prior intention into an action, whereas it is difficult, if at all possible, to stop the execution of an intention in action. This example recalls Wittgenstein's query about what is left from a voluntary movement when the movement itself is subtracted: 'When I raise my arm, my arm goes up. And the problem arises: what is left over if I subtract the fact that my arm goes up from the fact that I raise my arm?' (Wittgenstein 1953, 1, paragraph 621). In theory, the

Wittgenstein query has at least one possible answer. Suppose my arm is paralyzed by a peripheral block (e.g. a block of the neuromuscular transmission which leaves intact the neural commands but prevents the muscle from contracting): what will be left if I try to raise my arm, and the movement itself is 'subtracted' by the paralysis, is the internal processes (including the intention) which should have normally resulted in moving my arm. This answer goes far beyond a mere theoretical assumption; it also has an empirical counterpart. If, as we will see elsewhere, my brain is scanned during the attempted movement of raising my arm, brain areas corresponding to the generation of a voluntary movement and to the formation of an intention will be activated and become visible through the neuroimaging technique.

In the subsequent sections of this book, I will use the term *motor intention* as an alternative for intention in action. In my view, the term motor intention (Jeannerod 1994) better captures the proximity of the intention to its direct consequence, a goal-directed movement. Another reason for this choice is that the term motor intention seems to account better for the notion of 'intention' as it is generally used by physiologists and neuroscientists to designate the early stages of action generation.

1.1.3 Conceptual and non-conceptual action representations

The goals of our actions are specified by many different sources of information, both from inside and from outside. Internal cues arise from within our mental states, like our desires, beliefs or preferences. External cues arise from the outside world through the sensory systems. Both of these internal and external cues contribute to the conceptual content of our action representations.

To clarify the problem of the conceptual content of action representations, let us return to the comparison we made earlier between perceptual representations and action representations. A perceptual representation of a visual object, for example, first goes through a stage (the visual percept) where this object is encoded with all its visual properties (e.g. color, contrast, contours, texture, etc.). The visual percept thus has a rich informational content about the object, but has no conceptual content: it remains non-conscious and is ignored by the perceiver. If visual processing were to stop at this stage, as may occur in pathological conditions (Jacob and Jeannerod 2003), the object could not be categorized, recognized or named. It is only at the later stage of the processing that conceptualization occurs. The representation of a goal-directed action operates the other way around. The conceptual content, when it exists (i.e. when an explicit desire to perform the action is formed), is present first. Then, at the time of execution, a different mechanism comes into play where the representation loses its explicit character and runs automatically to reach the desired goal. Take for example the conceptual representation of the action of making a phone call. The first visible step of this complex sequence is to grasp the telephone. Thus, motor commands are generated such that the corresponding arm, hand and finger movements match the geometrical properties of the object to be grasped and handled (its location, size, shape and orientation). Simply observing the grasping hand reveals that this process is largely anticipatory and pertains to an action representation, not to a mere on-line adaptation of the motor commands to the object. First, the hand pre-shapes during reaching such that, at the time of contact with the object, the fingers are positioned to make an accurate and stable grasp. The pre-shaping of the hand includes the well-known phenomenon of 'maximum grip aperture' (MGA), whereby the finger grip opens more than required by the size of the object, but proportionally to it (Jeannerod 1981). Secondly, the whole pattern of grasping is preserved when the subject executes the action with his hand out of sight. Finally, the motor commands quickly adapt (within less than one reaction time) if and when the target object in displaced during the movement, until the goal is reached (Paulignan *et al.* 1991) (Figure 1.1).

At first sight, this fast and automatic action of grasping seems to correspond to the definition we gave for actions resulting from motor intentions, i.e. one-step actions embedded within a larger action plan. This segment of the global representation of the action, because it is largely dominated by its visual input, can be called a 'visuomotor' representation. Note that visuomotor representations share properties with both perceptual representations and action representations. First, because they encode visual properties of objects, they resemble perceptual representations, or at least that part of perceptual representations that has no conceptual content (the visual percept). Secondly, because they anticipate the state of the visual world that will take place when the action is executed, they resemble action representations: the function of visuomotor representations is not to acquire explicit knowledge about the visual world, it is to feed in intentions for acting on the visual world. Finally, because they have no conceptual content, they can operate rapidly and automatically, as shown in Figure 1.1.

At this point, action representations can be seen as including a vast group of representations with and without conceptual content. They all have in common that they encode goals, i.e. they anticipate the effects of a possible action directed to a specific goal. Action representations with a conceptual content are those where the goal is explicitly represented, e.g. in planning a complex action, imagining oneself executing an action or observing an action performed by someone else with the intent to replicate it. Action representations

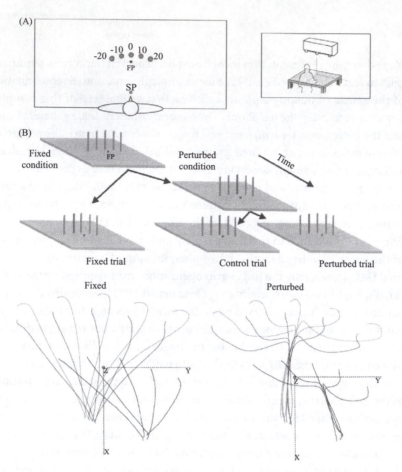

Fig. 1.1 Automatic functioning of visuomotor representations. The upper part of the figure describes an experiment in a group of normal subjects. The subjects were requested to grasp rapidly and accurately plastic dowels placed in front of them at reaching distance (A). The signal for the reach to grasp movement was the illumination of the dowel. In the 'fixed' condition, only one dowel was illuminated. In the 'perturbed' condition, the central (0°) dowel was illuminated but, on some trials, the light was shifted to another dowel at the onset of the movement (B). The lower part of the figure describes the subjects grasping performance in this task. The spatial paths of the wrist (dark grey lines), the thumb (middle grey lines) and the index finger (light grey lines) are represented as seen from above. On the left, is the performance during 'fixed' trials, with movements directed at each of the dowels presented during the experiment. Note that the grip formed by the thumb and the index finger first opens to a maximum grip aperture (MGA) and then begins to close well ahead of contact with the object. On the right, is the performance during the 'perturbed' trials. Note that all movements are first directed to the central dowel and, after a short delay (~150 ms), are redirected to the location of the new dowel presented at movement onset. The rearrangement of the whole movement pattern testifies to the existence of a representation of the action which 'pulls' the fingers towards their goal. Rearranged from Farné et al. (2000).

with low or no conceptual content are those where the goal is present in front of the agent and where the action, if and when it is executed, can be performed automatically. The former type is probably more accessible to introspection and more liable to philosophical study, whereas the latter is clearly more accessible to experimental investigation and can be described in terms of its neural implementation. This distinction between action representations, based on their conceptual content, directly challenges the influential Two Visual Systems Theory defended by Milner and Goodale (e.g. 1995). As is well known, this model postulates a duality of visual processing between the dorsal and the ventral cortico-cortical visual pathways. Accordingly, the dorsal visual pathway, which includes the parietal lobe and is connected to the motor system, underlies the visuomotor transformation, i.e. it accounts for the fast and automatic transformation of visual information about object attributes into motor commands. In contrast, the ventral pathway underlies visual perception, i.e. the conscious identification and recognition of objects. Although this model does capture one of the most obvious divisions of labor between visual pathways, it tends to overlook the above distinction between types of action representations. As we saw, the automatic, non-conceptual type represents only part of the information processing for actions: they are embedded in higher level representations, those which have a conceptual content. The critical point here is that higher level action representations also rely, at least partly, on parietal lobe functions. Indeed, neuropsychology offers a wealth of clinical observations of patients with posterior parietal lesions whose higher level representations for visually goal-directed actions are altered. Although these patients appear to have intact visuomotor representations (e.g. they correctly grasp objects), their difficulties typically arise in situations where they have to use these objects as tools for achieving a task on a visual goal. They also fail in tasks such as pantomiming an action without holding the tool, imitating an action performed by another agent, judging errors from incorrectly displayed actions or imagining an action (see below, page 12).

As an alternative to the purely visuomotor function of the dorsal visual pathway, it can be proposed that the processing of visual information in the dorsal stream shares a common functional organization with that of the ventral stream. To repeat what we said above, action representations which result from processing in the dorsal stream include different levels of complexity. Like perceptual representations in the ventral stream, action representations can have a non-conceptual as well as a conceptual content. What distinguishes the two streams, beyond the anatomical separation between a ventral and a dorsal pathway, is the functional opposition between a 'semantic' and a 'pragmatic' mode of visual processing. The semantic/pragmatic dichotomy, better than the classical model, accounts for two equivalent processing routes for perception and action, respectively. In the perception route, the non-conceptual visual percept feeds into conceptual perceptual representations where the semantics of the visual world are encoded. In the action route, conceptual action representations built from internal and external cues end up with non-conceptual visuomotor transformation to interact with the external world (Jeannerod 1994; Gallagher and Jeannerod 2002; Jeannerod and Jacob 2005).

1.2 Neural models of action representations

Now, we turn to more concrete aspects of action representations and, primarily, to their neural implementation. The problem is 2-fold. First, it consists of understanding how an abstract goal can be transferred into an appropriate sequence of movements. Secondly, it consists of identifying the neural structures where the representation is formed prior to execution of the action. We will look at this problem by following a historical thread.

The history of the concept of action representations starts at the end of the nineenth century, when motor physiology was dominated by the sensory-motor theory of action generation. This model, however, turned out to be unsatisfactory for the generation of voluntary movements. In contradistinction to reflex actions which are responses to the occurrence of external stimuli, voluntary actions should remain independent from external events. However, if actions are to be generated from within, their generation should require the existence of an internal state where they can be encoded, stored and ultimately performed independently from the external environment: this requirement for an internal state (a representation) is far from clear in physiology.

1.2.1 The demise of the sensory-motor theory of action generation

The view that actions were, in one way or another, reactions to changes in the external environment was supported, among other arguments, by the famous deafferentation experiments in monkeys (Mott and Sherrington 1885). These authors had observed that, following a section of the dorsal spinal roots on one side, an operation which suppresses sensory input from the corresponding limb to the central nervous system, the deafferented limb became useless and almost paralyzed. The animal could only produce awkward movements with that limb when forced to use it. Hence Mott and Sherrington concluded that movements owed much to the periphery for what concerned both their initiation and their execution.

The Sherringtoninan theory of action generation, which was for a time the dominant theory, met strong opposition. Karl Lashley was the main proponent of an alternative view. Lashley (1917) had observed a patient with a deafferented leg following a gunshot injury of the spinal cord. Despite the complete absence of sensations from that leg, the patient was capable, even when blindfolded, of bending his knee at a given angle, or placing his foot at a height indicated by the experimenter. In subsequent papers, Lashley noted that a great number of our movements are executed too rapidly for any sensory control to intervene. He pointed out that, during the playing of a musical instrument, for example, finger alternations can, in certain instances, attain the frequency of 16 strokes/s, which exceeds the possibility of any sensory feedback influencing the command system. Thus, the succession of such rapid movements had to be centrally encoded before they were executed (see Lashley 1951). Further clinical observations, since Lashley, have confirmed this point of the independence of the central command from the periphery. A patient suffering a severe sensory neuropathy, and who had lost all somatosensory cues from his limbs, was studied by Rothwell *et al.* (1982). In spite of his sensory impairment, this patient, when blindfolded, was able to perform a wide range of motor tasks such as tapping, fast flexion extension movements of the elbow, drawing figures in the air, etc. Furthermore, the electromyographic (EMG) pattern of these movements was closely similar to those observed in normal subjects. In Chapter 4, we will examine for a different purpose the case of another completely deafferented patient.

Among neurophysiologists, the Sherringtonian view was maintained throughout the first half of the last century until deafferentation experiments were repeated by Emilio Bizzi and his colleagues in the late 1960s. They showed that a monkey with bilateral deafferentation of the forelimbs could perform reasonably accurate monoarticular elbow movements directed to a visual target, in the absence of sight of the limb. The entire structure of the movements was preserved, including not only their initial, ballistic, phase but also their low-velocity phase up to the end-point (Bizzi *et al.* 1971). This finding opened up a new field in motor research, by resurrecting the notion of a central action representation. The theory of action representation proposed by Bizzi, based on the theoretical work of Feldman (1966), assumed that the position of a joint was pre-determined by the central nervous system as a single point of equilibrium between the tension of the muscles attached to that joint (the 'equilibrium point model'). For displacement of the limb, a new equilibrium point was specified, and the movement automatically stopped at a new position corresponding to the desired position of the limb. EMG recordings from the biceps and triceps muscles of the monkey showed that relative shifts in background activity of the two muscles correlated with the target positions in space. The early version of the theory was limited to simple, monoarticular, movements, but it was later expanded to multijoint movements (e.g. Gomi and Kawato 1996). The equilibrium point model had also been proposed for explaining the production of speech, a rapid succession of movements which also exceeds the critical frequency for feedback to take place. The idea (MacNeilage 1970) was that each phoneme is centrally represented as a point of equilibrium between the muscles that comprise the vocal tract. In order ot move from one phoneme to another, a single command is given, whatever the configuration of the vocal tract. Thus, a given phoneme can be obtained without having to take into account the initial configuration of the musculature. The equilibrium point model of action representation is an interesting one, because it does not require the intervention of sensory systems for coding a movement. It should not be taken literally, however: the fact that movements can be coded in the absence of sensory feedback does not mean that one does not take advantage of sensory feedback when it is present.

Among neuroscientists, the most widely accepted modality of action representation was that of the 'motor program' described by Steven Keele as 'a set of muscle commands that are structured before a movement sequence begins, and that allows the entire sequence to be carried out' (Keele 1968, p. 387). For a single-joint movement, the muscular command takes the shape of the triphasic EMG pattern, with an EMG burst of the agonist muscle, followed by a burst of the antagonist muscle, and finally a second burst of the agonist muscle. This alternating pattern, which accounts for the displacement of the limb and its stopping at the desired location, is entirely of a central origin, because it persists after suppression of sensory afferences (see Jeannerod 1988). Indeed, this pattern can also be observed by recording the activity of nerve stumps in the isolated spinal cord in invertebrates (Grillner 1985). Motor programs of that sort, however, the expression of which lasts only a few hundred milliseconds, are minimal forms of representations of action: although they fulfill the criterion of independence with respect to peripheral influences, they are far too simple to capture the complexity of actions under consideration here. We need to conceive a form of representation that would penetrate deeper into the covert stages of action.

1.2.2 Central neural mechanisms for action representation and generation

Assuming the existence of voluntary actions generated in the absence of sensory input does not solve the problem of how these actions are generated. Lively debates arose among neurologists and psychologists of the mid-nineteenth century about how to conceive the central origin of actions. The literature of the time offers a wide range of concepts accounting for the production of an action.

Charlton Bastian, for example, supported the concept of 'kinesthetic images'. According to him, these images were formed from sensory traces left by a prior movement, stored in the motor cortex, and revived when the same movement was executed again (Bastian 1897). William James thought that they could represent a 'mental conception' of the movement, an 'idea' which was transformed into an action at the moment of execution. 'When a particular movement, having once occurred in a random, reflex or involuntary way, has left an image of itself in the memory, then the movement can be desired again, proposed as an end, and deliberately willed' (James 1890, vol. II, p. 487).

Hugo Liepmann, starting from a different background, that of clinical neurology, went one step further (see Fig. 1.2). He proposed the concept of *Bewegungsformel*, which can be translated into English as 'movement formula'. Liepmann, based on the observation of patients with action generation problems (for which he coined the term apraxia, see below), thought that movement formulas were partial representations of an action and its goal: in other words, they were units of action. Several movement formulas were assembled into a more general representation, which itself encoded the succession and the rhythm of the partial representations (Liepmann 1900). Nicholas Bernstein had an interesting analogy for explaining this mode of organization. He thought that the representation of an action must contain, 'like an embryo in an egg or a track on a gramophone record, the entire scheme of the movement as it is expanded in time. It must also guarantee the order and the rhythm of the realisation of this scheme; that is to say, the gramophone record . . . must have some sort of motor to turn it' (Bernstein 1935/1967, p. 39).

Later authors, although they replaced the term movement formula by 'engram' (Kleist 1934), 'schema' (Head 1920) or 'internal model' (Bernstein

Fig. 1.2 Portrait of Hugo Liepmann. Hugo Liepmann (1863–1925) was first the assistant of Karl Wernicke at Breslau for 4 years (1895–1900). Then, he was appointed as a psychiatrist at the Dalldorf Hospital in Berlin, where he conducted his work on apraxia.

1935/1967), retained the notion of a hierarchical organization. In one of the most recent versions of the theory (Arbib 1981), motor schemas are described as recursive entities which are both decomposed into more elementary ones, and embedded in more complex ones. For example, the motor schema 'drink' which accounts for the action of drinking can be decomposed into simpler motor schemas such as 'reach' for a glass and 'grasp' it; the motor schema 'grasp' includes still simpler ones (e.g. 'close fingers'). At the other end, the motor schema 'drink' is embedded in a more complex one (e.g. 'have dinner'), and so on. Most of the above theories hold that schemas or engrams are stored in one way or another. This notion should be looked at with caution. Indeed, the same movement is rarely, if ever, replicated twice. Initial conditions of the limb change, the goals are different and the kinematics must be re-computed. For this reason, it would be inadequate to store static and pre-organized units of action: schemas should be plastic and adaptable rather than fixed, in order to adapt the movements to the conditions of each single action. According to this view, action representations should be assembled in response to immediate task requirements rather than depend exclusively on stored information.

The way Liepmann and his followers conceived the representation of an action offers a possibility to transfer the concept of representation into neural mechanisms. Here, we will leave aside the difficult question of how action representations (be they called engrams, schemas or otherwise) are implemented at the neuronal level: this would require a detailed description of single neuron activity in the many cortical and subcortical areas encoding goal-directed movements, which is beyond the scope of this book. Extensive studies of these neuron populations have led to the notion of a 'motor vocabulary' where actions are encoded element by element. In Chapter 5, we will examine some specific aspects of the neuronal coding of action representations.

1.2.3 Neuropsychological evidence for neural representations for action: apraxia

As we mentioned in the above paragraph, the term apraxia was coined by Liepmann to account for higher order motor disorders observed in patients who, in spite of having no problem in executing simple actions (e.g. grasping an object), fail in actions involving more complex, and perhaps more conceptual, representations. There have been many attempts to describe and specify the basic impairment of these patients. Along with Liepmann (1905) and Heilman *et al.* (1982) who respectively assumed that apraxic patients had lost movement formulas or motor engrams, we will define apraxia as the consequence of a disruption of the normal mechanisms for action representations. According to this definition, the deficit of an apraxic patient should show up better in skilled actions requiring the use of a tool. A tool is an object with a 'pragmatic' meaning, and its use is constrained by the representation of the corresponding action. The manipulation of a tool includes but does not reduce to mere grasping. One does not grasp a hammer, a screwdriver or a violin and a bow in a single fashion: knowing how to use them contributes to grasping them. Thus, the manipulation of tools includes a higher level processing of the visual attributes of an object than either reaching or grasping. Grasping is necessary but it is not sufficient for the correct use and skilled manipulation of a tool. It is not sufficient because one cannot use a tool (e.g. a hammer, a pencil or a screwdriver, let alone a microscope or a cello) unless one has learnt to use it, i.e. unless one can retrieve an internal representation of a recipe (a schema) for the manipulation of the object (see Johnson-Frey 2004).

However, the above definition of apraxia as an impairment of action representations also implies that an apraxic patient should be impaired in more abstract versions of the same action, such as pantomiming the use of a tool when the tool is absent. Thus, Clark *et al.* (1994) tested apraxic patients when pantomiming the action of slicing bread (in the absence of both bread and knife). They found that the kinematics and spatial trajectories of the patients' movements were incorrect: patients improperly oriented their movement, and the spatiotemporal coordination of their joints was defective. Ochipa *et al.* (1997) made similar observations in patient G.W.: when asked to pantomime the use of 15 common household tools, G.W. failed in every case. She failed using either hand and she failed in a variety of conditions: when she was verbally instructed, when the tool was visible but not used and when she was asked to imitate the action of an actor. She committed mostly spatial errors: for example, the direction of her movements was generally incorrect. Handling the object did not help G.W. very much: her success rate increased from 0/15 to 3/15. Despite her deep impairment in pantomime, G.W.'s detached knowledge of the function of objects was preserved: she could correctly distinguish objects according to their function. Finally, intertwined with her pantomiming deficit, G.W. was also impaired in imagining actions: for example, she could not answer questions about the specific postures her hands would have taken while performing a given action. Tasks involving action imagination ('motor imagery' tasks) are currently used for testing action representation deficits in patients. Motor imagery and its contribution to our knowledge of action representations will be the topic of Chapter 2.

If the above impairment is the consequence of altered action representations, then it should not be restricted to the preparation and execution of skilled actions. Nor should it only impair the ability to pantomime actions in the absence of the relevant tool: it should also impair the ability to recognize actions either executed or pantomimed by others. This is what Sirigu *et al.* (1995b) observed in their patient L.L. Not only was L.L. impaired in positioning her fingers on a tool when grasping it for manipulation, such as grasping a spoon in the action of eating soup, but she also consistently failed when asked to sort out correct from incorrect visual displays of another person's hand postures, and was unable to describe verbally hand postures related to specific uses of an object. This type of impairment is directly responsible for the failure, frequently observed in apraxic patients, in tasks requiring imitation. Recent work by Bekkering *et al.* (2005) suggests that the problem encountered by such patients in imitating should not be in programming or executing the observed action, but rather in the selection of the different elements of a goal-directed action: this would account for the fact that the deficit is more marked for complex or meaningless sequences of movements. We will come back to this point when we discuss the mechanisms of imitation in Chapter 5.

Most of the patients described above have lesions which include the parietal lobe. Parietal lesions are usually located in the angular and supramarginal gyri (the inferior parietal lobule), i.e. more anterior and ventral than those, in the superior parietal lobule and in the intraparietal sulcus, which typically produce visuomotor impairments such as optic ataxia (Perenin and Vighetto 1988, Binkofski *et al.* 1998, Rossetti *et al.* 2003). Indeed, as already stated, apraxic patients with a lesion of the inferior parietal lobule have no basic visuomotor impairment: they can correctly reach and grasp objects. Furthermore, parietal lesions responsible for apraxia are more often localized in the left hemisphere, a lesional lateralization which is irrelevant to optic ataxia. In other words, the superior parietal and the intraparietal sulcus would monitor action 'on' the objects, such as pointing or grasping, whereas the inferior parietal lobule would be concerned with action 'with' the objects, such as tool use. The impairments in representing actions shown by apraxic patients do not result from a general difficulty in visual recognition: Sirigu and Duhamel (2001) reported the cases of two patients whose impairments in visual recognition tasks and in motor representations were dissociated. One apraxic patient with a left parietal lesion was unable to perform motor imagery tasks but had normal scores in visual imagery tasks. Conversely, another patient with agnosia for faces and visual objects had no visual imagery but normal motor imagery. A similar dissociation between impaired motor imagery and preserved visual imagery was also observed by Tomasino *et al.* (2002) in one patient with apraxia following a left parietal lesion.

I will borrow the conclusion of this clinical description from the recent study of Buxbaum *et al.* (2005). They examined a group of apraxic patients with relatively large lesions of the left hemisphere resulting from stroke, which, in all cases, involved the inferior parietal lobule. The dorsolateral prefrontal cortex was also involved. The patients were tested in a motor imagery task. They were requested to judge what the position of their hand would be on a rod, if they had to grasp it. No movement was allowed (this task is fully described in the next chapter). Patients were deficient in this task. Indeed, they were also impaired in other tasks involving action representation, such as imitation of meaningless gestures or pantomiming the use of an object when it was shown to them. In contrast, the patients performed correct grasping movements: during the action of grasping cubes, their MGA was normally scaled to the cube size. These results taken together confirm the hypothesis that apraxia reflects deficient generation of internal models of object-related actions.

The clinical observations of apraxic patients stresses the role of the parietal cortex in monitoring action representations. While the superior parietal lobule is mainly involved in the automatic control of visually guided actions towards objects, the inferior parietal lobule (particularly on the left side) is involved in the planning of actions involving the retrieval of complex representations thought to be formed precisely in that region (see Glover 2004). This function of the inferior parietal lobule is consistent with the results of monkey studies showing its role as a multimodal association area where sensory signals (visual, acoustic and somatosensory) are integrated with signals arising from the commands for action generated by the motor system (Mountcastle 2005). In normal human subjects, neuroimaging experiments show that action representation tasks consistently activate areas in the posterior parietal lobe (Decety *et al.* 1994; Grafton *et al.* 1996), and especially on the left side (Johnson *et al.* 2002; Mühlau *et al.* 2005). Raffaella Rumiati and her colleagues ran a neuroimaging study in normal subjects, using the same tasks as those used for testing apraxic patients, such as imitating an observed pantomime or pantomiming the use of an object shown. They found that these tasks, when the confound effects of perceptual, motor, semantic and lexical factors were controlled, consistently activated the left inferior parietal cortex (Rumiati *et al.* 2004).

The parietal lobe, however, is not the only site where actions are represented and processed. Parietal areas, together with areas in the motor system (e.g. premotor cortex), account for what we have called 'pragmatic' representations. These are responsible for representing self-generated (overt as well as covert) actions, and the actions of other agents, when these actions have to be understood, learned, replicated or imitated. Other brain areas are also involved in perceiving and recognizing actions of other people. Seeing a meaningful action with the instruction to recognize it later activates areas in the infero-temporal cortex (Decety *et al.* 1997). Infero-temporal lesions can indeed affect the recognition of pantomimed actions. Rothi *et al.* (1985)

described in two patients what they called 'pantomime agnosia' following a left temporal lesion. Both patients could execute pantomimes upon verbal request and could imitate gestures of others. However, they were impaired in naming the gestures performed by the examiner. These patients with lesions in the ventral stream, although they had retained the ability to use and assemble motor engrams, had lost the ability to extract the meaning of the gestures they saw others making. We will devote a full section to the dual mode of action perception/understanding in Chapter 5. Note that we are dealing here with representations of actions, not of objects. Apraxic patients, although they fail in action representation tasks, usually remain unimpaired in tasks evaluating their conceptual knowledge about objects or tools (for a discussion of this point, see Mahon and Caramazza 2005). This dissociation between 'actions' and 'objects' stresses the limitation of theories based on motor simulation to explain conceptual knowledge. This difficulty further illustrates the validity of a distinction between semantic and pragmatic processing, where semantic processing provides knowledge about what things are, and pragmatic processing provides the means to use them. The two are relatively independent of one another: after all, you may know everything about a violin (shape, size, weight, number of strings, etc.) without being able to play a single note on it.

1.3 Functional models of action representations

In this section, we concentrate on understanding the functional organization of action representations and their relationship to the mechanisms of execution. Action representations, as already said, do not necessarily end in an executed action. Yet they play a critical role during action execution: the fact that they are anticipatory allows them both to set the desired goal and to check that this goal has effectively been reached. In other words, the anticipated representation of the goal acts as a reference with which the result of the action can be compared: it is when the results matches the anticipation that the goal has been attained.

1.3.1 Early conceptions of action regulation

The notion of reference is borrowed from the field of engineering. Engineers during the early part of the nineteenth century had invented devices for controlling the action of machines. The regulation system invented by Maxwell for steam engines, for example, was based on monitoring the speed of rotation of the engine. When the speed went above a certain reference value, a brake was activated to reduce the speed; conversely, when the speed decreased below this value, the brake was released. The same concept of regulation based on a reference value also appeared in nineteenth century biology. It was used by Claude Bernard and his followers to explain the constancy of the *milieu intérieur*. Claude Bernard thought that the *milieu intérieur* was held constant by the operation of self-regulating (later called homeostatic) systems. The regulation of blood glucose, for example, proceeds from a pre-determined reference value which is maintained in spite of metabolic changes. Homeostatic regulation, both in machines and in organisms, is an ensemble of mechanisms which automatically detect errors between the actual value of a given parameter and the reference value assigned to this parameter.

The concept of regulation was also used to understand motor control. Edward Pflüger, in agreement with Claude Bernard, considered that spinal reflexes obeyed a pre-determined purpose, in the sense that they were apparently organized so as to preserve the integrity of the animal in response to external aggressions.[1] Later, under the influence of cybernetics, the same concept was extended to the representation of goal-directed actions. Bernstein (1935/1967) proposed that, during a grasping movement, the desired final position of the hand on the object is pre-determined in the motor command system, and compared during execution of the movement with its actual position, as detected by the sensory receptors. The continuously changing difference between the actual and the desired positions, Bernstein suggests, is used as a driving signal to the muscles until the system self-stabilizes. Craik (1947) used this model extensively for describing actions such as tracking a moving target by hand. In such situations, according to Craik, the human operator behaves as an intermittent correction servo, where errors with respect to the target are corrected by small ballistic movements. Monitoring its own output was thus considered by cybernetics as a basic principle of the functioning of any machine, mechanical or otherwise. A comparison between the desired output of the machine and its actual output is needed because machines (and organisms as well) are non-linear. Non-linearities in the execution of an action cannot be anticipated entirely by the command generation mechanism: hence the need for the command to be updated by signals arising from the execution.

The main contribution of cybernetics to the functioning of action representations was provided by Von Holst and Mittelstaedt in 1950. These two authors assumed that each time the motor centers generate an outflow signal for producing a movement, a copy of this command (the efference copy) is retained in a short-term memory. The reafferent inflow signals (e.g. visual, proprioceptive) generated by the movement are compared with the

---

[1] References about the history of the reflex theory and the concept of regulation can be found in Jeannerod (1983).

efference copy. Von Holst (1954) later suggested that the reafference of the movement should be a mirror image of the efference copy stored in the representation. If the two corresponded, he thought, they would cancel each other out in the same way as the positive and the negative of the same photograph are canceled out when they are superimposed. Conversely, should the execution not correspond to the expected outcome (or should the movement not be executed, because of some peripheral block, for example), a mismatch would arise between the reafference and the efference copy. This mismatch would signal that the actual movement departed from the desired movement.

Note that the equilibrium point model of Bizzi/Feldman, which was developed in the late 1960s, was clearly posterior to the models described in the above paragraph. The equilibrium point model, along the same lines as Lashley, rejected the idea of a feedback control of movements, whereas the cybernetic models explicitly stated the role of feedback control for action regulation. The two types of model, however, did not address the same purpose. The equilibrium point model was designed to account for simple movements involving one single joint, whereas the cybernetic models have been generalized successfully to the control of complex actions.

1.3.2 Disentangling self-produced versus externally produced changes in the world

In fact, the outcome of the comparison process in the von Holst and Mittelstaedt model carries much more information than simply signaling movement completion. It is also a crucial mechanism for disentangling the changes in the world arising from self-produced movements from those produced by external forces[2]. The key paradigm for the distinction between self-produced and externally produced changes in the world is that of the stability of the visual world during eye and head movements. Each time the eyes move, the visual scene sweeps across the retinas: yet, no displacement of the visual scene is perceived. Conversely, a displacement of the visual scene is attributed to an external change, not to a self-produced eye movement.

---

[2] The distinction between self-produced and externally produced changes in the external world is not to be confounded with the distinction between real and illusory self-displacement in a visual scene. In certain circumstances, displacements of the visual scene may create an illusion of displacement of the self (e.g. when you are sitting in a stationary train next to another train that starts to move). These illusions of self-displacement, called *vection*, are due to the fact that the low-level processing of visual motion involves cerebello-vestibular circuits. In the absence of a stationary reference in the visual field, i.e. when the whole visual field is seen in motion, the vestibular nuclei are strongly activated and the stationary self is perceived in motion.

A tentative explanation for this phenomenon was proposed by Roger Sperry in a paper published in the same year as that of von Holst and Mittelstaedt (Sperry 1950). Sperry had observed that a fish with inverted vision (caused by a surgical rotation of the eyeball by 180°) tended to turn continuously in circles when placed in a visual environment (Sperry, 1943). He interpreted this circling behavior as the result of a disharmony between the (normal) mechanism generated to stabilize visual perception during the movements of the animal and the (abnormal) retinal input produced by these movements. This mechanism, as proposed by Sperry, was a centrally arising discharge that reached the visual centers as a corollary of the motor commands resulting in movement: hence the term 'corollary discharge' used by Sperry to designate this mechanism. In this way, the visual centers could distinguish the retinal displacement related to a movement of the animal from that produced by a moving visual scene. Visual changes produced by a movement of the animal were normally cancelled by a corollary discharge of a corresponding size and direction, and had no effect on behavior. If, however, the corollary discharge did not correspond to the visual changes (e.g. after inversion of vision created by rotation of the eyeball), these changes were not canceled out and were read by the motor system as originating in the external world. Thus, the animal moved in the direction of this apparent (non-canceled) visual displacement as if it were tracking a moving scene. A similar cancelation mechanism is suggested by experimental findings in monkey and man. In monkeys, Müller-Preus and Ploog (1981) found that the spontaneous vocal utterance of the animal inhibited the activity of auditory cortical neurons: thus, the self-produced auditory stimulus could not be confounded with an externally arising stimulus (e.g. the vocal utterance of another monkey). Similar results have also been found in humans by Blakemore *et al.* (1998). They compared brain activity in normal subjects during the processing of externally produced tones and tones resulting from self-produced movements. Using neuroimaging techniques, they found that the activity of the auditory recipient areas in the temporal lobe was higher when the tones were externally produced, suggesting that cortical activity was inhibited by the volitional system when the tones were self-produced.

The functions of the von Holst and Mittelstaedt's efference copy and the Sperry's corollary discharge clearly overlap. Both mechanisms are predictive and are suited for anticipating the sensory effects of a self-produced movement. As a consequence, any detected change in the external world unaccompanied by a centrally arising discharge is likely to be due to an external cause. This distinction between self-produced and externally produced sensory effects represents a first step for the critical function of self-recognition. As such, however, this would represent a rather crude mechanism, simply based on a default distinction between self and non-self. Motor cognition, as we shall emphasize in later chapters, allows much more refined distinctions, for identifying one's own actions, for perceiving, understanding and reproducing those of others and for attributing actions to their real agent.

1.3.3 Action representations as internal forward models

A more complete description of the functioning of action representations is offered by the concept of forward models. This concept arose from the field of engineering where forward models were designed for the control of complex systems. Engineers involved in the control of machines are concerned by the fact that information about the action of the machine arising from peripheral receptors alone is inadequate to make an accurate estimate of the desired state of the machine: information arrives too late and is corrupted by noise. The main advantage of forward models is that they can estimate the desired state of the machine ahead of its action. This can be achieved by monitoring the commands sent to the effectors, without waiting for feedback information about execution. Feedback information, when it arrives, is combined on-line with forward information for estimating the current state and predicting errors due to a possible drift of the motor command signals. Thus, forward models capture the causal relationship between actions and the resultant change in the motor system. A full description of these models is available in papers by Daniel Wolpert and his colleagues (Wolpert *et al.* 1995; Wolpert and Ghahramani 2000). Forward models can thus be considered as advanced versions of the early models of motor control using the efference copy or the corollary discharge concepts (Figure 1.3). However, they also have the critical property of predicting the sensory outcome of the action without actually performing it. In other words, they include an emulator, i.e. a device that implements the same input–output function as the execution mechanism (Grush 2004). When the emulator receives a copy of the control signal (an efference copy), it emits an output signal closely similar to the feedback signal produced by the execution mechanism. The advantage of the signal emitted by the emulator compared with the execution feedback signal is that it has almost no delay with respect to the control signal. The idea of an emulator is close to what one would expect from a mechanism accounting for representation of an action, as has been proposed in this chapter. We will meet this concept again within the framework of the Central Monitoring Theory of action recognition, in Chapter 4.

In the above paragraphs, we have dealt with representations of actions as more or less empty structures. The notion of an internal forward model, the most advanced conceptualization for action representations, captures the idea of a structure with an internal organization, where endogenous and exogenous

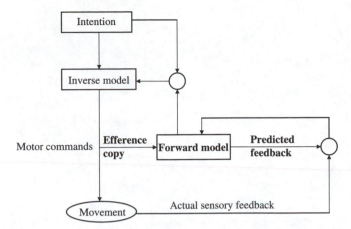

Fig. 1.3 Principle diagram explaining the functioning of an internal model. This highly schematic diagram depicts the main property of models of this family, their anticipatory nature. Note that the intention, the inverse model, the motor commands, the efference copy, the forward model and the predicted feedback all pre-exist movement occurrence. Internal and external feedback loops make it possible to check the effectively executed movement against the intention and the forward model. This is in part the basis for the motor simulation idea that will be developed throughout the book. Inspired from Wolpert *et al.* (1995).

signals can interact. This notion easily accounts for short-term storage of action information and anticipation of forthcoming changes of the motor system and in the external world. Finally, it also accounts for off-line functioning during simulation of an action without executing it. However, because we cannot be satisfied with an abstract concept, or with an empty vehicle, the next step will be to assign internal models a content, in terms of rules and instructions on how to operate in order to produce the desired action. This will be the objective of the next two chapters.

Chapter 2

Imagined actions as a prototypical form of action representation

We now turn to the content of action representations. In the previous chapter, we have defined the different forms an action representation can take; we have tried to describe the mechanisms through which an agent can consciously access his/her own actions and intentions; and we have made a distinction between action representations and intentions with and without conceptual content. However, we have not addressed the question of the content itself of these representations. Here we will attempt to look inside the representation, in the absence of execution. In other words, we will consider the covert part of the action, uncontaminated, so to speak, by the processes that lead to overt execution. For this purpose, we will report experiments using a specific methodology combining the resources of cognitive psychology with those of cognitive neuroscience. This approach, partly based on introspection and mental chronometry, but also on the monitoring of physiological variables and brain metabolism, gives access to purely mental states related to actions.

This paradigm for studying action representations in fact corresponds to a classical paradigm in cognitive psychology, that of mental imagery. Mental imagery and, more specifically, visual imagery, has been studied extensively in the past three of four decades by researchers in the field of perception and memory, and has greatly contributed to our knowledge of visual cognition. In the field of motor cognition, motor imagery, the ability to generate a conscious image of the acting self, began to be seriously considered only in the late 1980s. One of the reasons for this delay is that, unlike in visual imagery, there is no clear reference in motor imagery with which the image can be compared: motor images are private events in the sense that they can hardly be shared (if at all) by the experimenter, whereas visual images refer to perceived scenes or objects which pertain to external reality and are common to other perceivers. Still, the importance of motor imagery for the study of representational aspects of action was already envisaged more than a century ago. Alfred

Binet, for example, had claimed that mental images in general resulted from excitation of the same cerebral centers as the corresponding actual sensation. In the domain of motor images, he made the remark that the state of the motor centers influences the possibility of generating a motor image. For example, he found it impossible to generate the image of pronouncing the letter *b* if he kept his mouth wide open: this was because the motor system, he thought, cannot be engaged in two contradictory actions at the same time (Binet 1886, p. 80).

Like visual imagery, however, motor imagery can also be studied objectively. These studies reveal that motor images, as classically characterized by their conscious nature (a property that they share with mental images in general), represent only a small part of the phenomenon that we are considering here. As a matter of fact, the content of motor images extends far beyond what can be consciously accessed by the agent. We will discover that, in addition to their conscious content, imagined actions involve an unconscious content that retains many of the properties which are observed in the corresponding real actions when they are executed. The objective description of these states is thus a critical step for understanding the content of action representations. In the subsequent sections, we will take motor images as a privileged way to access action representations in general. We will describe first the 'kinematic' content of action representations, as revealed by mental chronometry experiments with motor images (Section 2.1). Subsequently, we will describe the physiological changes which can be observed during experimental manipulation of this kinematic content (Section 2.2). We will devote a special section (Section 2.3) to the functional anatomy of action representations, as revealed by neuroimaging techniques during motor imagery and other action-related mental states. Finally, Section 2.4 will examine some of the consequences of the embodiment of action representations for learning and rehabilitation (Jeannerod 2004b).

2.1. **The kinematic content of motor images**

Can the term 'kinematic', which applies to the properties of executed movements, also be used to characterize a mental state such as motor imagery? In this section, we describe properties of motor images which resemble those of overt movements. Motor imagery, by definition, is not static; it involves dynamic changes in the content of the image over time, corresponding to the unfolding of the action which is being imagined. In that sense, as we will argue throughout this book, the mental action can be considered as a *simulation* of the physical action. These dynamic changes are described under three headings: temporal regularities, programming rules and biomechanical constraints

2.1.1. The representation of temporal regularities

Already in 1962, Landauer had noticed that mentally reciting a series of numbers took approximately the same time as saying them aloud. This fact suggested to him that the two behaviors may involve many of the same central processes. Landauer's observation of an isochrony of the physical and the mental performances of the same action (Landauer, 1962) has been consistently replicated since then. In 1989, with Jean Decety and Claude Prablanc, we compared the time taken by subjects to walk either physically or mentally to targets located at different distances. The participants were instructed to look for 5 s at the specified target. Immediately afterwards, they were blindfolded and instructed to either walk, or to imagine walking to that target. In both conditions, they held a chronometer which they started when they began the task and stopped when they finished it. The main result was that the subjects took, on average, the same time to achieve the physical and the mental task. In the two conditions, the walking time was found to increase with the distance covered (Decety *et al.* 1989; see also Schott and Munzert 2002). Sirigu *et al.* (1996), using a task of reciprocally tapping two targets separated by a varying distance, also reported a temporal scaling of movement duration to distance in the mental condition similar to that observed in the condition of overt execution (see also Cerritelli *et al.* 2000; Papaxanthis *et al.* 2002; Sabaté *et al.* 2004).

2.1.2 The representation of programming rules

In view of the above results, one should also expect that the difficulty of the motor task should influence the duration of the mental performance to the same extent as it does for actual execution. In physical execution, as expressed by Fitts law (named after Fitts 1954), the duration of a task requiring accuracy increases with the demands for accuracy. For example, the duration of the movement of pointing at a visual target increases when either the size of the target decreases or the distance to the target increases. As early as 1987, Georgopoulos and Massey had designed a situation where Fitts law appeared to hold also in mentally executed movements. They requested subjects to move a lever when a visual target appeared. The instruction was to move the lever, not in the direction of the target, but in a direction at a given angle with respect to the target. They found the duration of the reaction time before moving the lever in the requested direction to be a function of the amplitude of the angle. Their interpretation of this finding was that the reaction time was a 'mental movement time' during which the movement vector was rotated until it matched the direction of the mental target. The larger angle, the more difficult the task and the longer the duration (Georgopoulos and Massey 1987). Interestingly, the same relationship of movement duration to task difficulty also holds in a purely mental condition, where no actual execution is ever involved. Decety and Jeannerod (1996) created such a situation by using virtual reality. Their participants were instructed to walk mentally through gates of different widths and positioned at different distances. The gates were presented within a virtual reality helmet which prevented the subject from referring to a known physical environment. Participants had to indicate the time they started walking mentally and the time they mentally passed through the gate. In accordance with Fitts law, mental movement times were found to be affected by the difficulty of the task, i.e. they took longer for walking through a narrow gate placed at a greater distance. In a recent experiment, Stevens (2004) found that visual imagery could not explain this type of data. Stevens got her subjects to walk physically or mentally on wooden paths of different lengths and different widths. Again, the same trade-off between movement duration and task difficulty was observed in both conditions. In addition, when the subjects imagined the displacement of an object along the same paths (a visual, not a motor, imagery task), the duration of the imagined motion was simply a function of path length, but was not influenced by the path width, i.e. was unrelated to the task difficulty. These findings support the view that functional rules which govern the execution of goal-directed actions, such as Fitts law, also apply to mentally executed actions and, therefore, pertain to the representation of these actions.

2.1.3 The encoding of biomechanical constraints

Another set of rules which also contribute to both the temporal and the spatial characteristics of goal-directed actions are based on optimization principles that operate during execution. One typical example of such principles is the organization of the spatial trajectory of arm movements during the action of grasping. As shown by David Rosenbaum and his group, the arm trajectories appear to be organized so as to minimize the discomfort of the final posture of the limb. In other words, the trajectory which is spontaneously selected for grasping an object will be that which avoids extreme joint rotations and allows the most efficient posture of the hand for object manipulation and use (the concept of 'posture-based motion planning', see Rosenbaum *et al.* 2004). In the situation described by Rosenbaum *et al.* (1990), the participants, using their right hand, were instructed to grasp a horizontally placed bar with the instruction to place either the right or the left end of the bar on a stool. The posture of the hand which was used for grasping the bar appeared to be conditioned by the instruction: an overhand posture was selected for placing the right end on the stool, and an underhand posture was selected for placing the left end. In both cases, these postures resulted in the same, comfortable final position of the hand. The selection of this final hand position must in fact be made prior to the initiation of the movement, i.e. at the level where the action is represented and prepared. Indeed, in another study where the movement trajectory was recorded, the wrist rotation for placing the hand in its final position was found to begin very early in movement time (Stelmach *et al.* 1994). Motor imagery experiments based on the same paradigm fully confirm this point. Johnson (2000) used a situation inspired by that of Rosenbaum *et al.* (1990), where the bar was presented in different orientations, but where no movement was executed: the subjects only had to indicate verbally which grip posture (underhand or overhand) they would select for a given orientation of the bar. The time taken by the subject to give the response increased as a function of the angle at which the bar was presented, i.e. as a function of the angular distance the subject's hand would have to cover to reach the selected posture via the shortest biomechanically plausible trajectory. Thus, the selection of the final hand position in the task of mentally grasping the bar follows the same optimization rules as during real grasping.

Similar findings were reported from experiments based on the concept of 'mental rotation'. The concept of mental rotation is borrowed from the study of visual imagery. In the original experiment of Shepard and Metzler where this concept was first used, subjects had to compare an object (the test object) visually presented in different orientations, with another object (the reference object) presented in its canonical orientation. The time to give the response (e.g. were the two objects the same or different?) was a function of the angle of rotation of the test object (Shepard and Metzler 1971). Can these results, obtained with the mental rotation of a neutral visual shape, be reproduced with the mental rotation of a body part, e.g. a hand? Lawrence Parsons designed a hand recognition task, inspired by the task of Shepard and Metzler, where a test hand (right or left) presented in a picture in different orientations had to be compared with a reference hand presented upright. Unlike for the rotation of neutral visual shapes, however, the response time for comparing the two hands was influenced not only by the angle of rotation between the two hands, but also by the direction of the rotation: the response time in fact depended on the trajectory that the hand would have had to follow if it had actually been moved, as if the subjects mentally rotated their own hand into the stimulus orientation for comparison (Parsons 1994). Indeed, whereas visual shapes can be rotated freely in any direction, the rotation of one's hand is limited by the biomechanical constraints of the arm. The Parsons' hand recognition task thus turns out to be a motor imagery task, not a visual imagery task. We will see several confirmations of this point below.

Along the same lines, other situations have been designed where the subject, in order to give a response to a visually presented display, has to simulate an action on objects. As in the above grip selection or hand recognition tasks, the subject is not specifically requested to make a mental movement, but only to make a prospective judgement about a potential action. An example of such a situation was described by Frak *et al.* (2001): the subjects were simply requested verbally to judge the feasibility of the action of grasping an object. The object (e.g. a cup) was shown in different orientations, some of which afforded an easy grasp and others an awkward one. Again, the time to give the response ('easy' or 'difficult') was a function of the orientation of the object, suggesting that the subjects unknowingly simulated a movement of their hand into an appropriate position before they could give the response. This interpretation is supported by the fact that the time to make this estimate was closely similar to the time taken physically to reach and grasp an object placed in the same orientation (Frak *et al.* 2001; see also de Sperati and Stucchi 1997). This type of implicit motor imagery seems to be widely used in preparing actions in everyday life. For example, the time taken to judge whether an object can be grasped by the right or the left hand is influenced by the orientation in which the object is shown. The response times are consistent with the classical stimulus–response compatibility effects which are observed during real movements (Tucker and Ellis 1998). Even the mere inspection of graspable objects and tools, or pictures of them (but not the picture of other object types, such as a house or a car, for example) seems to elicit in the observer the covert action of using them!

The situations described above, involving tasks such as grip selection, mental rotation or decision about the feasibility of an action, depart from the canonical concept of motor imagery. In these situations, in contradistinction to motor imagery proper, no conscious image is formed, and no explicit strategy is used. The subjects tend to 'simulate' the potential action spontaneously, even when they have not received specific instructions to perform it or to imagine it. These covert actions, which retain characteristics of executed movements (such as the speed–accuracy trade-off and the integration of biomechanical limitations), are therefore, as we said, in direct continuity with the implicit preparation processes that normally take place prior to executing everyday actions.

2.2 Dynamic changes in physiological parameters during motor imagery

The assumption developed in this section is that imagining a movement relies on the same mechanisms as actually performing it, except for the fact that execution is blocked. This assumption of a functional equivalence of dynamic imagery and overt action generates a specific prediction, namely that one should find in motor imagery and related phenomena physiological correlates similar to those measured during real action.

2.2.1 The encoding of simulated effort

Active execution of a movement implies the production of muscular force. The production of muscular force, in turn, implies metabolic demands which require adaptation of the organism. Covert actions, like motor images, do not involve muscular activity and therefore should not require adaptation mechanisms to come into play. In fact, adaptation to effort has a central component, in addition to its well-known reflex component. Motor images offer a unique possibility for investigating this central component. In our experiment on the duration of mentally walking to targets at different distances, reported above (Decety *et al.* 1989), we had noticed that, when the subjects imagining walking to the targets were loaded with a heavy weight (25 kg), their mental time increased by up to 30 per cent with respect to the non-loaded condition. In contrast, in the condition where the subjects walked physically with the weight, they took the same time walking to targets as when they were not loaded: they achieved this by spontaneously putting greater muscular force into the loaded task. The surprising result of an increased mental walking time with a load was later confirmed by Cerritelli *et al.* (2000) in a task of mentally pointing at targets of different widths with a hand-held stylus loaded with a 2 kg weight: again, mental movement time in the loaded condition was longer than in the non-loaded condition, by about 30 per cent.

Although the precise interpretation of this result remains unclear, it suggested to us that muscle force was indeed encoded at the representational level. More precisely, it suggested that this encoding should reflect physiological variables normally involved in adaptation of the organism to an increase in metabolic demands during muscular effort. Our hypothesis was that the autonomic system responsible for heart and respiration adaptation to effort, not submitted to voluntary control, should present visible changes during motor imagery involving graded changes in mental effort. Earlier work in the field of physiology of exercise had revealed the existence of a central patterning of vegetative commands during preparation for effort: heart and respiration rates show an almost immediate increase at the onset of exercise, or even prior to exercise (Krogh and Lindhard 1913; Adams *et al.* 1987). As this effect precedes the increase in muscle metabolism, it can only be due to central commands anticipating the metabolic change. Similarly, situations where the level of motor command can be manipulated but where muscular exercise is kept constant demonstrate the existence of a central activation of the autonomic system (Goodwin *et al.* 1972; for a review, see Requin *et al.* 1991). In our experiments involving motor imagery, highly consistent changes in heart and respiration rates were found during motor imagery of running at an increasing speed (Decety *et al.* 1991) or pedaling at an increasing rate (Decety *et al.* 1993). The increase in heart and respiration rates correlated with the level of the mentally represented force (see also confirmatory results by Beyer *et al.* 1990; Wang and Morgan, 1992; Wuyam *et al.* 1995). In the experiments of Decety *et al.*, the mean increase in heart rate during mental simulation of running or pedaling at the maximum speed was about 30 per cent above the resting rate, to be compared with a mean increase of about 50 per cent during the corresponding physical effort. Respiration rate also increased during mental simulation, to an even higher rate than during the corresponding physical effort. The absence of muscular activity during mental simulation was verified by measuring end-tidal P_{CO2} and anaerobic muscle metabolism [using nuclear magnetic resonance (NMR) spectroscopy]. The logical conclusion is that the autonomic activation during motor imagery pertains to the same phenomenon of central activation as that observed during preparation for action. An additional argument in this direction is provided by an experiment by Simon Gandevia and his colleagues. They observed graded cardiovascular changes in artificially paralyzed subjects attempting to produce muscular contractions at different intensities. As the paralysis was complete, these changes could not be due to residual muscular activity and had to be of a central origin (Gandevia *et al.* 1993).

The activation of the autonomic system during mental imagery of effort raises the question of its possible function. One possible answer is that the observed changes are the expression of the activation of an ensemble of mechanisms which prepare the organism for a potential action, to the same extent as activation of the motor pathways, which will be described in the next section. However, whereas activation of motor pathways during motor imagery is voluntarily blocked by inhibitory mechanisms, the activation of the autonomic system, which escapes voluntary control, becomes visible. In other words, the autonomic changes would represent an uncontrolled 'leaking' of the central processes involved in action representation. Another possible and complementary answer to the above question about the function of autonomic activation is that it would serve the purpose of 'somatic markers' (an expression borrowed from A. Damasio) providing the representation with visceral cues about the degree of effort involved in the represented action. This possibility will be discussed again in the context of another type of action representations, those which arise as a consequence of the observation of actions performed by other agents: in that case also, changes in respiration rate which map the degree of effort involved in the observed action can be measured

(Paccalin and Jeannerod 2000; see also Mulder *et al.* 2005). If correct, this hypothesis could bridge the gap between action representations and emotions, where emotion-specific autonomic changes are seen during both experiencing emotions and watching the emotions of other people (see Chapter 6).

2.2.2 Changes in excitability of the motor pathways

Measuring the changes in excitability of the motor pathways during various forms of action representation can also provide further information on the involved mechanisms. Indeed, it is a frequent finding that some degree of background EMG activity persists in the muscular groups involved in the simulated action (e.g. Jacobson 1930; Wehner *et al.* 1984; Gandevia *et al.* 1997). This finding suggests that during motor imagery, motor commands to muscles are only partially blocked, and that motoneurons are close to the firing threshold. Bonnet *et al.* (1997) confirmed this point by measuring spinal reflexes during motor imagery tasks. They instructed subjects either to press isometrically on a pedal or to simulate the same action mentally. Two levels of strength (weak and strong) were used. The H-reflexes in response to direct electrical stimulation of the popliteal nerve and the T-reflexes in response to a tap on the soleus tendon were measured. Both types of reflexes increased during mental simulation, and this increase correlated with the force of the simulated pressure (see also Gandevia *et al.* 1997).

The excitability of the corticospinal pathway can also be tested by using transcranial magnetic stimulation (TMS). This method allows measurement of the amplitude of motor evoked potentials (MEPs) produced in the muscles involved in mental simulation of an action, by a magnetically induced electrical stimulus applied to the corresponding area of the contralateral motor cortex. A consistent finding is that there is a specific increase of MEPs in those muscles involved in an imagined task (e.g. in the finger flexor muscles during imagination of hand closure), whereas no such increase can be seen in the antagonist extensor muscles (Fadiga *et al.* 1999; Hashimoto and Rothwell 1999; Rossini *et al.* 1999).

These results support the view that the motor system is involved during different types of mental representation of actions. Indeed, in a recent study, Clark *et al.* (2004) were able to compare MEP amplitude in the same subjects during explicitly imagining, observing and physically executing the same hand gestures. They found that observation and motor imagery conditions led to a similar facilitation in MEP amplitude in the relevant hand muscle. Although MEP facilitation was weaker during action representation than during physical execution of the same action, the existence of a facilitation in the two conditions calls for a unitary mechanism operating during action representation and execution.

2.3 The functional anatomy of motor images

In view of the results demonstrating the activation of physiological correlates pertaining to action execution during motor imagery, the next logical step is to examine the changes occurring at the level where the motor commands are generated. The description of the functional anatomy of these representations of action has greatly benefited from the neuroimaging techniques developed during the last two decades. Following the pioneer papers by Ingvar and Philipsson (1977) and Roland et al. (1980), the pattern of cortical activity during motor imagery has been extensively investigated.

From the wealth of published results, two main points emerge: first, there is a remarkably consistent pattern of activation common to the different forms of motor imagery; secondly, this pattern of activation largely overlaps that corresponding to motor execution. A meta-analysis of the data accumulated during the years 1994–2000, but still valid (Grèzes and Decety 2001), reveals a broad consensus between different laboratories for the activation of areas in the premotor cortex and in the posterior parietal cortex. The data concerning the involvement of motor cortex proper, however, are still controversial and will be treated separately.

2.3.1 The premotor–parietal network during action representation and execution

A joint activation of the frontal and parietal lobes during motor imagery is one of the most conspicuous findings across all studies. Decety et al. (1994) first found a large activation of the dorsal and ventral parts of lateral area 6 during imagined hand movements, as well as in parietal areas caudal and ventral to the primary parietal cortex. These findings were subsequently replicated in many studies dealing with either consciously imagined movements (Stephan et al. 1995; Grafton et al. 1996; Gérardin et al. 2000; Hanakawa et al. 2003) or unconscious perceptually based decisions (Parsons et al. 1995; Kosslyn et al. 1998). Simple visual presentation of graspable objects (Chao and Martin 2000) and even hearing action words (Hauk et al. 2004), two situations which may involve motor imagery, yield the same effect. Note that the network activated during motor imagery is clearly distinct from that activated during visual imagery. This point was verified during experiments comparing the two types of imagery, e.g. comparing the Parsons' hand recognition task with a task of mentally rotating neutral visual objects (Kosslyn et al. 1998; Richter et al. 2000; de Lange et al. 2005).

The areas activated during motor imagery overlap with those activated during motor execution. Apart for primary motor cortex (see below), this is true for lateral premotor cortex, where a large overlap was found by Rizzolatti *et al.* (1996), Lotze *et al.* (1999), Gérardin *et al.* (2000) and Hanakawa *et al.* (2003). The same degree of overlap between conditions of covert and overt actions exists for the supplementary motor area (SMA). However, SMA activation during imagined movements seems to be more rostral than during executed movements (e.g. Stephan *et al.* 1995; Grafton *et al.* 1996; Lotze *et al.* 1999; Gérardin *et al.* 2000). This rostral part of SMA, or pre-SMA, is more specifically involved in selection of a response among others possible, or in the endogenous generation of responses (Lau *et al.* 2004a; Rushworth *et al.* 2004). It is therefore not surprising to see it activated in motor imagery. Activation of the ventral area 6 in the inferior frontal gyrus, which is so clearly found in conditions of covert actions, is less frequently mentioned during execution. Finally, a large overlap is also observed for the parietal areas. A systematic comparison of activated areas during imagined and executed finger movements (Hanakawa *et al.* 2003) confirmed this overlap between the two conditions. According to these authors, cortical areas that were equally activated during the two conditions were found in the dorsal premotor cortex, the rostral SMA, the ventral lateral premotor cortex, the intraparietal sulcus and the supramarginal gyrus. Cortical areas that were more activated during imagery than during execution were in the posterior superior parietal cortex and in a zone anterior to the lateral premotor cortex and to the pre-SMA. Finally, cortical areas that were more activated during execution than during imagery were located in the motor cortex, in the posterior part of the lateral premotor cortex, in the posterior part of the SMA, in the parietotemporal operculum and in the anterior parietal cortex (see also de Lange *et al.* 2005). This finding of a large, but partial overlap of areas involved in both imagined and executed actions will be of a great theoretical importance at a later stage of our discussion. We will see that the same areas are also partially involved in other aspects of motor cognition, including identifying one's own actions, attributing actions to their real agent and understanding the actions of others.

2.3.2 The controversy about the involvement of primary motor cortex in action representation

The classical view of primary motor cortex holds that it is an area devoted to transferring to motor execution messages that have been elaborated upstream in the cerebral cortex. Anatomically, primary motor cortex is the site of convergence of inputs from premotor cortex and basal ganglia; it is also the main site of origin of the pyramidal tract and of direct cortico-motoneuronal connections. Early functional studies using direct cortical stimulation had concluded that the role of the motor cortex is limited to selecting the proper muscular addresses and encoding muscular force for executing a movement. To quote Penfield's Ferrier Lecture, 'Movement produced by stimulation of the motor cortex takes place most often in those members of the body which are capable of dextrous and complicated voluntary activity, and yet the movements thus produced are never dextrous nor purposeful', and, in addition, 'The conscious patient is never deceived into believing that he made the movement himself. He knows he did not plan it' (Penfield 1947, p. 344). This finding, which is confirmed by the everyday practice of TMS, contrasts with the effects of stimulation of other more rostral motor areas. Stimulation of lateral area 6 by Penfield and Boldrey (1937), although it elicited no overt movements, frequently elicited an intense 'desire to move' (see also Fried *et al.* 1991).

More recently, however, experimental data have pointed to the fact that the relationship of motor cortex activity to the production of movements is not as simple as it was thought on the basis of early stimulation experiments. This revision of motor cortical function originated from two main lines of research, dealing first with the plasticity of the somatotopic organization of primary motor cortex and, secondly, with its involvement in cognitive functions.

2.3.2.1 Plastic changes in the motor cortex

The somatotopic organization of primary motor cortex is unstable. It can be radically altered in a number of situations, such as peripheral changes in neuromuscular connections or motor learning and training. It has been known for over 10 years that motor cortical somatotopy is subject to a vast amount of reorganization following amputation of a limb or peripheral nerve lesion (e.g. Donoghue and Sanes 1987). In man, like in rats, the cortical territory controlling the amputated joints tends to shrink, whereas the territory controlling remnant adjacent joints tends to expand (e.g. Pons *et al.* 1991). For example, following amputation of a hand, the territory of the fingers will be invaded by more proximal joints of the same limb (e.g. elbow and shoulder), or even by the face. As it was suspected, but not proven until recently, this plastic phenomenon seems reversible. One case of hetero-transplantation of the two hands several years after bilateral amputation at the level of the mid-forearms was studied by Giraux *et al.* (2001), using functional magnetic resonance imaging (fMRI) for mapping activation of motor cortex. Before surgery, the areas corresponding to the two hands were mapped by asking the subject to 'extend' or 'flex' his (missing) fingers. Execution of these movements was controlled by palpating finger extensors and flexors at the level of the stump.

Six months after surgery, the hand areas were mapped during movements of the grafted hands. The comparison of activation before and after surgery revealed that the hand areas on either side, which were initially reduced to the most lateral part of the normal hand area close to the face area, re-expanded medially to reoccupy its full territory. Similarly, the elbow area, which had invaded a large section of the hand area, was pushed back medially to its normal anatomical location.

Motor cortical reorganization following amputation is associated with subjective sensory phenomena, such as phantom pain (Flohr *et al.* 1995; Lotze *et al.* 2001). Partial restoration of the normal topography by training reduces phantom pain. Lotze *et al.* (1999) showed that the extensive use of a myoelectric prosthetic device by the amputee, by preventing cortical reorganization, has a positive effect on phantom pain. Giraux and Sirigu (2003) also showed that re-expansion of the hand area by training resulted in a decrease in phantom pain. The visuomotor training method used by Giraux and Sirigu consisted of transferring, by way of mirrors, the image of the normally moving limb at the location of the paralyzed limb. After a few sessions, the patient imagined his paralyzed limb moving and this resulted in re-expansion of the atrophied corresponding primary motor cortex (see also Chapter 5).

Plastic modification of primary motor cortex somatotopy is not limited to peripheral changes such as amputation. It is also observed during motor training. Neuroimaging studies and studies using TMS show that long-term training of finger movements, e.g. in professional musicians, produces an increase in the amplitude of the activation and an enlargement of the finger cortical area (Karni *et al.* 1995; Pascual-Leone *et al.* 1995; Jancke *et al.* 2000; Nordstrom and Butler 2002). Although this effect of training can be partly explained by peripheral factors (e.g. the increase in reafferent input from the moving limb during repetitive movements; see Johnson 1982), it is also clearly influenced by central factors. Indeed, the same effect can be observed during mental training in the absence of overt movements from the trained limb (see page 41). Thus, primary motor cortex is liable to long-term changes in its intrinsic arrangement and connectivity, an experimental fact which would not be expected from a system devoted to transmitting executive commands, and opens up new possibilities for reinterpreting its role in motor functions.

2.3.2.2. Cognitive functions of motor cortex

The second set of data which leads to reconsideration of motor cortex function arises from experiments showing the implication of motor cortex in cognitive activities related to motor function, but where no movement occurs. Apostolos Georgopoulos and his colleagues first demonstrated in the monkey the existence of orderly changes in activity of primary motor cortex neurons during a cognitive operation. In this experiment, a monkey was instructed to perform an arm movement directed to a virtual target, different from that shown to her. During this process of target selection preceding execution of the movement, the activity of the neuronal population coding for the direction of the movement (the population vector) progressively changed from the direction of the target shown to the monkey to the direction of the virtual target, suggesting that the animal was performing a mental rotation of the population vector until it matched the instructed direction (Georgopoulos *et al.* 1989).

According to Georgopoulos (2000), primary motor cortex should be considered as a cognitive area, i.e. an area involved in cognitive motor processes, rather than simply as an area devoted to motor execution and control of the spinal level. In the following paragraphs, we will examine the role of motor cortex in motor imagery and related states, an ensemble of cognitive operations where no action is overtly executed. We will progressively discover in this and further chapters that primary motor cortex activation during cognitive motor operations is part of the neural process of simulation which serves as the basis of action representations.

The above two paragraphs have set the stage for examining the activity of M1 during the cognitive phenomenon of mental imagery. The anatomical and functional plasticity of motor cortex, emphasized by these recent findings, clearly departs from the rigid organization that one would expect for a purely motor mechanism. Thus, the participation of motor cortex in motor imagery should not really be a surprise. Many studies, using functional neuroimaging with metabolic methods [positron emission tomography (PET)] and fMRI have dealt with this problem since 1995 (Kim *et al.* 1995; Leonardo *et al.* 1995; Grafton *et al.* 1996; Lotze *et al.* 1999; Porro *et al.* 1996; Roth *et al.* 1996). Typically, primary motor cortex activation is not consistently found in every subject and, when present, is less intense than during motor execution of the same movement (e.g. Hanakawa *et al.* 2003). However, this activation is usually significant at the group level (Michelon *et al.* 2006). The activated zones overlap those activated during execution, with the same voxels involved in the two conditions (e.g. Porro *et al.* 1996) (Figure 2.1). Finally, primary motor cortex activation during motor imagery seems to be transient: it culminates during the first few seconds of the imagination task and subsequently tends to vanish (Dechent *et al.* 2004). The involvement of primary motor cortex during motor imagery can also be detected with the magnetoencephalographic (MEG) technique; in this case, the activation of the motor cortex is inferred from a specific change in cortical activity, the suppression of the 20 Hz rebound induced by a peripheral nerve stimulation. This phenomenon is observed in the precentral gyrus during manipulative finger movements, and also during motor imagery of the same movements (Schnitzler *et al.* 1997). As we will discuss elsewhere, these MEG findings represent a direct demonstration of the existence of a cortical system for matching execution, imagination and observation of the same movements.

In nearly all the above studies, great care was taken by the investigators to control for the absence of small movements or EMG discharges during the imagery task, with the idea in mind that, if EMG activity was recorded, this would mean that the subjects were not doing the task properly, and this would

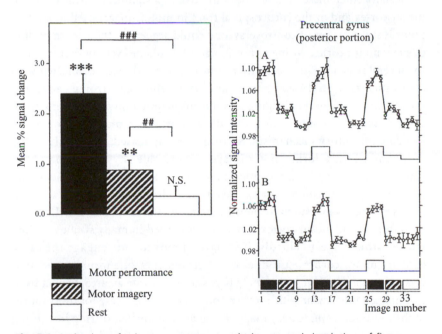

Fig. 2.1 Activation of primary motor cortex during mental simulation of finger movements. Normal subjects were instructed alternatively to either move their fingers (motor performance, black marks) or mentally simulate finger movements (motor imagery, dashed marks) during brain scanning with a functional magnetic resonance imaging (fMRI) device. Right: (A) signal intensity (in number of pixels) in the motor cortex during a sequence of episodes with motor performance, followed by motor imagery and by rest; (B) alternation of motor performance and rest. Left: mean percentage signal change from motor performance to motor imagery and rest. Note the decreased activation from motor performance to motor imagery and the significant difference between motor imagery and rest. Rearranged from Porro *et al.* (1996).

count as execution, not imagination. This argument is also used for discussing the issue of motor imagery in amputees. Amputees who imagine moving their amputated limb show an activation of their motor cortex (e.g. Ersland *et al.* 1996; Lotze *et al.* 2001). This finding raises the intriguing question of whether motor images in amputees are represented actions to the same extent as they are in normal subjects, or are real actions, such that, if the muscles were still there or were still connected, they would contract. One way to verify this point would be to check for possible muscle contractions at the level of the stump: if they were present, cortical activation would relate to execution of a 'movement' with the amputated limb; if they were not, the observed cortical activation would pertain to a motor image. This remains to be tested.

Taken together, these findings speak in favor of a significant involvement of motor cortex and of the corticospinal tract in motor imagery. Although this point is still a matter of controversy, one could argue that the reverse finding (a silent motor cortex during motor imagery) would be even more surprising, for several reasons. First, recall that motor cortex is directly connected with areas, such as the SMA and premotor cortex, which are strongly activated during motor imagery: blocking this monosynaptic input converging from several areas to the motor cortex would require a complex and potentially insecure inhibitory mechanism. Secondly, the increased excitability of the corticospinal tract during motor imagery (as revealed by TMS) can only be explained by an increased synaptic activity at the level of the pyramidal tract cells in the primary motor cortex: this increase in synaptic activity, which is precisely what is measured by neuroimaging methods such as fMRI, readily accounts for the motor cortex activation observed in many studies dealing with motor imagery. Thirdly, if imagined movements engage the same primary motor cortex neurons as overt movements, one would expect that imagining a movement with a body part should activate an area distinct from imagining a movement with another body part, as is the case for overt movements. Ehrsson *et al.* (2003) mapped the areas activated during imagining movements with the hand, the mouth or the foot, and found that this activation followed (on a voxel to voxel basis) the same topographical organization as during overt movements.

2.3.3 The problem of motor inhibition during the representation of actions

An essential aspect of motor imagery is that the imagined action remains covert. Classical authors (e.g. James 1890), within the framework of the Ideomotor Action Theory, had made the remark that what they called 'ideas of action' were not readily transformed into action. This was because, they thought, an active suppression process opposed the spontaneous tendency to move. The same speculation might apply to motor images. Earlier in the present chapter we showed that imagined actions are indeed actions in their own right: they involve a kinematic content, they activate motor areas almost to the same extent as executed actions, they involve the autonomic system as if a real action was under way and yet they remain invisible. This suggest that the neural commands for muscular contractions, although they are effectively present during motor imagery, are simultaneously blocked at some level of the motor system by an active inhibitory mechanisms. It is indeed critical that action representations, not only during motor imagery, but also during action observation, can operate 'off-line'. This is a basic requirement for the possibility to simulate actions without executing them. We will come back to this point in Chapter 6.

In fact, considering the above body of data about the activity of the motor system during imagined actions, there are two possible explanations for this absence of overt motor output. The first explanation postulates that the transfer of the information elaborated within premotor or supramotor cortical areas (e.g. dorsal and ventral premotor cortex and parietal cortex) would be blocked before entering motor cortex. The prefrontal cortical areas, which are also active during motor imagery (e.g. Decety *et al.* 1994), could represent a possible site of origin for this inhibition, in line with the well known role of prefrontal cortex in behavioral inhibition in general. This point was specifically investigated by Marcel Brass and his colleagues in a neuroimaging experiment with normal subjects. Participants were instructed to perform finger movements while they were observing another person executing either congruent or incongruent movements. When the observed movements were incongruent with respect to the pre-instructed movements, the subjects had to inhibit their spontaneous tendency to imitate the movements of the other person. This task resulted in a strong activation of the dorsolateral and frontopolar areas of prefrontal cortex (Brass *et al.* 2001a). Indeed, an impairment of this inhibitory function of prefrontal cortex has often been invoked as an explanation for psychiatric cases of dysfunction of voluntary actions (see Chapter 3). An observation by Marshall *et al.* (1997) of a patient with a hysterical paralysis of the left side of her body lends additional support to this explanation. When this patient was instructed to move the right 'good' leg, a normal activation (mapped with PET) of the left sensorimotor cortex was observed. No such activation, however, was observed on the right side during unsuccessful attempts to move the left 'bad' leg. Instead, the right anterior cingulate and orbitofrontal cortices were strongly activated. This suggests that these prefrontal areas exerted a state-dependent inhibition on the motor system when the patient formed the intention to move her left leg. The hypothesis of a cortico-cortical inhibition originating in prefrontal cortex, however, is not compatible with the very fact that motor cortex is activated during action representation: this should not be the case if motor cortex were under the inhibitory influence of prefrontal areas. It is more likely that prefrontal cortex is involved during motor imagery, not in inhibiting the execution of represented actions, but rather in selecting the appropriate representation (e.g. Shallice 1988). While executing a pre-instructed action incompatible with an observed one, as in the experiment by Brass *et al.* (2001b), one has to select the endogenous representation and to ignore that arising from the outside or, in other words, to prevent oneself from being distracted by an external event. This is indeed what patients with frontal lesions cannot do (see Chapter 3).

The second hypothesis to account for the empirical data showing both the involvement of motor cortex and the lack of overt execution in motor imagery is that the inhibitory mechanism should be localized downstream of the motor cortex, possibly at the spinal cord or brainstem level. Many observers have reported incomplete relaxation of muscular activity during imagination of actions, which has been accounted for by the variability in subjects' strategy during motor imagery. In fact, a more likely explanation would be that residual muscular activity observed in these subjects results from incomplete inhibition of downstream volleys from motor cortex to the motoneurons. Our hypothesis to account for both motor cortical activation and motor inhibition during motor imagery would thus be that a dual mechanism operates at the spinal level. The subthreshold tendency to move, reflected by the increased corticospinal tract activity, would be paralleled by an inhibitory influence for suppressing the overt movement. The posterior cerebellum may play an important role in this inhibitory process (Lotze *et al.* 1999). Whereas during action execution, the activated cerebellar areas are located in anterior and lateral regions, those activated during imagery and action observation are located in the posterior cerebellum (Parsons *et al.* 1995; Grafton *et al.* 1996). Another possibility would be that of an intraspinal inhibition. This possibility is suggested by an experiment in monkeys where the animal was instructed to wait for a go signal before a learned action. Prut and Fetz (1999) found that spinal interneurons are activated during the waiting period. Because the overt movement was suppressed during this period, Prut and Fetz hypothesized a superimposed global inhibition possibly originating in premotor cortex, and propagating to the spinal cord in parallel with the excitatory input. This hypothesis would account for both the increased motoneuron excitability and the block of muscular activity which are observed during motor imagery.

2.4 The consequences of the embodiment of action representations

2.4.1 Mental training

Already in the early 1960s, the sport psychology literature offered a wealth of studies reporting measurable effects of mental imagery on subsequent motor performance (for a review and meta-analysis, see Driskell *et al.* 1994; Feltz and Landers 1983, respectively). Nowadays, mental training is currently used by a wide range of motor performers, such as sport professionals and musicians: it has been shown to affect several aspects of motor performance normally thought to be specific outcomes of training, such as the increase in strength of muscular contraction (Yue and Cole 1992), improvement in movement speed and accuracy (Pascual-Leone *et al.* 1995), reduction of variability and increase in temporal consistency of movements (Vogt 1995).

One of the early explanations proposed for these phenomena highlighted the role of cognitive factors. For example, mental training could modify perceptual organization and provide a new insight into the action to be performed (for a review of these explanations, see Johnson 1982). Here, we will develop a different working hypothesis, based on the experimental data presented in this chapter. The study of motor images and related states has revealed that they are 'embodied' mental states. Our hypothesis proposes that representing an action and executing it are functionally equivalent. As we saw, many aspects of overt actions are centrally represented and motor images appear to encode rules and constraints inherent to executed actions. It is therefore not surprising that the changes occurring at all levels of the motor system during motor imagery affect subsequent motor performance. By covertly rehearsing the motor pathways, the activity of the motor system facilitates further execution. This facilitation represents a physiological basis for various forms of training (e.g. 'mental training') and learning (e.g. observational learning) which occur as a consequence of self-representing an action. Experimental data strongly support this explanation. Pascual-Leone *et al.* (1995) measured the changes in excitability of motor cortex (using TMS) during mental training of finger movements (piano playing). They found that the size of the excitable area devoted to finger movements increased as movements were repeated over training periods. The interesting point is that the same increase in the size of the excitable area was produced by purely mental training of the finger movements (Figure 2.2). More recently, Lafleur *et al.* (2002) showed that learning a motor task by using motor imagery induces a pattern of dynamic changes in cortical activation similar to that occurring during physical practice. In both conditions, a first phase is observed, with an increase in

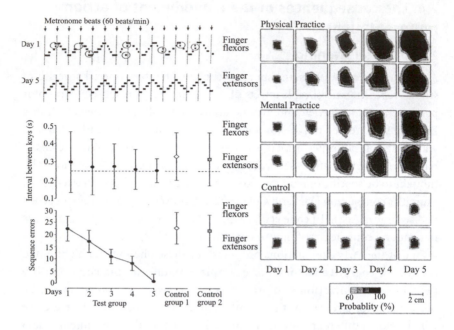

Fig. 2.2 Influence of mental training on motor cortical activity. Upper left: motor performance of naive normal subjects performing piano scales prior to (day 1) and after training (day 5). Lower left: mean scores of subject groups for regularity of intervals between notes and number of errors over the 5 days of training. Control groups correspond to subjects who watched the piano without performing the scales. Right: change in the mean cortical excitable area for producing motor evoked potentials in two groups of finger muscles (flexors and extensors) during the 5 days of training. From top to bottom, in subjects making physical practice, mental practice and in subjects from a control group without practice. Note the similar progressive increase in excitable area for both physical and mental practice groups. From Pascual-Leone *et al.* (1995).

activity in the premotor cortex, the parietal cortex and the cerebellum. Subsequently, this activation tends to disappear and to be replaced by activation in the basal ganglia and prefrontal cortex (in the orbitofrontal and anterior cingular regions). Hence the idea that mental training, alone or combined with physical training, might help in rehabilitating patients with motor impairments following central lesions (Jackson *et al.* 2004; Lacourse *et al.* 2005).

The simulation interpretation of the effects of mental training is confirmed by recent experimental evidence showing that subjects can learn voluntarily to increase the degree of activation of their motor cortex during an imagined manual action (deCharms *et al.* 2004). During the training period, subjects first receive ongoing information about the level of activation of their motor cortex, via a continuously updated fMRI signal taken from the cortical motor area. Subsequently, they become able to increase this level of activation without recourse to the feedback signal. According to deCharms *et al.*, this procedure yields a level of activity in the sensorimotor cortex similar to, or higher than, during actual manual action. Obviously, this type of result showing the possibility of increasing at will the activity in a specific brain area opens up a number of potential applications for designing new training techniques, not only in the domain of action, but also in the realm of the control of behavior in general. Rehabilitation procedures in patients with motor impairments of a central origin should greatly benefit from this possibility. In stroke patients suffering from hemiparesis on one side of the body, not only are the movements executed with the affected arm slowed down, but the imagined movements also appear to be slower than with the unaffected arm (Decety and Boisson 1990; Malouin *et al.* 2004). It is possible that systematic rehearsal of motor imagery in these patients would help them restore their motor output by activating substitutive mechanisms.

Finally, mental rehearsal could also be useful in patients with prolonged immobilization of one limb. Prolonged immobilization, which is typically followed by a long period of muscular weakness and motor awkwardness, is likely to reduce the activity of motor cortex. Motor imagery could be profitably used for maintaining motor cortical activity in the absence of overt movements, with the consequence of shortening the recovery period.

2.4.2 Coupling motor representations with neuroprosthetic devices

We have provided evidence showing that represented actions involve the orderly activation of the same neural structures that would be involved if the action were actually executed (the definition of action simulation). Following this line of thought, it seems logical to assume that, if neural activity in the motor areas of a subject imagining a movement could be properly monitored and coupled to an appropriate device, the imagined movement would become visible. This conjecture is the basis for building hybrid brain–machine interfaces that could be used to control artificial devices, with the ambition to substitute deficient motor function in patients with severe motor disabilities or paralysis (e.g. Nicolelis 2001; Cincotti *et al.* 2003; Mehring *et al.* 2003). A monkey has been trained to move a spot on a computer screen just by 'thinking' about the displacement of the spot. The monkey was implanted with an electrode for recording the activity of a small neuronal population in the primary motor cortex area controlling the animal's arm movement. The monkey first used a manipulandum for displacing a spot on the computer screen. Then the connection between the manipulandum and the computer was replaced by a connection between the output of the microelectrode and the spot: the monkey was immediately able to use the neural activity-based signal to carry out the task without any further training. During this time, the animal made intermittent arm movements or no arm movements. The importance of this finding (Serruya *et al.* 2002) is 2-fold. Not only does it show that non-human primates, like humans, can generate motor representations that have properties similar to real actions, but it is also of a high potential value for designing rehabilitation procedures. Considering that a human subject can learn to increase his cortical activity at will, as we saw in the previous paragraph (deCharms *et al.* 2004), it should be possible for this subject to train his motor cortical activity mentally so as to obtain any desired effect, provided he receives some feedback about the effect. Subsequently, this same subject should become able to manipulate a neuroprosthetic device as if it were his own limb. The issue of whether feedback would be necessary for producing the required cerebral activity is actually debatable. Rats acquire the ability to use their brain activity for producing movements of a robot arm if they have visual feedback from the movement and are rewarded when they complete the action successfully. When they have acquired this ability, however, they continue to generate the correct neural activity so as to be rewarded, but stop producing the movement! In other words, they generate a mental image of the action without taking the trouble to produce the overt action (see Nicolelis 2002).

Chapter 3

Consciousness of self-produced actions and intentions

We remain unaware of many of our own actions. It is common experience that when leaving home we ask ourselves questions such as: 'Did I lock the door'? Or 'Did I turn off the light'?, immediately after having done it. We may also drive the car back home and suddenly realize that we are at our destination without having the least idea of how we did it. However, on the contrary, there are situations where we remain fully aware throughout the action. When I do something for the first time, e.g. start a new laptop computer, I try to follow the instruction manual carefully and to control each step of the action consciously. In this chapter, we will be faced with a set of theoretical and empirical questions about how it is possible to evaluate the degree of consciousness involved in a given action, and what are the factors and the constraints for an action to be conscious or not. We will try to identify some of the neural mechanisms that are involved in this process of access or non-access to consciousness. Finally, we will extend our discussion to the consciousness of intentions and to the problem of volition.

3.1 Consciousness of actions

What is consciousness of action about? What is the content of consciousness when this term is referred to an action? Several possible answers to these queries come to mind. The first answer is that consciousness of action refers to what the action is about. Actions have goals. To be aware of the goal one is reaching for is one way of being conscious of the action undertaken to reach that goal. Being aware of the goal, however, does not imply being aware of how it is being reached. Woodworth stated that 'When I voluntarily start to walk, my intention is not that of alternatively moving my legs in a certain manner; my will is directed toward reaching a certain place. I am unable to describe with any approach to accuracy what movements my arms or legs are to make; but I am able to state exactly what result I intend to accomplish' (Woodworth 1906. Quoted in Kimble and Perlemuter 1970, p. 369). Another possible answer to the query of what consciousness of action is about is precisely that it refers to how that action is (or was) performed. This is indeed a crucial point in the situation of learning how to do something and how performance could be improved. Finally, a third possible answer is that consciousness of an action is about who is doing the action (Jeannerod 2003b).

Here, we will first concentrate on the questions of what and how. The third question of who refers to a slightly different problem: it refers to the agent of the action and not to the action proper. It is a question about the self. Being conscious of whether one is, or is not, the author of an action refers to the recognition of oneself as a causal self, as opposed to other selves. The discussion about this latter point will start at the end of this chapter in the section about volition and free will, and will continue in the next chapter about identification and attribution of self-produced actions.

3.1.1 Awareness of the goal of an automatic action

Most of our actions directed at external objects are prepared and executed automatically. Once started, they are performed accurately and rapidly (typically within less than 1 second). The brevity of execution time leaves little room for top-down control of execution itself. Rather, the representation that accounts for these movements or actions must automatically process those properties of the goal-object that are relevant to its potential interactions with the agent. In the action of grasping an object, for example, the object's shape and size are relevant to grip formation (maximum grip aperture and number of fingers involved), its texture and estimated weight are relevant to anticipatory computation of grip and load forces, etc. The term visuomotor representations has been proposed in Chapter 1 for qualifying this mode of representing objects as goals for action. The most striking characteristic of visuomotor representations is their implicit functioning and correlation, their non-conscious nature and their lack of conceptual content. For the purpose of the present chapter, which is to discuss the degree of consciousness attached to different forms of action, we have to examine the reasons why the processing of object-related actions turns out to be non-conscious.

One possible hypothesis for explaining the automaticity of fast object-oriented actions is that these actions are non-conscious because this is a prerequisite for their accuracy. The argument here is 2-fold. First, the representation coding for a goal-directed movement must have a short life span: in fact, it should not exceed the duration of the movement itself, so that the representation of that goal can be erased before another segment of the action starts. Secondly, consciousness is a slow process, such that the above temporal constraint does not leave enough time for consciousness to appear (more on this point below). As a consequence, a fast and accurate movement can only be executed automatically. It has been shown that delaying the onset of a goal-directed movement by only a few seconds after the presentation of the stimulus severely degrades the accuracy of the movement (Jakobson and Goodale 1991). In this condition, according to the above hypothesis, it is likely that the representation of the movement rapidly deteriorates and that the fast automatic mechanism cannot operate.

As a matter of fact, awareness of the goal and accurate performance seem to be controlled separately. Bruce Bridgeman and his colleagues showed that, if a visual target (e.g. a spot of light) rapidly changes its location immediately prior to a pointing movement of the arm toward that target (e.g. during the saccadic eye movement that precedes the pointing movement), subjects usually remain unaware of the target displacement: because of the phenomenon of 'saccadic suppression' which partly blocks vision during saccades, they see only one, stationary, target. Yet, in spite of their lack of awareness of the target displacement, they automatically point their hand at the correct location of the target (Bridgeman *et al.* 1981). In a later replication of this experiment, Pélisson *et al.* (1986; see also Goodale *et al.* 1986) confirmed that the subjects were able to point their hand at the displaced visual target, but also found that the movements to the displaced targets had the same duration as those to stationary targets. In other words, no additional time was needed to produce the correction, suggesting that the unconscious visual signals related to the target shift were used with a very short delay for adjusting the trajectory.

According to this view, generating a motor response to a stimulus and building a perceptual experience of that same stimulus can be considered as distinct processes. On the one hand, the motor response is controlled by a visuomotor representation operating rapidly and unconsciously. On the other hand, the perceptual awareness is controlled by another, slower type of representation whereby the goal is perceived as an entity with all its attributes, including those that are not immediately relevant for the movement (e.g. its color), and where objects are represented by their identity and their function, not as mere targets for the motor commands of reaching and grasping. Indeed, there are situations in everyday life where this dissociation between actions in response to visual events and conscious experience of the same events becomes clearly apparent. We respond first and become aware later. For example, when driving a car, we have to make a change in trajectory because of a sudden obstacle on our way: we consciously see the obstacle after we have avoided it. Castiello *et al.* (1991) designed a series of experiments where they measured this temporal dissociation. Participants were instructed to reach by hand and grasp an object (a vertical dowel) placed in front of them, as soon as it became illuminated. They also received the instruction to signal, by a vocal utterance, at what time they became aware of the illumination of the object. The onset of the hand movement aimed at the object preceded by a short time (approximately 50 ms) the vocal response signaling the subject's awareness of its change in visual appearance. This difference was not noticed by the subjects, who felt their hand movements coincided with their perception of the illumination of the object. In the same experiment, the illuminated object was shifted by 10° on either side at the time where the reaching movement started (see Figure 1.1 for a description of the experimental design). The first sign of correction of the hand trajectory appeared shortly (~150 ms) after the shift in target position. In contrast, the vocal utterance corresponding to this same event came much later, some 350 ms after the beginning of the change in movement trajectory. The subjects' reports were in accordance with this temporal dissociation between the two responses: they reported that they saw the object jumping to its new position near the end of their movement, just at the time where they were about to grasp the object (sometimes even after they took it).

The main result of this experiment is that the time to awareness of a visual event, as inferred from the vocal response, keeps a relatively constant value across different conditions. Under normal circumstances, when the target object remains stationary and no time pressure is imposed on performing the task, this time is roughly compatible with the duration of motor reaction times: when we make a movement toward an object, we become aware of this object near the time when the movement starts, or shortly after it has started, hence the apparent consistency between our actions and the flow of our subjective experience. This consistency breaks down when the motor reaction time shortens under conditions of time pressure, such as avoiding sudden obstacles or tracking unexpected object displacements, so that the conscious awareness becomes dissociated from the movement. One might suggest that the normally long reaction times (~300 ms) of reaching movements have the function of keeping our subjective experience in register with our actions. Imagine what life would be like if the above temporal dissociation were the usual case, and if our awareness of the external events were systematically delayed with regard to our actions in response to these events!

Observations made in patients with lesions of primary visual cortex and presenting the 'blindsight' phenomenon add further arguments for this notion of a dual processing of visual information (Weiskrantz 1986). These patients appear to reach consciously for non-conscious goals. For example, patient P.J.G. described by Perenin and Rossetti (1996) correctly adjusted his hand movements, which he unknowingly directed at objects presented in his blind hemifield, without being able to report consciously about the presence of these objects within his visual field.

The dissociation between motor responses and subjective experience, when it happens, as well as the more usual synchrony between the two, reflects the fact that different aspects of the same event are processed at different rates, such that the global outcome is constrained by the slowness of the process that builds up awareness. Consciousness is not immediate, it takes time to appear. This point has been emphasized by Benjamin Libet in his Time-On Theory. The theory states that the transition from an unconscious event to one that is consciously experienced is a function of a sufficient increase in the duration of appropriate neural activities. 'That is, Libet writes, appropriate neural activities whose duration is below some minimum substantial duration could mediate a mental function that remains unconscious; but when such activities persist for longer than a minimum time of up to about 500 msec, subjective awareness of the mental function can appear' (Libet 1992, pp. 264–265). The delay of about 350 ms that was found for the conscious report of a target change in the experiment by Castiello *et al.* (1991) described above is compatible with Libet's timing.

The slowness of consciousness, together with the rapidity of accurate movements, results in these movements being automatic. Indeed, it is common experience that goal-directed movements executed under conscious control are usually slow and inaccurate, something that amateur sportsmen realize during their first attempts at learning a new skill: leaving the automatic mode introduces delays in action execution, to the detriment of movement accuracy. This discussion of the temporal constraints of access to consciousness clarifies one controversial aspect of the classical dissociation between acting on visual objects and recognizing them, held by the Two Visual Systems Theory. Mel Goodale and his colleagues (Goodale *et al.* 1991; Milner and Goodale 1995) had postulated that the dorsal visual system, which is responsible for visuomotor transformation, works on a non-conscious mode, as opposed to the conscious ventral visual system, responsible for object recognition. This opposition seems misleading, however. Many arguments, both experimental and clinical, suggest that the dorsal system exhibits conscious functioning to the same extent as the ventral system (see a review of these arguments in Jacob and Jeannerod 2003). According to Libet's Time-On Theory above, the impression of unconscious functioning of the dorsal system is created by the rapidity of the visuomotor transformation which does not leave enough time for consciousness to appear. As Libet says, 'It may be that one controlling factor for the transition between the conscious and the unconscious features of information is simply the duration of appropriate neural activity, and that both features could . . . then be a function of the same cerebral areas' (Libet 1991, p. 195).

The above queries were about the awareness of the goal of an action. In that sense, the experiments showing the lack of awareness of the goal, as well as the temporal dissociation between the unconscious visuomotor adjustment and the conscious report of the goal, referred to perceptual awareness, rather than to motor awareness. In the next section, we concentrate on the awareness of the motor execution itself.

3.1.2 Awareness of how an action is performed

In the previous section, we left aside the questions raised by the consciousness of how the goal is reached. The reason for neglecting this aspect was that the types of actions under consideration, such as reaching and grasping objects, were automatically executed actions. The experimental situations we have described for testing the subjects' awareness of the goal did not ask questions about the action itself. Indeed, those are questions that we rarely ask ourselves. Questions about which cues we rely on to perform the correct trajectory, or which level of strength we have to apply, seem quite irrelevant in a normal situation. In this section, however, we will make an attempt to get into this normally hidden aspect of our action representations. To this aim, we will report the results of experiments which deliberately created conflicting situations. Those are situations where what the subjects see or feel from their own actions does not correspond to what they actually do. Such situations produce a conflict between the different signals that are generated at the time of execution of an action (e.g. visual signals, proprioceptive signals or signals arising from central motor commands) and that are normally congruent with each other. Subjects' reports about their feelings in situations where these signals become mutually incongruent thus provide a direct insight into their ability consciously to monitor these signals.

Experiments dealing with subjects' behavior in situations of sensorimotor conflict have a long history. Such situations can typically be created by optical devices. Looking at one's moving hand through an inverting prism, for example, makes the movements appear inverted: in order to reach for a visual target seen on my right, I have to move my hand to the left (e.g. Stratton 1899). The main goal of these classical experiments was to study the process of adaptation, through which visuomotor coordination progressively rearranges to match the hand movements to the apparent location of the visual targets (see Held 1961). However, only a few systematic attempts were made at studying the subjects' motor awareness, i.e. their insight about how they performed their own movements when unknowingly faced with this type of conflict.

The research on motor awareness was initiated by Torsten Nielsen more than 40 years ago (Nielsen 1963). We will fully describe Nielsen's results in a different context, that of self-recognition (see Chapter 4). Here, we describe the results Pierre Fourneret and I obtained in a more recent version of the Nielsen experiment where we quantified what an agent can report about what he has just done in trying to reach for a visual target (Fourneret and Jeannerod 1998). Participants were instructed to draw straight lines between a starting position and a target, using a stylus on a digital tablet. The output of the stylus and the target were displayed on a computer screen. The participants saw the computer screen in a mirror placed so as to hide their hand. On some trials, the line seen in the mirror was made to deviate electronically by up to 10° from the line actually drawn by the subject. Thus, in order to reach the target, the subject had to deviate his/her movement in the direction opposite to that of the line seen in the mirror. At the end of each trial, the subjects were asked to indicate verbally in which direction they thought their hand had actually moved. There were two different results: first, the subjects were consistently able to trace lines that reached the target, i.e. they accurately corrected for the deviation. Secondly, they gave verbal responses indicating that they thought their hand had moved in the direction of the target, hence ignoring the actual movements they had performed. Thus, they were unable to monitor consciously the discordance between the different signals generated by their own movements, and falsely attributed the drawing of the line to their hand. In other words, they tended to adhere to the visible aspect of their performance, and to ignore the way it had been achieved (see Fig. 3.1).

Here, we are faced with an example of perceptual awareness without motor awareness. Subjects were aware of the goal and were able to reach for it: yet they ignored how this had been possible. This fits the Johnson and Haggard (2005) claim that perceptual and motor phenomena belong to different categories, and are processed separately. As for perceptual awareness, however, the access to motor awareness may be a matter of threshold. According to the above Time-On Theory, changes in certain critical factors beyond a certain level may make the agent aware of the strategy he uses to reach his goal. In the above experiment, the deviation of the line was limited to 10°, a deviation that apparently remained compatible with the possibility of an automatic correction, i.e. outside the subject's awareness. What would happen if the deviation were increased beyond the limit of 10°? Slachewsky *et al.* (2001), using the same apparatus as Fourneret and Jeannerod, introduced deviations of increasing amplitude up to 40°. They found that, as movement accuracy progressively deteriorated, the larger discordance between what subjects did and what they saw made them become aware of the deviation at an average value of 14°. Beyond this point, they were able to report that the movement of their hand erred in a direction different from that seen on the screen and that, in order to

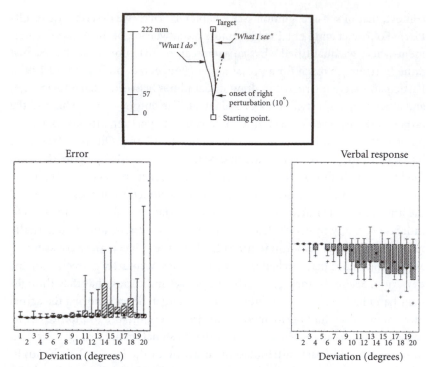

Fig. 3.1 A transition between automatic and conscious modes of action monitoring. Top box: subject's view of the experimental display. The subject holds a stylus with his unseen hand below a mirror. The mirror reflects the image of a computer screen where the displacements of the stylus are monitored. The subject is instructed to move the stylus on a graphic tablet, from a starting point to a target at 22 cm in front of him. On some trials, the visible trajectory of the stylus is electronically deviated by a certain angle (10° in the example shown). In order to fulfill the instruction of reaching the target ('What I see'), the subject has to deviate the stylus in the direction opposite to the deviation and by the same angle ('What I do'). Lower boxes: performance of a group of normal subjects in an experiment where the visible stylus trajectory was deviated by 1–20° according to trials. For each trial, the error with respect to the target was measured (error, lower left) and the subjects were asked to estimate the direction in which they thought they had moved their hand to reach the target (verbal response, lower right). Both results are in arbitrary units. Note that, up to around 10°, the deviation of the stylus is fully corrected, whereas the subjects remain unaware of moving their hand in a direction different from the straight ahead direction. Beyond 10°, however, note a brisk change in strategy. The subjects become aware of having to deviate their hand to reach the target, whereas their motor performance deteriorates. For further details see text. Rearranged from Fourneret and Jeannerod (1998) and Fourneret *et al.* (2002).

fulfill the instruction of reaching the target, they had to orient their hand movement deliberately in a direction different from that of the target.

Thus, the awareness of a discordance between an action and its sensory consequences emerges when the magnitude of the discordance exceeds a certain amount. This point was recently confirmed by Knoblich and Kircher (2004). In this experiment, the participants had to draw circles on a writing pad. As in the above experiments, they did not see their hand, but they saw an image of their movement, represented by a moving dot on a computer screen. The velocity of the moving dot was either the same as that of the subject's movement or it could be unexpectedly accelerated by a variable factor of up to 80 per cent. In order to compensate for the change in velocity and to keep the dot moving in a circle, as requested by the instructor, subjects had to decrease the velocity of their hand movement by a corresponding amount. They had to indicate any perceived change in velocity of the moving dot. Although they failed to detect the changes in velocity when they were of a small amplitude, their detection rate increased for faster velocity changes. Yet, subjects were found to be able to compensate for all changes in velocity, including for those that they did not consciously detect. Knoblich and Kircher conclude that 'Many movements are carried out unconsciously, and these movements also affect the sensitivity for detection of changes in visuomotor coupling. In a sense, the unconscious adjustment of movements conceals certain influences affecting action. It could therefore be said that the conscious system is deceived about the amount of control it exerts' (2004, p. 665). This conclusion also applies to the results obtained with deviated lines. Subjects compensated for deviations of which they were unaware, and their access to consciousness coincided with larger deviations. In other words, the visuomotor discordance became perceptible to them when the automatic compensation became impossible.

3.1.3 Factors that determine conscious access to actions

The results reported in the previous section indicate that a normal subject, even when involved in a conscious task such as reaching for a difficult target or tracing lines in an unusual condition, tends to ignore in which direction and at which velocity he actually moves. Yet, these aspects of his action may become consciously accessible if and when the discordance between the different signals generated by his movement or, more generally, between the aim of his movement and its outcome, exceeds a certain value.

Let us take a few examples to illustrate this point. Consider first the situation where you are engaged in the complex action of getting a cup of tea. You go through all the constituent actions in the proper sequence: you walk to the room while talking to a colleague, get to the place where the teapot is on the table, reach over it with your right arm and grasp it. Suppose the teapot handle is too hot: at the time of contact with your hand, you stop the grasping movement and withdraw your hand. Although the sequence was unfolding automatically, it is now interrupted because of the failure of one of its constituents. In the meantime, you become aware of the cause of the failure, of the fact that you were indeed in the process of getting a cup of tea, and that you will have to start another sequence to overcome the problem of the hot handle.

Another possible situation is that where you have mild tennis elbow at your right arm. You experience no pain when your arm is immobile with the elbow flexed in a relaxed position. While looking at your computer screen, you reach for your cup of tea on the right side of the computer. Pain arises during the completion of the movement. You suddenly become aware of the fact that you were reaching for the cup and that you cannot do it because it would be too painful. You use your left arm to take the cup and drink, and transfer the cup to the left of the computer to avoid repetition of the same painful experience.

Finally, consider a third situation. It is borrowed from the neuroscientist Alf Brodal who described his own experience following a stroke which had affected the movements of his left arm. He reported in a paper (Brodal 1973) the difficulty he experienced in carrying out skilled actions such as tying his bow tie. Whereas before the stroke, he says in this paper, the action was executed rapidly and automatically, after the stroke he felt as if his fingers did not know the next move. What was apparently defective in the action of tying, Brodal continues, was not the triggering off of the act. There appeared to be a lack of capacity to let the movements proceed automatically when the pattern was triggered because they could not be performed at the usual speed.

What is common to these three situations is that a goal-directed movement, a constituent of a broader intentional action, cannot reach its goal because of an intervening or unexpected event: an obstacle to completion of the movement in the first situation, an abnormal sensation in the second one and an incomplete paralysis in the third one. In all three cases, the action was unfolding automatically and outside the subject's awareness. The failure triggered a *prise de conscience* of the ongoing action, and a reconsideration of the strategy to obtain the final goal (or, in the case of paralysis, a detailed introspective analysis of the sensations arising from the attempt to move). The impression one gets from these observations is that the agent, who suddenly becomes aware of an action that he was doing automatically immediately before, has shifted to a different state of consciousness, as if the intervening event had acted as a 'stimulus' and triggered consciousness of the action as a 'response' to that stimulus.

Let us develop this tentative explanation. Situations where an action is delayed, incompletely executed or blocked typically create a mismatch between the desired motor output and its observed result. This mismatch would represent the stimulus which triggers the conscious experience. In fact, we now begin to understand how this mechanism operates. The recording of brain activity using neuroimaging techniques shows the activation of a relatively limited cortical area in the posterior and ventral parietal cortex on the right side when a mismatch is created between an action and its sensory consequences (Fink *et al.* 1999). The activity of this area increases as a function of the degree of the mismatch. Conversely, the activity of another area, in the posterior insula, decreases as a function of the degree of mismatch (Farrer *et al.* 2003). It is thus likely that the changes in activity of these areas reflected the incongruence between normally congruent signals from central or sensory origin generated during these movements: the central command signals generated for moving the hand in a certain direction were contradicted by the visual signals showing a movement in a different direction. The role of the right parietal lobe in monitoring action-related signals is supported by clinical observations. Patients with a lesion in this region show striking neuropsychological symptoms that testify to an alteration of self-consciousness and consciousness of action: neglect of contralateral space, neglect of the corresponding half of the body, denial of ownership or even denial of the frequently associated hemiplegia (anosognosia) (e.g. Daprati *et al.* 2000). These observations about the involvement of the right parietal lobe in consciousness of actions will be re-examined in the next chapter in the context of self-attributing one's own actions.

Our next task will be to examine in greater detail the mechanism that leads to the conscious experience of how a movement is performed to reach its goal. We will try to determine what are the respective contributions of the sensory (afferent) and the central (efferent) signals that are generated by the execution of a movement.

3.1.4 Is consciousness of action an afferent or an efferent phenomenon?

Several sources of information are potentially available to make a conscious judgement about one's own motor performance. Among the sensory sources are the visual and the kinesthetic signals. Visual signals are directly derived from vision of the moving limb, or indirectly from the effects of the movement on external objects; kinesthetic signals are derived from movement-related mechanical deformations of the limb, through receptors located in the skin, joints and muscles. Non-sensory sources are mainly represented by central signals originating from various levels of the action generation system. These different types of signals do not have the same status. Visual cues are of an uncertain origin: they cannot differentiate a self-generated from an externally generated visual change. In contrast, the central cues and, to some extent, the kinesthetic cues clearly relate to a self-generated movement: they are 'first-person' cues in the sense that they can only conceivably arise from the self.

There is a longstanding controversy about the respective roles of the two main first-person cues in conscious knowledge about one's actions. This issue was the topic of the classical 'Two Williams Debate', where Wilhelm Wundt held that our knowledge is based on *a priori* efferent information of a central origin, whereas William James defended the opposite opinion that all that we know about our movements is based on *a posteriori* information from sensory organs (see Jeannerod 1983 for historical references). Experimenters have consistently failed to resolve this issue, mainly because of the methodological difficulty of isolating the two sources of information from one another. There are no reliable methods for suppressing kinesthetic information arising during the execution of a movement. Alternatively, it is possible to prevent muscular contractions in a subject who is attempting to move, e.g. by using a curarizing agent (i.e. an agent that blocks neuromuscular transmission) to paralyze one limb: if the subject reports sensations from his attempts to move his paralyzed limb, these sensations should result from outflow motor commands, not from proprioceptive inflow. The available evidence shows that no perception of movement arises in this condition. However, experiments where an arm is only partially curarized (the arm is not paralyzed, but muscular force is weakened) suggest a more balanced conclusion: subjects requested to estimate the heaviness of weights that they attempt to lift with their weakened arm report an increased perceived heaviness (McCloskey *et al.* 1974). This illusion was interpreted as reflecting the increase in motor outflow needed to lift the weights (Gandevia and McCloskey 1977). This result provides indirect evidence as to the possibility for central signals to influence conscious experience.

A more direct solution to this problem is to examine patients with a pathological loss of haptic sensations, e.g. following a sensory neuropathy. One such patient, patient G.L., has been extensively studied by several experimenters (Cole and Paillard 1995). Patient G.L. has no haptic information about the movements she performs. Thus, provided visual feedback from her movements is suppressed, the only information on which she can rely to form an experience about her own action must be derived from central signals during the action generation processes. This point was examined by using the apparatus already described for the Fourneret and Jeannerod (1998) experiment and explained in Figure 3.1. G.L. had to draw a line with her unseen hand while the line was made to deviate to the right by an angle increasing from 1 to 20° over successive trials. Like a normal subject, G.L. performed the task without difficulty: she was able to compensate for the deviation and to reach the target. When asked, at the end of each trial, to estimate verbally the angle by which she thought her hand had deviated to the left to bring the line to the target, G.L. never explicitly reported a feeling of discordance between what she had seen and the movement that she thought she had made. Remember that, in this task, normal subjects become clearly aware (albeit by underestimating it) of a displacement of their hand towards the left to compensate for the disturbance when the discordance exceeded a certain value. Instead, G.L. consistently gave responses indicating that she thought she had drawn the line in the direction of the target. In spite of expressing perplexity at the end of some trials, G.L. never became aware of the discordance and, consequently, of any strategy of correction she had to apply to correct for the deviation. When asked to describe her feelings, she only mentioned that she found the task 'difficult' and that it required an 'effort of concentration'. Conversely, control subjects examined in this task were able to report their conscious strategy (Fourneret *et al.* 2002).

Another experiment with the same patient also addressed the question of a possible role for the efferent processes in motor consciousness, by exploring the production and the perception of muscular force. When muscular force is applied isometrically (with no change in muscle length), kinesthetic input is limited, because there is no displacement of the limb: thus, this condition should maximize the role of the central commands in the conscious appreciation of the exerted force. When instructed first to apply isometrically a certain degree of force with one hand, and then to match this degree of force with the other hand, G.L. performed with a close to normal accuracy (Lafargue *et al.* 2003): this result indicates that she was able to produce accurate central commands. Yet, she was unable to report any conscious feeling from her effort, neither did she experience fatigue when a high degree of muscular contraction had to be maintained.

The central, non-sensory cues which are still available in patient G.L. appear to be of little use for consciously monitoring her own movements, except for the vague feelings of effort and difficulty that she reported in one of the tasks. However, a mere opposition between peripheral and central sources of information in providing cues for consciousness (which was the core of the Two Williams Debate) may be misleading because it does not take into account the complete set of events arising during the voluntary execution of a movement. In normal conditions, not only are the central signals used as a reference for the desired action, but also the reafferent sensory (e.g. kinesthetic) signals arising from the executed movement have to be matched with this reference.

In patient G.L., because no reafference resulted from her executed movement, this matching process could not take place. Here we propose that the conscious information about one's movements is normally derived, not directly from the reafferent signals themselves, but from the output of the matching process, for which the presence of both central and peripheral reafferent signals is required. In the case of G.L., it was the lack of kinesthetic input from movement execution or isometric force generation which severely impaired the possibility to monitor the efferent signals consciously.[1]

The same explanation holds for the lack of conscious feelings during attempted movements in completely paralyzed subjects (produced by curarization, for example). In spite of the generation of intense motor commands for fighting against the paralysis, the absence of corresponding kinesthetic reafferent signals prevents the matching process from taking place. Conversely, when reafferent signals are present, but do not match the central signals, the matching process generates signals proportional to the degree of mismatch between the two. This would account for the conscious sensations of effort reported by subjects with an incomplete paralysis, where kinesthetic signals are still preserved (Brodal 1973), and in normal subjects during lifting weights with incompletely paralyzed arms. Finally, this could also account for the appearance of consciousness in situations where a movement cannot reach its goal. When an automatic movement is blocked or delayed by an external cause during its normal course, the agent becomes aware of the intention that was being fulfilled, but that he/she ignored prior to the block or the delay.

The picture of consciousness that arises when it is studied in its relationship to action is that of a *post hoc* phenomenon. First, consciousness of action (and probably other forms of consciousness as well) is a lengthy process, which can only appear if adequate time constraints are fulfilled. Secondly, consciousness of action is bound to *a posteriori* signals arising from the completion of the action itself, not to central signals that arise prior to the action. As we will emphasize at the end of this chapter, consciousness should not play a causal role, either in planning an action or in organizing its execution, simply because it comes too late.

3.2 Consciousness of intentions

The first part of the chapter was about whether we consciously monitor our own actions and how we eventually become aware of them. The response to

---

[1] This is not to say that outflow signals are not used for other purposes. The sense of agency, which is critical for self-attributing one's own actions (see Chapter 4), largely relies on outflow signals.

these questions was rather unambiguous: we remain unaware of most of our actions, unless an unpredicted event interrupts their course and brings them to consciousness.

In the second part of the chapter, we deal with another, distinct though connected, aspect of consciousness related to action, namely consciousness of intentions. This aspect is important for at least two reasons. First, as we already discussed in Chapter 1, intentions are part of the representations of actions, they contribute to the stream of processing which goes from the early part of the representation to the action execution, when it occurs. Determining experimentally whether intention stands as an individuated step in this processing or, on the contrary, cannot be distinguished from the rest of the representation/execution continuum may thus provide important insight into the functioning of motor cognition. The second reason is more speculative: the concept of a conscious intention seems to relate, at least implicitly, to the highly debated issue of whether our actions are caused by our own conscious choices, deliberations and free will. We will provide a tentative answer to this question.

3.2.1 Are we aware of our own motor intentions?

First, remember the distinction we made in Chapter 1 about motor intentions (Searle's intentions in action) and prior intentions. The latter have a conceptual content, the former do not. Motor intentions are closely linked to action execution; they are part of an automatic process which, by definition, should not be open to conscious choice or deliberation. It has been shown to be possible, however, to concentrate on one's intention during the process of executing a movement, and to make objective measurements of this phenomenon. However, before we go through the real experiments where subjects' awareness was effectively measured, there is no better way to illustrate our hesitation about the meaning of these responses than to quote an introspective description of the phenomenon of 'intention' made by the novelist Ian McEwan:

> 'She raised one hand and flexed its fingers and wondered, as she had sometimes before, how this thing, this machine for gripping, this fleshy spider at the end of her arm, came to be hers, entirely at her command. Or did it have some little life of its own? She bent her finger and straightened it. The mystery was in the instant before it moved, the dividing moment between not moving and moving, when her intention took effect. It was like a wave breaking. If she could only find herself at the crest, she thought, she might find the secret of herself, the part of her that was really in charge. She brought her forefinger closer to her face and stared at it, urging it to move. It remained still because she was pretending, she was not entirely serious, and because willing it to move, or being about to move it was not the same as actually moving it. And when she did crook it finally, the action seemed to start in the finger itself, not in some part of her mind. When did it know to move, when did she know to move it?

There was no catching herself out. It was either–or. There was no stitching, no seam, and yet she knew that behind the smooth continuous fabric was the real self—was it her soul?—which took the decision to cease pretending, and gave the final command' (McEwan, *Atonment*, 2001, pp. 35–36).[2]

Arguably, actions such as aimlessly moving one's finger are of little relevance in everyday life. Those are actions with no real goal and little impact on the external world: yet, they may represent a starting point for experimental studies. It is by using this type of actions that several authors have attempted to make subjects aware of the transition between intending and doing, of 'the dividing moment between moving and not moving'.[3] These authors used a situation where the subjects were instructed, while they voluntarily moved one finger, to concentrate on their 'urge to move' and to give an indication about when this occurred. Benjamin Libet made the first successful attempt. He instructed subjects to perform simple hand movements *ad libitum* and to report the instant (W) at which they became aware of wanting to move. In order to do so, subjects reported verbally the clock position of a spot revolving on a screen. EMG recordings were made from arm muscles to measure the precise onset of the movement: the W judgement was found to precede EMG onset by 206 ms. In addition, electroencephalographic (EEG) potentials were recorded from the subject's skull. The *readiness potential*, a DC potential that appears during preparation for voluntary action,[4] was found to anticipate W by about 345 ms. This striking result (Libet *et al.* 1983) shows that the intention (in the sense of 'wanting to move' or 'feeling the urge to move') can be perceived as distinct from execution itself; it also shows that the subject's

---

[2] I am pleased to thank Patrick Haggard for drawing my attention to McEwan's novel.

[3] The term intention used here is in fact a confound for several different aspects of the process of executing a movement, which may or may not be distinct from one another. In the experiment where a subject has to extend his/her right index finger at the moment of his/her choice, and is instructed to report the point in time at which he/she became aware of willing to carry out the movement, what will the response be about? Will it be about the awareness of having 'decided to move' or about the awareness of having released the action from the prior state of 'having decided to move, but not immediately'?

[4] The Readines Potential (RP) was first described by Kornhuber and Deecke as a negative potential recorded at the vertex of the skull during the preparation of a voluntary movement (*Bereitschaftspotential*, Kornhuber and Deecke 1965). It was shown later that there are two components in the readiness potential: the potential recorded at the central midline is influenced by the complexity of the motor task, irrespective of the hand used during the task, whereas a later component, recorded on lateral parts of motor cortex, is influenced by the performing hand. It is thought that the the midline potential arises from the SMA, whereas the lateralized component arises from motor cortex itself (Lang *et al.* 1989).

declarative awareness of this phenomenon does not correspond to the actual onset of movement preparation, which starts much earlier. The conclusion drawn by Libet from this latter result will be examined later.

Libet's findings have now been replicated several times (Keller and Heckenhausen 1990; Haggard and Eimer 1999; Sirigu et al. 2004). Haggard and Eimer (1999) took advantage of the variability between subjects' responses concerning the instant W. They found that the instant W reported by the subjects correlated with the onset of the lateralized component of the readiness potential (LRP), not with the onset of the readiness potential itself. This suggests that there is a tight relationship (if not a causal one) between the LRP and the subjective report. Patrick Haggard and his colleagues made a further observation which indirectly confirms the validity of such subjective estimates in determining the time course of covert events related to the generation of one's actions. Haggard et al. (2002) instructed subjects to make a simple voluntary movement (a key press) at a time of their choice. The action of pressing the key caused an auditory signal to appear after a fixed delay of 250 ms. In separate sessions, the subjects were asked to report the position of a clock hand, either at the time they thought they had pressed the key or at the time where they heard the auditory signal. Haggard et al. found that the time interval between the two estimated events was shorter than what it should be, i.e. shorter than 250 ms. Subjects tended to perceive their key press occurring later, and the auditory signal occurring earlier, than was actually the case. This shrinkage of perceived time between the two events did not happen in a control situation where the finger movement was not voluntary but was caused by a magnetically induced stimulation of motor cortex. The authors conclude that intentional action binds together the conscious representation of the action and its sensory consequences (see also Tsakiris and Haggard 2003). Although this experiments does not directly demonstrate awareness of the intention to do the key pressing, it shows that the intentional action modifies the conscious awareness of external events surrounding that action (see Fig. 3.2).

The Libet's paradigm not only reveals the possibility of attending to one's own mental states preceding action, it also provides important information on the brain areas involved in this conscious process. A specific region of dorsal premotor cortex (the region corresponding to the supplementary motor area, SMA) was consistently found to be activated in conjunction with the feeling of an urge to move. First, the readiness potential which in the experiments by Libet and his colleagues and by their followers precedes the subject's report of the feeling (the W judgement) is thought to originate from the SMA. Secondly, electrical stimulation of a small area immediately anterior to the SMA (the pre-SMA) induces a feeling of an urge to move, as reported by patients during

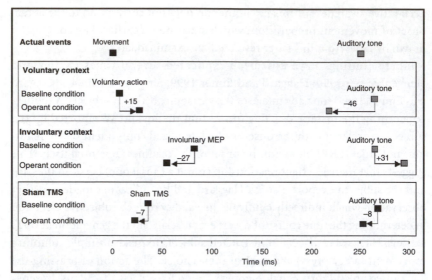

Fig. 3.2 Perceptual shift of time interval between a voluntary movement and an external event. Each time the subject makes a voluntary finger movement, an auditory tone occurs after a fixed time interval of 250 ms. In separate sessions, the subject is instructed to determine either the time at which he made his voluntary movement, or the time at which he heard the tone (upper box). Put together, the results show that the time of movement execution is estimated later than the real execution, and the time of the tone occurrence is perceived earlier than its actual occurrence, so that the perceived time interval between the two events is reduced by >60 ms. This shrinkage of perceived time is not observed when the movement is artificially produced by a transcranial magnetic stimulus (TMS) applied to the motor cortex (middle box). This effect reflects the tendency to over-attribute external events to oneself when they are consequences of self-produced actions. From Haggard *et al.* (2002), with kind permission of the first author.

direct low intensity electrical stimulation applied to this area during neurosurgical operations. The pre-SMA and the SMA are relatively closely connected to motor cortex: indeed, increasing the intensity of the stimulus produces muscular contractions in the body part where the feeling was resented (Fried *et al.* 1991). Finally, a recent fMRI study of normal subjects attending to their intentions showed that the W judgement made by these subjects was associated with activation of the pre-SMA and of the dorsolateral prefrontal cortex (Lau *et al.* 2004b). The dorsolateral cortex, as will be emphasized below, is known to be involved in willed actions.

3.2.2 The issue of volition and conscious will

In the previous section, we saw that 'simple' intentions, such the intention to move one's finger, can be consciously perceived in certain conditions. In this section, we deal with another type of intentions, those which are formed consciously. These intentions, which correspond to Searle's prior intentions, are about actions more complex than simple aimless movements of one's finger. They involve sequences of elementary actions with intermediate goals, aimed at achieving a final goal. The reason why these intentions are discussed here is that they are a constituent of the common feelings of intending, wanting, wishing, choosing or, in other words, of the feeling of conscious will. The term 'conscious will' as well as the closely related word 'volition' are not easy to define. Consulting a computerized dictionary (which analyzes the sense of English words into clusters of contexonyms, i.e. words which lie within the same semantic field; Ji *et al.* 2003) reveals that the semantic field of 'will' can be divided into several clusters. A large cluster refers to the 'force of will' (e.g. 'willpower', 'strength of will', 'mind'). A smaller cluster, which includes 'volition', overlaps with 'pleasure'. The semantic field of the word 'volition' itself includes words such as 'discretion', 'option', 'choice' or 'preference'. It also includes 'will' and 'free will'. Thus, it appears that volition and will are associated with the notion of willing or considering doing something in relation to a deliberate and free choice, but are clearly dissociated from the transfer of this choice into an intention or an executive force. Finally, the semantic field of the word 'intention', which is directly related to the anticipation of an action, includes neither 'volition' nor 'will'.

In classical philosophy, the concept of will is associated with the subjective impression of causing an action to appear. David Hume wrote that 'by the will, I mean nothing but the internal impression we feel and are conscious of, when we knowingly give rise to any new motion of our body, or new perception of our mind.' Similarly, Thomas Reid, in his *Essays on the active power of the human mind* (1788), wrote that 'every man is conscious of a power to determine, in things which he conceives to depend upon his determination. To this power, we give the name of will.' (See full references in Berrios and Gili 1995.) In psychology, the view of the will as an independent mental function, which was quite popular during the nineteenth century, came under attack from behaviorism. It is now regaining interest in psychiatry and neuropsychology, as will be emphasized in the final section of this chapter, on disorders of volition (see page 67).

The issue I want to raise here is that of the relationship between the conscious sense of willing to act and the forthcoming action. As we saw earlier, the representation of an action cannot be considered the cause of that action: the representation and the execution of an action are part of a continuum, such that the representation can eventually become an executed action. This is what is meant by Libet in a rather provocative interpretation of his results. His results, he says, 'lead to the conclusion that cerebral initiation . . . of a spontaneous voluntary act . . . can and usually does begin *unconsciously*'. 'The brain "decides" to initiate or, at least, to prepare to initiate the act before there is any reportable subjective awareness that such a decision has taken place' (Libet 1985, p. 536). Let us assume that what is true for 'simple' intentions such as those studied by Libet is also true for complex intentions. Whatever the interpretation about 'who' decides, the fact that consciousness follows, and does not precede, the process of action generation is hardly compatible with the notion of a causal role for the conscious sense of will. We are therefore faced with a paradox: whereas we feel and we strongly believe that our thoughts determine our behavior, we realize that conscious free choice and conscious will are consequences, not causes, of the brain activity that itself causes the actions to appear or the choices to be made. The fact that brain activity is ahead of our mental states, and not the reverse, is not a surprise. The surprising thing, however, is the discordance between this very fact and our subjective experience.

At this point, the problem of the consciousness of our own intentions clearly merges with that of self-consciousness. The ability to identify oneself as the agent of a behavior or a thought—the sense of agency—is the way by which the self builds up as an entity independent from the external world and from other agents. Without anticipating further discussions on this point of self-identification, however, we have to realize that there are several modalities of expression for the self. A first modality seems to correspond to what Shaun Gallagher calls the 'minimal' self, i.e. 'a consciousness of oneself as an immediate subject of experience, unextended in time. The minimal self almost certainly depends on brain processes and an ecologically embedded body . . .' (Gallagher 2000, p. 15). Thus, the minimal self is an embodied self. As an embodied self, I am the owner of a body and the author of actions. The type of consciousness (or non-consciousness) of actions and intentions that is linked to the experience of the embodied self is discontinuous: it operates on a moment-to-moment basis, it is bound to particular bodily events. As we saw for automatic actions and for intentions in action, the embodied self mostly carries an implicit mode of consciousness, where consciousness becomes manifest only when required by the situation. The related information has a short life span and usually does not survive the bodily event for very long. In other words, as far we are concerned here, the embodied self is an acting self in relation to the behaving body.

The other modality of the expression of the self is the 'narrative self' (Gallagher 2000). As a narrator, we obviously know who we are, where we are, what we are presently doing and what we were doing before. Unless we become demented, we have a strong feeling of continuity in our conscious experience. We rely on declarative memory systems where souvenirs (albeit distorted) can be retrieved, and can be used as material for describing the sequence of our prior intentions and actions. The concept of self-consciousness as understood here requires the ability to experience oneself consciously as an acting being, which enables one to attribute to oneself one's own actions.

Obviously, the two modalities of the self do not carry the same information about our intentions and actions. The embodied self, by avoiding conscious introspection, reaches simple and relatively straightforward conclusions about who is the agent of an action by monitoring on-line the degree of congruence between central and peripheral signals generated by the action. In contrast, the conscious sense of will arises from the belief that our thoughts have a causal influence on our behavior. While we tend to perceive ourselves as causal, we actually ignore the cause from which our actions originate. Because the conscious thought and the observed action are consistently associated, even though they may not be causally related, the narrative self tends to build a cause-and-effect story. Therefore, conscious free choice, like conscious will, may not be a direct perception of a causal relationship between a thought and an action, but rather a feeling based on the causal inference one makes about the data that do become available to consciousness. In conclusion, according to Wolfgang Prinz, 'There appears to be no support for the folk psychology notion that the act follows the will, in the sense that physical action is caused by mental events that precede them and to which we have privileged access'. 'Experimental evidence suggests that two different pathways [. . .] may be involved in action—one for the generation of physical action and one for the mental awareness of its causal antecedents. If anything, the second follows the first, and not vice-versa [. . .]' (Prinz 2003, p. 26; see also Wegner 2002).

The role of consciousness should rather be to ensure the continuity of subjective experience across actions which are—by necessity—executed automatically. Because it reads behavior rather than starting it, consciousness represents a background mechanism for the cognitive rearrangement after the action is completed, e.g. for justifying its results, or modifying the factors that have been at the origin of an action which turned out to be unsuccessful, as in learning a new skill, for example. This mechanism could have the role of establishing a declarative cognitive statement about one's own preferences, beliefs or desires. However, the fact is that what we know about our mental content does not match its actual functioning, that which determines the causal relationships of our behavior. When asked questions about these causal relationships, we tend 'to tell more than we can know' (to paraphrase Nisbett and Wilson 1977) and to build explanations based on incomplete information.

This tendency unavoidably creates a dissociation between what we believe we do and what we actually do.

Take naive physics, for example: our conceptual knowledge of physical laws does not match the way we automatically adapt our motor behavior. When catching a falling ball, we can accurately intercept its trajectory, which implies that our motor system takes into account the fact that the ball is progressively accelerated by gravity. Yet, if asked to make a judgement about when the hand should start to move to intercept the falling ball, we will make systematic errors, as if our cognitive system 'believed' that a ball falls at a constant speed. Zago and Lacquaniti (2005) explain this striking dissociation by the fact that the cognitive system mostly relies on vision, whereas the motor system also relies on touch and proprioception. Because, they conclude, 'vision sees massless objects, but the hand feels gravitational and inertial mass', 'motor competence of gravity might then result cognitively impenetrable' (2005, p. 186). This is yet another example of the broader distinction we made earlier between a semantic and a pragmatic mode of processing of external events. The semantic processing yields representations with a conceptual and declarative content; the pragmatic processing yields representations with an automatic functioning. Though connected, the two types of representation carry different types of information and fulfill different purposes (see Gallagher and Jeannerod 2002).

3.2.3 **Neuroimagery of free will**

Neurophysiological studies of the brain correlates of will have focused on the role of prefrontal cortex. We have already mentioned its role in carrying out intentions and motor plans, conscious or not, and in inhibiting concurrent activity. Christopher Frith and his colleagues went further in monitoring brain activity in normal subjects during what they consider as the hallmark of free will, i.e. tasks involving a voluntary choice between two different actions. In one condition, the subjects were instructed to move, using their own choice, either their right index finger or their right thumb. In the other condition, they had to utter a word, e.g. beginning with *s*. Brain activity measured with PET was found to be specifically increased in an area corresponding to the lateral prefrontal cortex corresponding to Brodmann area 46: in the condition of finger movement, the activation was bilateral; in the condition of word choice, it was limited to the left side (Frith *et al.* 1991). Note that this same area is involved irrespective of the modality of the intention, i.e. when the task consists of choosing which of two fingers will be moved or which word will be uttered, or even which of two phonemes (e.g. *la* or *ba*) will be pronounced (Spence and Frith 1999; see also Lau *et al.* 2004).

The primacy of lateral prefrontal cortex with respect to other areas involved in an action, such as primary motor cortex for example, appears best in a study measuring brain activity in subjects who were free to choose not only which finger to move but also when to initiate the move. Hunter *et al.* (2003), using event-related fMRI, confirmed that initiation of a willed action was associated with an activation of the prefrontal cortex on both sides, predominating in the middle prefrontal gyri (Brodmann area 10, just anterior to and partly overlapping with area 46). In addition, however, they added new evidence by measuring the temporal response dynamics of several areas in the frontal lobe in the free decision task. They found that the lateral prefrontal cortex was activated first, followed by the SMA and finally by primary motor cortex. As stated by the authors, this earlier activation of lateral prefrontal cortex can only be interpreted parsimoniously to suggest a hypothesis regarding causality of willed action in this part of the executive system.

3.2.4 Disorders of volition

A short section on disorders of volition may be useful here, as it may shed light on the debate about the role of conscious will in behavior. Considering the definition of volition given in the previous section, the expression 'disorders of volition' should refer to those pathological conditions where the ability to make choices, to express preferences or possibly to experience pleasure and freedom in making these choices or expressing these preferences are affected. Théodule Ribot, in his book on the diseases of the will, considered two opposite sides, the negative and the positive, of the alterations of the will (Ribot 1883).

Several terms have been used to describe such pathological conditions. On the negative side, *aboulia*, a pure disease of the will according to Ribot, has been defined as an impairment to execute what is in mind. In this condition, there is no paralysis, no disorder of the muscular system, there is no lack of desire, but the transition from desire to execution becomes abnormally difficult. An extreme example of aboulia has been described clinically under the term *athymhormia*: such patients show loss of drive and of a search for satisfaction, lack of curiosity, lack of taste and preferences, and flattened affect. This condition, clearly distinct from depression, can be observed in schizophrenia and may also be caused by lesions in the basal ganglia (Habib and Poncet 1988). Another example is the 'chronic fatigue syndrome' (CFS), defined by persistent or relapsing unexplained fatigue. CFS patients were tested in motor imagery tasks while their brain activity was monitored with fMRI. Patients were found behaviorally to be slower than controls. In addition, an area in their anterior cingulate cortex, known to be involved in error monitoring (Carter *et al.* 1998), remained inactive when they made errors.

These results support the notion that CFS may be associated with defective motor planning (de Lange *et al.* 2004).

On the positive side are found conditions where the deficient will cannot block impulses to act: the power to control and to inhibit, which Ribot considered as the highest level of the will, is impaired. An anecdotal illustration of the lack of inhibition of responses to stimuli is that of the 'jumping Frenchmen of Maine'. First described by G.M. Beard in 1880 in a small population in the American state of Maine, this familial disorder begins in childhood, persists throughout life and is characterized by violent jumps in response to sudden noise. In addition, some of these people present echolalia and respond automatically to a loud command by repeating the command and executing the order even though it might be dangerous or humiliating. One such case (by no means a Frenchman) was described in Siberia by Dr W. Hammond in 1884, in a steward working on a river boat. This man 'was afflicted with a peculiar mental or nervous disease, which forced him to imitate everything, suddenly presented to his senses. Thus, when the captain slapped the paddle-box suddenly, he seemed compelled against his will to imitate it instantly, and with remarkable accuracy. To annoy him, some of the passengers imitated pigs grunting, or called out absurd names [. . .] and the poor steward, suddenly startled, would echo them all precisely . . .' (reported in Stevens 1965).

At a different level, a well known example is that of some patients with frontal lobe lesions, who exhibit typical impairments demonstrating their inability to monitor their performance consciously and to over-ride their automatic responses. These patients tend compulsively to imitate gestures or even complex actions performed in front of them by another agent; when presented with common graspable objects, they cannot refrain from using them. This striking behavior, termed *imitation* or *utilization behavior* (Lhermitte 1983, 1986; Shallice *et al.* 1989), may be explained by an impairment of the normal suppression, by the prefrontal areas, of inappropriate actions triggered by external stimuli. Such patients can be said to have lost the ability to transfer their intentions into meaningful actions: as a consequence of this impairment, their behavior is dependent on external events. One such patient exemplified this typical behavior by putting pairs of spectacles on his nose each time he was presented with a new pair, ending with several pairs on top of each other!

As we will fully discuss in another chapter dealing with imitation (Chapter 5), the imitation behavior observed following frontal lesions suggests that the mere observation of an action would evoke a tendency to execute that action: this imitative tendency, however, would normally be inhibited in everyday life situations. Compulsive imitation in frontal patients would result from an impairment of this inhibitory mechanism. Following this idea, Brass *et al.* (2001a) have studied brain activity in normal subjects who were instructed to execute a simple pre-defined finger movement (e.g. lift one finger) in response to the onset of an observed movement executed by an experimenter. When the observed movement was congruent with the movement the subject was instructed to perform, the response was given with a short latency; in contrast, when it was incongruent (e.g. the subject had to lift his finger in response to an observed tapping movement), the latency was increased. In addition, in incongruent trials, the lateral prefrontal cortex in the middle prefrontal gyri was strongly activated. It is therefore conceivable that a prefrontal lesion involving the lateral prefrontal cortex impairs the possibility to refrain from imitating other people. Lhermitte (1986) has used the term 'environmental dependency syndrome' to designate the tendency of these patients to stick to external events, to the detriment of their own free will.

Chapter 4

The sense of agency and the self–other distinction

How do we recognize ourselves as an agent and how do we distinguish ourselves from other agents? In this chapter, we examine theoretical and experimental evidence for a set of mechanisms by which we attribute our own body and our own actions to ourselves. These mechanisms are important to consider, for the reason that the ability to recognize oneself as the owner of a body, i.e. the sense of ownership, and the agent of a behavior, i.e. the sense of agency, is the way by which the self builds up as an entity independent from the external world and from other selves (see Gallagher 2000). One of the main conclusions of this chapter will be that our body is a behaving body and that self-identification primarily relies on the recognition of one's own actions. Thus, the distinction between self-generated actions and actions produced by other agents, and the corresponding ability to attribute an action to its proper agent will appear to be key functions for the self–other distinction.

The identification of oneself as the origin of an action may seem a relatively simple task when movements are overtly executed. In this condition, sensory signals arise from the moving limbs and from the effects of the movement on the external world: these signals can be compared with those resulting from the action generation mechanism, and the outcome of this comparison can be used to label the action as self-generated. What makes self-identification and the role of the sense of agency less easy to understand is the existence of a number of situations where the action generation mechanism is activated, but where the action remains covert. One of these situations is that of imagined actions (motor images) which we have already considered in Chapter 2. Yet, imagined actions, as well as other mental states involving covert actions, such as intending or thinking about an action, are clearly self-attributed in spite of the lack of overt execution, and the lack of the corresponding sensory signals. In addition, as we will discuss in Chapter 5, actions performed by the people that we observe are also encoded in representations closely similar to those where our own actions originate. Thus, our task as an agent is not only to recognize our own actions, it is also to disentangle our own actions from those of other agents. This is true not only for actions we and other agents execute, but also for those that remain at the representational stage (Jeannerod 2003a).

4.1 Sense of ownership and sense of agency in self-identification

In this section, we will describe the constituents of self-identification in adult subjects. Everybody can experience that recognizing one's own body (including one's own face) is not always simple (Kircher *et al.* 2001). Consider, for example, a situation such as seeing oneself in a mirror. If there is discontinuity between the body part we see and the rest of the body, the body part seen in the mirror can only be self-attributed if it is referred to a representation of our body as a whole, what Shaun Gallagher calls our 'body image'. The body image is a representation (sometimes conscious, sometimes not) of an owned body, one that belongs to the experiencing self (Gallagher 1995). Again, however, situations may arise where this recognition becomes less than obvious. In social interactions, several people may participate in the same action and interact rapidly with the same object. Consider the example of two surgeons operating jointly in the same surgical theater and seeing their respective hands through a magnifying lens. There are several moving hands visible in the scene, which may not appear to be directly connected to the corresponding body. Yet, these hands and the corresponding movements are correctly attributed to their authors. What is meant by this example is that attributing to oneself both the ownership of a body part and the authorship of a movement must be based on specific mechanisms, sufficiently accurate to allow unambiguous self-identification in everyday life. At the level of the self which is under consideration here, that of a minimal, embodied self, according to the terminology we used in the previous chapter, both the sense of ownership and the sense of agency concur with self-identification: it is as essential to identify oneself as the owner of one's body as it is to identify oneself as the agent of one's actions.

4.1.1 The cues for self-identification

Several potential sources of information contribute to self-identification. First, the synchrony of visual, tactile and proprioceptive signals originating from the same body parts powerfully contributes to a cross-modal sensory image of the body, i.e. a representation of the whole body to which body parts can be referred. Secondly, the congruence between one's intentions and the effects of the corresponding actions contributes to the sense of the self as an agent.

As stressed by many experimental results, vision has a prevalent role over other senses in this process: we feel our hand where we see it, not the converse. Optical distortion of the visually perceived position of a limb with respect to its felt position (e.g. by wearing laterally displacing prisms) produces no alteration of the sense of ownership: the position sense is actually recalibrated to conform with the visual information (Harris 1965). This prevalence of vision is further illustrated by experiments using a rubber hand. Botvinick and Cohen (1998) positioned a realistic rubber hand in front of subjects, while their real arm, hidden by a screen, was moved aside: tactile stimulation was applied simultaneously to the real and the rubber hands. After some time, the subjects experienced an illusion in which they felt the touch at the locus of the rubber hand (that they could see) not of their real (hidden) hand. In other words, the tactile stimulus was felt at the place where it was seen, at the expense of a distortion of the felt position of the real arm. In addition, subjects spontaneously reported experiencing a clear sense of ownership for the rubber hand. According to other authors who replicated this experiment, the illusion of displacement of the tactile stimulus and the illusion of owner-ship both disappear if the rubber hand is not properly aligned with the subject's body (Farné *et al.* 2000) or if the hand shown (e.g. a left hand) does not correspond to the subject's hand (Tsakiris and Haggard 2005).

There are other tricks for confusing the subject about who is the owner of the limb he sees. For instance, simply looking at a moving limb optically superimposed on one's own limb (by way of a mirror) creates a strong impres-sion of having willed the movement and of being its author. Observations have been reported in amputees who experience having a phantom limb. When their valid limb is optically transposed to the amputated side, and when they produce movements with that limb, they experience a strong feeling of voluntary movement of the phantom limb. The same happens if the visually transposed limb is that of an experimenter (Ramachandran and Rogers-Ramachandran 1996). As argued by Daniel Wegner, these observations reflect the tendency, that we have already mentioned, to perceive oneself as causal (Wegner 2002).

A special mention can be made here of the role of proprioception. Proprioception or, more generally, kinesthesia, the ensemble of sensory signals which accompany a movement, has been said to be the first-person cue par excellence. This suggests that kinesthetic cues might be sufficient by them-selves for signaling a self-produced movement and, by extension, for self-identification. Like other haptic (e.g. tactile) cues, kinesthetic cues generate 'private' information, in the sense that they originate from the body and cannot be attributed to anyone else. They have limitations, however: first, they may not originate from a self-produced movement if, for instance, my arm is moved by an external force; secondly, they are transient, and decay rapidly after the end of the movement; thirdly, as we pointed out earlier, they are absent from self-produced, but covert, actions. Also, we have examined in the previous chapter several situations where the information provided by kinesthetic cues was of a limited significance for recognizing one's actions. In the Fourneret and Jeannerod (1998) experiment, for example, the contribution of kinesthesia to the detection of the direction of the movements was neglected and dominated by the contribution of visual cues. Patient G.L., who lacked haptic cues, was unable to describe how she managed to reach for a target, but she never questioned the fact that the movements were hers. We concluded from this latter observation that haptic cues (among which are kinesthetic cues) are not sufficient by themselves to provide the sense of ownership. Kinesthesia can tell: 'this arm which moves is mine' (an ownership information), but cannot tell: 'I am the one who makes this arm move' (an agency information).

Body ownership is only part of the solution to self-identification. The self most of the time is an acting self. Body parts are moving with respect to one another and with respect to external objects, as the result of self-produced actions. One major factor of self-attribution of our own actions is the congruence between the expected effects of these actions and the flow of resulting (visual and kinesthetic) signals. This matching process provides the agent of an action with the sense that he is causing that action. As is illustrated by the famous mirror scene in the Marx Brothers' film, *Duck Soup*, an efficient means to determine whether the body or the body parts we see are ours is to move: if the image of a body I see in a mirror in front of me moves when I move and the two movements are congruent, then the image must be an image of my body. In the scene of the film, a mirror breaks, and Harpo imitates Groucho, move for move, to postpone the discovery of the broken mirror.

This congruence criterion for self-attributing body parts and actions begins to be used very early in life. Infants at 5 months of age are able to discriminate their own leg movements displayed in a mirror from those of another infant, presumably by making use of a perceived contingency between their own behavior and its effects (Bahrick and Watson 1985). As infants grow older, their behavior will increasingly testify to their development of a conscious self-representation. Infants at 15–20 months of age, for example, will typically resolve the task of wiping a red spot stuck on their face, when they see themselves in a mirror (for a review, see Bahrick 1995). In the following sections, we will examine experiments in adults where this notion of congruence was measured and manipulated.

4.1.2 **The Nielsen paradigm for studying the recognition of self-generated actions**

A set of pioneering experiments will be reported first, as they have set the stage for more recent investigations of the sense of agency. These experiments were undertaken in the 1960s by Torsten Nielsen working at the Psychological Laboratory of the University of Copenhagen. One of the phenomena Nielsen thought of great importance for self-awareness and self-identification was the volitional experience, i.e. the experience of volitional or intentional control of perceived events. Nielsen considered that an essential task for approaching this problem was to create situations in which the experiences of intentional control versus lack of control could be experimentally manipulated. To this aim, he created several varieties of a *substitution* paradigm, where the subjects received a false feedback from their own actions: in fact, what the subjects perceived was the effect of the actions of another person, which were substituted for their own.

In one of Nielsen's experiments (Nielsen, 1963), the experimental subject was facing a box placed on a table top. He placed his hand holding a pencil on the table below the box, and looked at it through the box. The box was equipped with a mirror which could be displaced by the experimenter between trials, without the subject knowing, so that the subject either saw his own hand or the hand of another person (the alien hand) through the mirror. The mirror was placed in such a way that the subject thought that he was looking directly at his own hand whereas in reality he was presented with the alien hand, lying at the same location on the table as his own. Finally, to ensure that the subject had no cues to identify the hand he saw, the two hands were made indistinguishable by wearing identical gloves. During the experiment itself, the subject was requested to draw a straight line in the sagittal direction on a piece of paper. In those trials where the subject saw the alien hand, the alien hand was also doing the same task at about the same rate. In some trials, however, the alien hand carried out a movement that diverged from that which the subject was carrying out at the same time. The latter condition generated a conflict between what the subject saw and what he kinesthetically felt from what he was doing. In order to solve this conflict, the subjects tended to deviate the trajectory of their own (unseen) hand in the direction opposite to that of the alien hand, so as to fulfill the instruction they had received to draw a straight line.

According to Nielsen, all the subjects in the conflict trials experienced that they saw their own hand moving involuntarily in the wrong direction. They remained unaware of having themselves performed a movement departing from the instruction, by erring in the direction opposite to that of the alien hand to compensate for the conflict produced by the movement they saw: when shown their own deviant performance, they tried to explain it by factors independent from their volition, such as fatigue or inattention. In Nielsen's terms, some subjects reported impressions of loss of voluntary control, 'as if driving one's car on an icy road'. Thus, this experiment revealed that subjects were poor at recognizing their own hand movements and tended to misattribute to themselves movements that were not theirs. The cues arising from the visual perception of the hand of the other person dominated the kinesthetic cues arising from the subject himself in determining self-awareness

Two years later, Nielsen together with his colleagues published the result of a second experiment based on the same substitution paradigm, but using volitional performance in a different domain, that of vocal utterance. In this experiment (Nielsen *et al.* 1965), subjects were equipped with headphones. A note at around 400 Hz was displayed to them by a sine-wave generator and they were instructed to match this note by singing. After 3 s, the generator was turned off and the subjects heard their own voice. They were instructed to hold the same note for several seconds. On some trials, however, the subject's voice was replaced by the voice of an assistant initially singing at the same frequency but then continuously falling by 10–30 Hz. This situation generated from the subject a 'compensatory' increase in the frequency of his own singing. The rise in frequency of the subject's voice was about equal to or even greater than the fall in frequency of the assistant's voice. When asked to comment on their experience during those trials, nearly all subjects commented that they were hearing their own voice with an unexplained falling pitch. Furthermore, when listening to the records of their own performance, they were surprised to hear the rising pitch of their voice and described that they were not aware of doing this during the trials. The same compensatory behavior was observed in the reverse situation, i.e. when the subjects heard an assistant's voice with a continuously increasing pitch: they decreased their own singing frequency and, even after hearing their performance, did not give up the idea that, during the trial, they had heard their own voice with a rising pitch. As a rule, the subjects experienced their own performance as involuntary and mentioned that they tried to correct the changing pitch of the voice, but could not succeed.

Nielsen *et al.*'s conclusion was that the subjects had no distinct kinesthetic awareness of their own vocal movements and that 'the auditory voice perception dominated the kinesthetic voice awareness' (1965, p. 206). Concerning the experience of loss of voluntary control reported by the subjects, both in the experiment with hand substitution and in the voice substitution experiment, Nielsen stated that 'Usually, people are not explicitly aware of volitional aspects of their own performance until they meet difficulties in carrying out an intentional act. The present experiments created difficulties in such a way that they suddenly became conscious of the volitional aspects of singing a note' (1965, p. 208). This observation refers to observations about consciousness of action that we made in the previous chapter.

Finally, Nielsen performed yet another experiment, which basically transferred the previous substitution paradigm to the movements of the whole body (Nielsen 1978). The subject standing on a platform looked at a reflection of his body in a mirror placed below his feet and was instructed to sway his body straight ahead. On some trials, the mirror was removed without the subject's knowledge and the subject was now looking down at a dummy (an 'alien body'): when the subject moved straight ahead, the alien body was made to move in a different direction, e.g. to the right. Subjects consistently reported that they experienced that their own body was pulled to the right. As stated by Nielsen, 'When the dummy swayed toward the right, [subjects] were quite certain that they were looking at themselves, and the visual impression actually shaped their postural body consciousness to such a degree that they also felt that they were being forced over to the right, against their will' (1978, p. 259). Indeed, some subjects moved to the left in an attempt to rectify the rightward movement.

Nielsen's experiments were embedded in a conceptual framework aiming at a formal description of how humans can act and reflect on their acts. His main idea was to present an alternative to psychological theories which are based on a deterministic and objectified view of human action. Humans, he thought, rather than the psychologist, must provide themselves answers to the questions of how they understand their own actions.

4.1.3 Recent implementations of the Nielsen paradigm

Except for the fact that subjects were poor at recognizing their own movements and tended to misattribute to themselves movements that were not theirs, Nielsen's experiments carried no detailed information as to self-recognition. In order to explore this point specifically on a trial by trial basis, the same substitution paradigm was used in several slightly different versions. One of these versions has already been described in Chapter 3 about conscious monitoring. In this experiment (Fourneret and Jeannerod 1998), subjects tended to ignore the true trajectory of their hand in making a conscious judgement about the direction of their hand: instead, like Nielsen's subjects, they based their report on visual cues and tended to adhere to the direction seen on the screen, thus ignoring non-visual (e.g. kinesthetic) cues.

Keeping this fact in mind, we will now describe another set of experiments initiated by Daprati *et al.* (1997) which explored the factors of self-attribution of a moving hand. A situation was created where the subjects were shown movements of a hand of an uncertain origin, i.e. a hand that could equally probably belong to them or to someone else. Subjects were instructed to determine explicitly whether or not they were the authors of the hand movements they saw. In order to give such a response, they had to use all available cues for comparing the current movement of their unseen hand with the movement that was displayed in a mirror placed in front of them. During the experiment, the subject's hand and the hand of an experimenter were filmed with two different cameras. By changing the position of a switch, one or the other hand could be briefly (5 s) displayed to the subjects. They positioned their right hand on the table, below the mirror. The display allowed the experimenter to match the image of her hand exactly with that of the subject's hand before the beginning of each trial. Thus, looking at the mirror, the subjects got the impression that they were watching their own hand. The experimenter's and the subject's hands were covered with identical gloves, in order to minimize the effects of gross morphological differences (see Figure 4.2, page 95).

The task for the subjects was to perform a requested movement with their right hand, and to monitor its execution by looking at the image in the mirror. Once the movement was performed and the screen was blank again, the subject was asked whether the hand that he just saw was his or not. One of three possible images of the hand could be presented to the subjects in each trial: (1) their own hand; (2) the experimenter's hand performing a different movement; and (3) the experimenter's hand performing the same movement.

Subjects were able to determine unambiguously whether the moving hand seen on the screen was theirs or not, in conditions (1) and (2). First, when they saw their own hand in condition (1), they correctly attributed the movement to themselves. Secondly, in condition (2), when they saw the experimenter's hand performing a movement which departed from the instruction they had received, they denied seeing their own hand. In contrast, their performance degraded in the third condition, i.e. in trials where they saw the experimenter's hand performing the same movement as required by the instruction: in this condition, they misjudged the hand as theirs in about 30 per cent of cases. Indeed, subjects' judgement had to rely on slight differences in timing and kinematics between their intended movement and that which they perceived on the screen: when these differences were below a certain threshold, they tended to be neglected. This is consistent with the above observation of Fourneret and Jeannerod (1998) where a small discordance between the movement and its visual consequences was ignored. One further finding of Daprati and her colleagues was that, when the subjects incorrectly recognized the hand shown to them, they tended to attribute that hand to themselves, and not to an alien agent. One possible explanation for this effect could be that, because subjects saw only one hand and because they had moved their fingers during the presentation, the hand was automatically attributed to the author of the movements: when the movements were clearly those of somebody else, the subjects discarded the idea that it was their own hand; when the movements were theirs, or similar to theirs, they attributed the hand to themselves.

To avoid this possible confound, a different situation was used, which combined uncertainty about ownership of the subject's hand and uncertainty about authorship of the movements performed with that hand. This situation (van den Bos and Jeannerod 2002; see also Knoblich 2002) involved simultaneous presentation of two hands, one of which was the subject's hand, the other being an alien hand. This situation is more realistic than the one used in the previous experiments, since it involves interaction between two people, in which problems of self versus other identification are most likely to arise. The question in this situation was therefore not whether an observed action corresponded to the action one had performed, but rather which of two observed actions was the one corresponding to the action performed by the self. The subject and the experimenter sat at the opposite sides of a table. The subject was facing a screen. Both the subject and the experimenter placed their right gloved hand below the screen. A mirror attached to the back of the screen reflected the image of the two hands to a video camera connected to a computer. A program processed the digitized video image in real time (within 20 ms) and sent an image of the hands onto the screen. The program allowed the image displayed on the screen to be rotated by − 90°, 90° and 180°. So, the subject could see his or her own hand at the bottom of the screen, where it would be in reality (0° rotation), at the top of the screen (180° rotation), at the left of the screen (90° rotation) or at the right of the screen (−90° rotation), while the experimenter's hand was always in the opposite direction. Different angles of rotation were combined across trials with different movements. At the beginning of each trial, the subject was instructed to extend either the index finger or the thumb, or to make no movement. During the trials where the subject was instructed to make a movement, the experimenter would either make the same or the alternative movement. Once the movements were performed, the screen returned dark within about 1 s. Then a pointer was placed at the position where one of the two hands had been. Subjects had to determine whether the hand indicated by the pointer was theirs or that of the experimenter (see Fig. 4.1).

This experiment first allowed the role of the apparent positions of the hands in self-identification to be studied. When the two hands appeared on the screen at positions corresponding to their real positions, the subjects showed relatively little difficulty in recognizing their own hand. However, when the

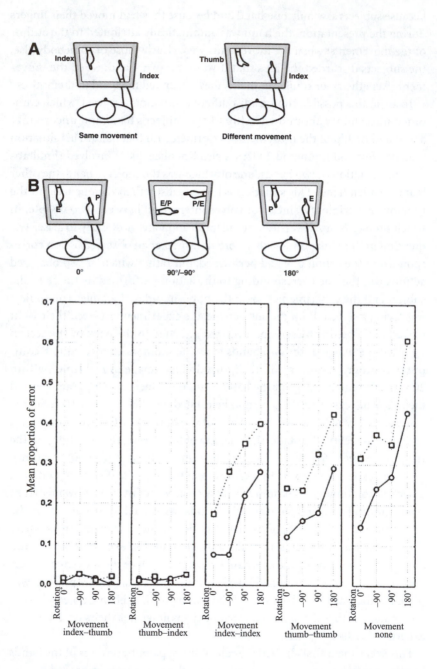

apparent locations of the hands were interchanged with respect to reality, they made attribution errors. This confirms that the contingency between visual and proprioceptive signals (kinesthesia and position sense) plays a role in self-identification. However, the most critical factor for correct attribution was shown to be the presence of finger movements. When finger movements were present and these movements were clearly attributable to the self (i.e. they differed from those of the experimenter), no attribution errors were found. This result replicates the findings of Daprati *et al.* (1997), where subjects correctly attributed the hand they saw when the finger movements were theirs or when the hand was that of the experimenter performing a different movement. The surprising finding in the present experiment is that accurate self-identification was possible for all orientations of the display, including the 180° rotation. In other words, when distinctive movements are available, subjects tend to recognize actions, not just hands. In contrast, when the two hands performed the same movements or no movements, the error rate increased as a function of the degree of rotation.

Finally, the direction of errors in this experiment is important to consider: when movements were not discriminative (e.g. when they were the same or absent), subjects misattributed the indicated hand more often to themselves than to the other person. Thus, along with the observations made by Nielsen himself and with the results of Daprati *et al.* reported above, subjects tend

Fig. 4.1 The role of self-produced movements in determining the sense of agency and the sense of ownership. Top: subject's view of the experimental display. (A) The subjects sees for 5 s the image of his own hand and the image of the hand of an experimenter. Both hands are hidden below a computer screen, and are filmed by a TV camera. At the beginning of the trial, the subject receives an instruction of either moving the index or the thumb, or making no movement. At the same time, the experimenter produces movements that can be either congruent or incongruent with those of the subject. (B) The two hands can be shown in an anatomically plausible situation (0°) or rotated by 90 or 180°. After each trial, after the image on the screen is turned off, a mark appears at the location of one of the two hands. The subject is asked to indicate whether that hand was his or not. By courtesy of G. Knoblich, in Knoblich (2002). Bottom: results of the experiment. Attribution errors made by the subjects are plotted as a function of the experimental situation combining the occurrence of movements (incongruent movements, first two boxes; congruent movements and no movement, last three boxes) and the rotation of the image. Errors are shown as overattribution to the self (squares) or overattribution to the other (circles). Note the virtual absence of errors when the movements of the two hands are distinctive, whatever the degree of rotation of the image. In contrast, note the increasing number of errors with the degree of rotation when the movements are not distinctive or absent. Also note the larger number of errors by overattribution to the self. From van den Bos and Jeannerod (2002).

consistently to attribute to themselves movements that they see when the signals for self-recognition are weak. This finding has important implications for understanding the pattern of misattribution in pathological conditions that will be mentioned in the last section of this chapter.

4.2 The nature of the mechanism for self-identification

The predominance of action recognition over other possible cues for self-identification, which was clearly highlighted by the above experiments, generates a number of empirical and theoretical questions. The main hypothesis that accounts for this dominant role of action is the Central Monitoring Theory of action recognition. This theory holds that the comparison between efferent signals at the origin of an action and those which arise from its execution (the reafferent signals) provides cues about where the action originates. We examined its basic principles in Chapter 1 when we discussed the functional aspects of action representations. The original idea is that each time the motor centers generate an outflow signal for producing a movement, a copy of this command (the 'efference copy') is retained. In the simplest form of the model, the reafferent inflow signals generated by the movement (e.g. visual, kinesthetic) are compared with the efference copy. A predictive component can be added to the model, which predicts the sensory consequences of the movement. In the case of a self-produced movement, the actual sensory feedback will match the prediction. In contrast, signals arising in the absence of a self-produced movement will be referred to an external event. A sensory signal will therefore be perceived differently whether it arises from a self-produced movement or it is externally produced (see Wolpert *et al.* 1995; Blakemore *et al.* 1998). This model of the control of action can be directly applied to the problem of self-identification. Below, we examine experimental and clinical data which lend support to this model.

4.2.1 Experimental support for the Central Monitoring Theory

Several groups have used neuroimagery to map the brain activity in situations where the processing of externally produced stimuli and stimuli resulting from self-produced movements could be compared. The situations used in these experiments typically involve an incongruence between the action performed by the subjects and the sensory signals received as a consequence of the action. In the experiment of McGuire *et al.* (1996a), for example, the subjects were reading aloud while they heard either their own voice or an alien voice (a replication of one of the Nielsen's experiments). The latter, incongruent situation yielded an increased neural activity in the auditory temporal cortex. This finding is complemented by that of Blakemore *et al.* (1999): in subjects hearing tones, the neural activity in the temporal lobe is greater when they hear the tones passively than when the tones arise as a consequence of their own movements. Taken together, these results suggest that the processing of auditory signals in the recipient temporal cortical area is different according to their origin. Self-produced signals activate the temporal cortex less than passively received external signals and less than odd signals. The interpretation proposed for this difference is that the predicted consequences of an action are attenuated, or even possibly canceled, at the input level, whereas unpredicted consequences are fully processed. This mechanism would be adequate for disentangling whether a sensory event is produced by one's own action or by an external agent (and, ultimately, if an action is self-produced or not). A behavioral experiment by Sato and Yasuda (2005) confirms this point, in showing that the sense of agency depends on the degree of discrepancy between the predicted and the actual sensory feedback (a tone) of a self-produced action. In their experiment, the sense of agency decreased when the tone was unpredictable in terms of its timing or frequency; conversely, subjects experienced an illusory sense of agency when the tone was presented at a time compatible with the predicted feedback of the action, even if it was not the consequence of the subjects' action.

Other experiments have concentrated on the activity of the parietal lobe during visuomotor conflicts. A visuomotor conflict is another situation where the actual sensory feedback resulting from a self-produced movement does not correspond to the expected feedback, for example when the sensory feedback is spatially distorted or temporally delayed. We have already mentioned earlier in this chapter several examples of situations corresponding to this definition. The results emphasize the role of the posterior part of the parietal lobe. The contribution of the parietal lobe in matching a self-produced movement with its sensory consequences can indeed be suspected on the basis of its anatomical connections. In the monkey posterior parietal cortex, neurons located in the intraparietal sulcus (a sulcus which delimitates the superior and the inferior parietal lobules) receive abundant visual and somatosensory input. In addition, these neurons are activated during eye, arm and finger movements. Assuming that the organization of the human posterior parietal cortex is similar to that of other primates, this region appears as a likely candidate for the 'comparator' postulated in the Central Monitoring Theory: it can monitor the spatial and temporal congruence between the information it receives about the motor commands for a movement and the sensory information resulting from this movement.

Now consider the effects on the activity of the human parietal lobe, of a spatial incongruence between what you do and what you see: you move your hand straight ahead and you see it moving, say, to the right. In this situation, the normally correlated signals which arise at the time of a movement communicate different things: the motor command signals tell that the movement was intended to be in the straight ahead direction, the kinesthetic reafference confirms that the movement went in this direction, but the visual reafference is in conflict with the other two. Several authors have monitored brain activity during this type of visuomotor conflict. As we briefly mentioned in the previous chapter, Fink and his co-workers studied the effect of a conflict between self-produced finger movements and the visual feedback given to the subject about his movements When the executed finger movements no longer correlated with those shown to the subjects, an increased activity was observed in the posterior parietal cortex (Brodmann areas 40 and 7) bilaterally (Fink *et al.* 1999). More recently, Chloé Farrer and her co-workers devised an experimental situation where the visual feedback provided to the subjects about their own movements could be either congruent with the execution or distorted to a variable degree. The degree of distortion went up to the point where the movements seen were completely unrelated to the executed movements. The subjects were instructed to move a joystick continuously with their right hand. The hand and the joystick were hidden from their view. Instead, the subjects saw the electronically reconstructed image of a hand holding a joystick appearing at the precise location of their own hand. When the subjects moved, the electronic hand also moved by the same amount and in the same direction: subjects rapidly became familiar with this situation and felt the movements of the electronic hand as their own. Distortions were introduced in this system, such that the movements seen by the subjects were rotated with respect to those they actually performed by 25° and 50°, or finally were completely non-correlated with them (they were actually produced by an experimenter). Subjects were instructed to concentrate on their own feelings of whether they felt in control of the movements they saw. The task of observing one's own movements in this unusual situation activated the posterior parietal lobe, predominantly in the right hemisphere. The peak activation was located in the inferior parietal lobule, in Brodmann area 39. The important point, however, was that the less the subjects felt in control of their own movements, due to larger and larger degrees of distortion, the more the right inferior parietal lobule was activated (Farrer *et al.* 2003). This first suggests that the processes underlying the sense of agency are not all-or-none processes: rather, they rely on continuous monitoring of the different movement-related signals, from sensory (kinesthetic, visual) and central (motor command) origin. However, this also suggests that the mismatch between these normally congruent signals requires an increased level of processing, hence the progressive increase in activity observed by Farrer *et al.* (2003). As we saw, this was also the case for incongruent acoustic feedback signals.

Now consider the effects of temporal incongruence between what you do and what you see: you move your arm and you see it moving after a delay. Leube *et al.* (2003) instructed subjects to move their fingers rhythmically, by opening and closing the hand several times in a row. However, the visual presentation of their performance was delayed, such that they could either move their hand without seeing it, move it and see it moving or see it moving while it was not moving. According to the authors, this procedures creates the bizarre sensation of having an 'anarchic' hand. Mapping brain activity during these tasks showed that when the congruence between moving and seeing the movement was violated, a right fronto-parietal network was activated. The parietal activation predominated in the superior parietal lobule (Brodmann area 7). This result is to be compared with that reported by Shimada *et al.* (2005). They monitored brain activity in subjects who had their arm passively displaced, while the visual feedback corresponding to these passive displacements (a video image of their arm) could be delayed by up to 300 ms. Subjects were instructed to indicate, by key pressing, whether the felt and the seen displacements of the arm were synchronous or not. Note that in this situation, the temporal incongruence is between visual and proprioceptive feedbacks, but that signals related to motor commands are not involved. The results showed that the feeling that the visual and the proprioceptive feedbacks from a limb displacement are synchronized (as they normally are) is related to an activation of a superior parietal zone on both sides. In contrast, when subjects detect an asynchrony between the visual and the proprioceptive feedbacks, the activation moves to a right inferior parietal zone.

4.2.2 Clinical support for the Central Monitoring Theory

Thus, there is experimental support for the idea that several areas in the right parietal lobe monitor the degree of congruence between the different signals which are generated in relation to the execution of a movement. When the signals are congruent (i.e. they all arise from the same locus in space and within a narrow time window), the subject experiences being the owner of the limb he moves and sees, and the agent of the movement of that limb. The question now is: what are the effects of pathological lesions in this area? There is a specific clinical entity, called *somatoparaphrenia*, attached to the lesions of the right posterior parietal cortex and the neighboring parieto-temporal areas. Patients suffering from such lesions frequently present delusions about their own left limbs, especially when they are also paralyzed. The patients may deny ownership of the affected limbs, even when faced with contradictory evidence from touch or sight; they may even attribute their affected limb to someone else, or complain about having an alien body or a cadaver lying in their bed (see Berlucchi and Agliotti 1997). The current explanation for this behavior is that in the absence of processing of movement-related signals by the right parietal lobe, patients are faced with an alien limb, lacking its connection with the rest of the body image. The delusions would represent an erroneous inter-pretation, by the patient, of this disconnection (Bisiach and Berti 1987). One such patient (patient P.A.) has recently been explored by Elena Daprati and her colleagues, using the previously described apparatus for hand attribution (see above). The patient suffered from a right thalamo-parietal lesion, as a consequence of a neurosurgical intervention. Immediately following the lesion, he presented a neglect for the left part of space, a left hemiparesis and an alteration of the position sense on the left side. He also presented somatoparaphrenic delusions about his left hand that he attributed to his son. One month later, although the left neglect was still present, he had partly recovered from the paresis and his delusions had disappeared. When tested for hand identification in the hand apparatus, a surprising behavior was observed. When shown his own left hand (the affected hand), not only did patient P.A. fail to recognize it in about 50 per cent of trials (normal subjects are close to 100% correct in this task), but also his delusions resumed: P.A. frequently denied seeing a hand, instead he reported seeing a spot, a string or even a star. No such behavior was observed when he was presented with his right, unaf-fected hand (Daprati et al. 2000). In this patient with a right parietal lesion, the self-recognition disorder was latent and was reactivated by the unusual situation used for testing his self-identification.[1] Somatoparaphrenia, after all, is not that strange: it simply reflects that if an action is not recognized as self-produced, it must pertain to someone else.[2]

....

[1] The rubber hand illusion, described earlier in this chapter, can be tentatively considered as a mild case of somatoparaphrenia, where normal people attribute to themselves an artificial hand. Ehrsson et al. (2004) explored brain activity in subjects while they were experiencing the feeling of ownership of a rubber hand. They found that the main focus of activity was localized in the ventral premotor cortex. The authors conclude that premotor cortex, together with parietal cortex, is part of a network for the multisensory integration of body-related signals.

[2] Hyperactivity of the parietal lobe also produces disorders of self-identification. Transient hyperactivity of the parietal lobe during epileptic fits may produce impressions of an alien phantom limb. Similarly, direct electrical stimulation of this region induces out of body experiences (Blanke et al. 2002). Finally, as we shall discuss at length elsewhere, hyperactivity of the inferior parietal lobule has been described in a category of psychotic patients who present difficulties in action attribution (see page 98).

Somatoparaphrenia is distinct from, though frequently associated with, another pathological phenomenon, *anosognosia*. Anosognosia is observed in some right brain-damaged hemiplegic patients who deny their motor impairment and claim that they can still move their paralyzed limbs. A recent study (Berti *et al.* 2005) has disclosed that anosognosia is best explained by lesions involving the motor and premotor areas. One of the patients studied by Berti *et al.* presented a pure form of anosognosia in the absence of parietal symptomatology: he had no somatosensory deficit and showed no denial of ownership of his paralyzed arm. His lesion was centered on primary motor cortex and premotor cortex, predominantly in its ventral part. The authors' interpretation of this case is that the patient, in spite of being unable to move, generated a distorted representation of his intended movements, which was responsible for the false belief of being able to move. This observation suggests that the sense of agency might arise primarily from activity of motor areas.

4.3 The problem of the self–other distinction

The Central Monitoring Theory offers a convincing explanation of how the monitoring of action-related signals can be at the origin of the feelings of being in control of an action and attributing it to oneself. The theory takes into account the existence of peripheral signals produced by the subject's motor activity, and their integration, by the parietal cortex, with the central action generation signals. However, for this same reason, it cannot explain the fact that the sense of agency also arises in many situations where an action representation is formed but no movement is executed.

4.3.1 The concept of shared representations

Thus, the existence of an overt behavior and of its consequences should not be a prerequisite for self-attribution. Indeed, situations where actions remain covert are ubiquitous in everyday life. Thinking is one: thinking has often been considered as a weaker form of behavior which does not activate muscles and is therefore invisible from outside (see Feinberg 1978; Hesslow 2002; Wegner 2002). Yet, people unambiguously self-attribute their own thoughts. This is even more striking for 'motor thoughts' like motor imagery. As we saw in Chapter 2, motor images include many of the components that are involved in an overt action, except for those which directly relate to execution of the action: in motor images, there is no output signal to the muscles and, consequently, no reafferent signals from the outside world, no proprioceptive signals and, therefore, no possibility for comparing execution with a desired output. Yet, the attribution of the motor representation is correctly made to the self.

Another situation is action observation. We spend a vast amount of our time watching the actions of others and draw from observing them an enormous amount of information about what these actions mean. In fact, observing an action is not far from doing it. Action observation triggers, in the observer's brain, a representation very similar to the representation that the same person would build for preparing, executing or imagining the same action. The arguments regarding this similarity will be reviewed in the next chapter. What is important for the time being is that a subject may entertain in his own brain representations that, although they look alike, can refer to himself as well as to another agent. If, in addition, these representations are about actions that remain covert (e.g. a representation for a self-produced potential action) or are executed by someone else (a representation for the action observed from another person), the cues for disentangling the two representations, and the two agents, are not to be found in comparing signals arising from the subject's body or the outside world. They have to be found inside the subject's brain.

The hypothesis that we entertain in our brains representations for both our own actions and those of others has at least two logical consequences. First, the two modalities of action representation (self-produced and observed from others) should share the same neural structures, those which are activated in both conditions. Secondly, and critically, this overlap between action representations of different origin should not be complete. Indeed, this is a necessary condition for disentangling the respective origin of each representation: a complete overlap between the two would not allow the attribution of one or the other to its real origin; in contrast, non-overlapping zones would specify each representation and would allow a distinction to be made between the two modalities. This idea of *shared representations* (Georgieff and Jeannerod 1998), although it is supported by experimental evidence, as we will show later, is still a working hypothesis. The nature of the signals which could arise from those non-overlapping zones and would allow the attribution of a given representation either to the self or to the observed other still remains to be determined (see Jeannerod and Pacherie 2004).

The important point here is that the shared representation hypothesis is a possible alternative to that of central monitoring for explaining the identification of the agent, with the additional advantage that it also proposes a solution for understanding the agent's action. The main problem for a theory of action recognition is that it cannot ignore the content of the action. The Central Monitoring Theory could only explain how action attribution is achieved, through the existence of action-related signals. By this mechanism, an action can only be attributed to another agent by default (e.g. 'if these signals do not belong to me, they must belong to someone else'), and not by way of a positive identification of what the agent of the action is doing. It is true that in one of its latest versions, the Central Monitoring Theory postulates that the internal model at the origin of an action can operate on a purely representational basis, and can estimate the current state of the motor command of a movement to predict the next state, by simulating the movement dynamics; in doing so, it can predict the sensory feedback that would result from the movement if it were actually executed (Frith *et al.* 2000). This improvement of the theory, however, although it answers the question of how non-executed actions can be self-attributed, does not fully take into consideration the fact that actions of other agents have a specific content to the same extent as our own. As we will see later, we get far more information from the actions of others than simply distinguishing their actions from our own. We observe other people, among other things, to understand their actions and possibly read their intentions, to learn and possibly replicate their actions.

4.3.2 **Perspective taking**

Trying to understand the actions of another person implies that one adopts her point of view on the external or the social world. Popular expressions such as 'putting oneself in the other's shoes' or 'in the other's skin' account for this idea of taking the perspective of the person one observes. By taking the other's place, one sees things as she would see them.

Perspective taking is thus part of the self–other distinction: putting oneself in the place of somebody else implies that the two selves have been identified as distinct from one another. At the same time, however, putting oneself in the other's place may involve the risk of confusing the two selves. As we saw above, one of the major challenges of the notion of shared representations is to explain how it can be possible to understand another self without losing the fact that the two selves remain distinct: we normally continue to be ourselves when we simulate another self, whereas the confusion of the two selves might create a strange situation. Here, we examine some of the correlates of this implicit strategy of perspective taking, using mental chronometry and neuroimaging.

Experiments are carried out by instructing subjects to represent to themselves an action performed by somebody else. For example, Wohlschläger *et al.* (2003) used the Libet paradigm (Libet 1983, see Chapter 3) for measuring the time at which a subject becomes able to detect when he/she intends to move a lever. Participants in the experiment first gave estimates about their own intention time. Subsequently, they gave an estimate of the intention time of another participant that they were observing. The estimates were found to be closely similar. In other words, intending one's own action and representing the intention of another person seem to activate the same mechanism, which would lead to the same time estimate. Another attempt was made by Anquetil *et al.* (work in progress). They asked subjects either to imagine themselves performing a grasping movement or to imagine another person facing them performing that movement. Again, the measure of the mental movement time in both conditions was of the same duration. In order to represent the actions of others the best way is to read representations of one's own actions in a third-person perspective, instead of the usual first-person perspective.

This issue of perspective taking is a critical one for understanding the actions of others: by simulating their actions (covert as well as overt) through our own representations, we come to experience 'how it would be if I were doing it'. Not surprisingly, studies using neuroimagery have focused on the posterior parietal cortex as the site for disentangling first-person perspective from third-person perspective processing (see the review by Vogeley and Fink 2003). In a previous section, we showed that introducing a conflict between a self-produced action and its consequences resulted in an increased level of neural activity in this area (e.g. Farrer *et al.* 2003). In another study by Farrer and Frith (2002), subjects were instructed to watch a screen where they could see a moving spot that reflected either their own action of moving a joystick or the action of someone else. When subjects attributed the action to themselves (first-person perspective), the main activated area was located in the anterior part of the insula; when they attributed the action to someone else (third-person perspective), the main activation was located in the posterior parietal lobes on both sides. Ruby and Decety (2001), in a study where they instructed subjects either to imagine themselves doing an action or to imagine that they were watching somebody else doing the same action, found different results. In the first-person perspective, the inferior parietal lobule in the left hemisphere was activated; in contrast, in the third-person perspective, activation was found in a symmetrical area of the right hemisphere. Although these experiments may seem to provide a relatively confusing picture of the brain mechanisms of self–other recognition, they all have in common the fact that they clearly point to the role of posterior parietal cortex. The fact that activation may predominate on the right or the left side reflects the complexity of the notion of perspective taking itself, and the different instructions given to the subjects. What seems the most consistent is that the left parietal region is predominant for action representation, whereas the right parietal region is predominant for representing body and space. It is likely that whether the subjects in these experiments focus their processing on the action or on the spatial coordinates in which this action is performed can influence the pattern of the results in activating predominantly the parietal cortex on one side or the other.

The relative similarity of brain mechanisms for the first-person and the third-person processing of actions suggests that action attribution may be a fragile process. Indeed, there are in everyday life ambiguous situations where the cues for the sense of agency become degraded and which obviously require a subtle mechanism for signaling the origin of an action. This is the case for situations created by interactions between two or more individuals, such as joint attention, matched actions or mutual imitation. This may also happen during man–machine interactions such as, for example, telemanipulation or virtual reality systems. As first shown by Nielsen, one can easily create situations where normal subjects fail to recognize their own actions and mis-attribute to themselves actions performed by another agent.

The principle of shared representations that we have proposed in this chapter clarifies this problem for what concerns the recognition of one's actions and the distinction between one's own actions and those of others. On the one hand, the neural representation of one's actions overlaps that of the actions of other agents: in that sense, self-produced actions and actions pro-duced by others share the same processing. On the other hand, however, as we emphasized, there are zones of non-overlap. Different non-overlapping zones are specific to self-produced actions and to actions produced by others, respectively. While changing from the first-person to the third-person perspective, or vice versa, one activates one or the other representation. How this ultimately generates an experience of either being the owner of one's own body and the agent of one's actions, or being the observer remains an unans-wered question. In the next section, we examine the sense of agency in the pathological condition responsible for schizophrenia, a disease where the self-merges with other selves and where the self–other distinction becomes problematic.

4.4 Failure of self-recognition/attribution mechanisms in pathological states

In this section, we investigate the effects of pathological conditions, as another potential source of information concerning the mechanisms of self-identification. Pathological conditions offer many examples of misattribu-tions: a typical case is that of schizophrenia. Misattributions are not evenly distributed among schizophrenic patients. This type of disturbance is prefer-entially observed in one particular class of patients who present the so-called 'first-rank symptoms'. According to Kurt Schneider, these symptoms refer to a state where patients interpret their own thoughts or actions as due to alien forces or to other people and feel that they are being controlled or influenced by others (Schneider 1955). First-rank symptoms (or *Schneiderian* symptoms, as they will be called here) reflect the disruption of a mechanism that normally generates consciousness of one's own actions and thoughts and makes possible their correct attribution to their author. Thus, a study of attribution behavior in schizophrenic patients would not only help us understand the factors responsible for misattribution in the patients but would also shed light on this critical function in normal life.

The pattern of misattributions in these patients is 2-fold. According to the French psychiatrist Pierre Janet, patients may either attribute their own actions or thoughts to others rather than to themselves (underattributions) or they may attribute the actions or thoughts of others to themselves (overattributions) (Janet 1937). A typical example of underattributions is hallucinations. Hallucinating schizophrenic patients may show a tendency to project their own experience onto external events. Accordingly, they may misattribute their own intentions or actions to external agents. During auditory hallucinations, the patient will hear voices that are typically experienced as coming from a powerful external entity, but in fact correspond to subvocal speech produced by the patient. The voices are often comments where the patient is addressed in the third person and also include commands and directions for action (Chadwick and Birchwood 1994). The patient may declare that he or she is being acted upon by an alien force, as if his or her thoughts or acts were controlled by an external agent. The so-called mimetic behavior observed at the acute stage of psychosis also relates to this category. Overattributions, which Janet (1937) called 'excess of appropriation', correspond for the patient to the illusion that actions of others are in fact initiated or performed by him/her and that he/she is influencing other people (the clinical picture of megalomania). In this case, patients are convinced that their intentions or actions can affect external events, for example that they can influence the thoughts and the actions of other people. Accordingly, they tend to misattribute the occurrence of external events to themselves. The consequence of this misinterpretation would be that external events are seen as resulting from their own intentions and actions.

4.4.1 Is there a failure of the action monitoring system in Schneiderian schizophrenic patients?

The most prevalent theory for explaining attribution difficulties in schizophrenic patients is that proposed by Christopher Frith and his colleagues. This theory, which was first formulated in the early 1990s (e.g. Frith 1992), has been recently reformulated within the framework of the action monitoring mechanism described earlier in this chapter (see also Jeannerod and Pacherie

2004). The general idea is that the delusion of influence arises from a lack of awareness of the predicted limb position. The reasoning is the following: 'Under normal circumstances the awareness of initiating a movement must depend on the predicted limb position because awareness of initiating a movement precedes the actual movement and any feedback about actual limb position. The patient with delusions of control is aware of his goal, of his intention to move and of his movement having occurred, but he is not aware of having initiated the movement. It is as if the movement, although intended, has been initiated by some external force' (Blakemore *et al.* 2002, p. 240). In terms of the Central Monitoring Theory, the key problem for these patients would be that, due to their pathological condition, the endogenous signals related to action generation (the so-called efference copy) would be either absent or not properly used by the nervous system (Frith *et al.* 2000).

These contentions are supported by experimental evidence showing that patients with Schneiderian symptoms fail to monitor the discrepancies between their intended and predicted limb positions. In these experiments, patients were shown moving visual targets that they had to reach by displacing a lever, in the absence of visual feedback from their movement. If the target moved in an unexpected direction, the patients tended not to correct their error when they had started their movement in the direction where they expected the target to appear. In contrast, the same patients had no difficulty making the correction when they were provided visual feedback on the displacement of the lever (e.g. Frith and Done 1989; Mlakar *et al.* 1994). This type of experiment, however, mostly stresses the automatic part of the action monitoring system, but tends to overlook the conscious part of this mechanism, that which makes it possible to give an explicit judgement on the action. In other words, the link between the experimentally proven inability to make corrections and the clinically observed misattributions of the action to its agent is not firmly established.

In order to establish this link, one needs first to address the issue of conscious awareness of the action in schizophrenic patients. With this aim in view, Fourneret *et al.* (2001) used a paradigm similar to that of Frith and Done (1989) for testing the ability not only to produce automatic corrections but also to make conscious judgements on the motor task. They used a modified version of the apparatus previously described in Chapter 3. The task consisted of drawing a line in the sagittal direction, while a fixed deviation of 15° to the right was introduced in the system. An opaque mask occluded the screen, such that the subjects could not see the line they drew except in the last one-third of the trajectory to the target. Twenty trials were performed. Patients with and without Schneiderian symptoms, as well as normal control subjects were tested. It took

approximately 10 trials for subjects from all three groups to learn to compensate gradually for the deviation and to maintain the same strategy of moving
the arm to the left throughout the task. This result indicates that the patients
were able, in the absence of visual feedback, to initiate a hand movement in
the proper direction to reach the target. This implies that they monitored their
central command signals, modified them so as to achieve the task and maintained this modification across the trials. In addition, most of the patients in
the group with Schneiderian symptoms were found to be able to describe
explicitly the strategy they had to use in order to reach the target. This experiment (Fourneret *et al.* 2001) therefore demonstrates that conscious action
monitoring can be found in these patients, provided they are tested with the
appropriate experimental design.

4.4.2 A specific attribution deficit in schizophrenic patients

These findings suggest that the explanation for the misattribution observed in
Schneiderian patients should be looked for at a level of action consciousness
directly related to their experience of agency, rather than at the level of the
conscious control of the action. To address this point, we will examine the
results obtained with groups of schizophrenic patients in experiments specifically designed for testing self-recognition and attribution. The basic methodology for these experiments, already described in this chapter, is to record
agency judgements about movements that are shown to the subjects and that
may correspond, or not, to their own movements. The first experiment of this
type was conducted by Daprati *et al.* (1997). Remember that subjects were
requested to make simple finger movements with their hidden right hand. At
the same time, they were shown on a screen the movements of a right hand of
an uncertain origin, i.e. a hand that could equally probably belong to them or
to someone else. Finally, the movements performed by that hand either could
be the same as, or different from, those the subjects had performed. In the
condition with the maximum uncertainty about the ownership of the hand,
Schneiderian patients made attribution errors in 80 per cent of trials, i.e. they
massively misattributed the movements of the alien hand to themselves. The
error rate in the same condition was only 30 per cent in control subjects and
around 50 per cent in non-Schneiderian patients (see Fig. 4.2). The results
thus reveal the existence of impaired attribution of action in schizophrenia,
especially in Schneiderian patients (see also Franck *et al.* 2001). In addition,
these patients tend to misattribute to themselves the moving hands they see
more often than to misattribute their own hands to other agents. As we saw
earlier, this effect is also clearly present in normal subjects. The exaggerated
tendency of schizophrenic patients to self-attribute alien actions testifies to

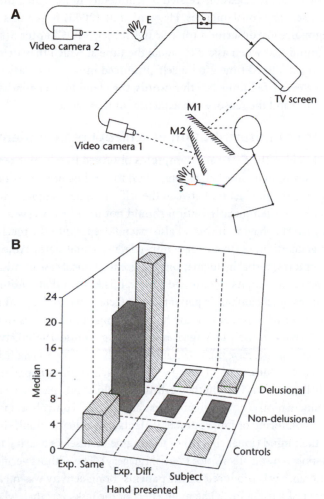

Fig. 4.2 Misattribution of one's own hand movements in schizophrenic patients. Top: experimental set-up for presenting the subject with either his own hand or an alien hand. This is done by switching either camera 1 (subject's hand) or camera 2 (alien hand) on the monitor screen reflected to the subject in mirror M1. Bottom: median value of attribution errors in three groups of subjects (from bottom to top: normal controls, non-delusional patients and schizophrenic patients with delusional syndrome), and in three conditions of hand presentation. In the condition Subject, the subject sees his own hand performing his own movements. In condition Exp. Diff., the subjects sees the alien hand performing a movement different from that which he was instructed to perform. In condition Exp. Same, the subject sees the alien hand performing the same movement as he was instructed to perform. The latter condition yields a significantly higher proportion of errors in the patients group than in the control group, and in the delusional patients group than in the non-delusional patients group. Reproduced from Jeannerod (2003b). Data from Daprati *et al.* (1997).

a perturbed sense of agency, possibly related to a difficulty in matching one's actions and their sensory consequences. Haggard *et al.* (2003) tested this by using a paradigm already described for normal subjects in Chapter 3(see Fig. 3.2). They found that when asked to signal the time at which they detect a sound occurring at a fixed time after a self-produced movement, patients tend to shrink the estimated time. In other words, they tend to over-bind the actions they produce and the sensory consequences of these actions.

4.4.3 The depth of misattribution in schizophrenic patients

According to Schneider, the first-rank symptoms observed in schizophrenic patients are the expression of false beliefs which lead to a feeling of depersonalization by impairing the distinction between the self and other people. If this assumption is correct, then misattribution should not only be observed for actions involving overt behavior; it should also extend deeper into the mechanisms of action generation, i.e. to covert action-related mental states. Among Schneiderian symptoms, verbal hallucinations represent a typical case of misattribution of covert behavior. As mentioned earlier, it is known that auditory verbal hallucinations in schizophrenic patients are in fact related to the production of inner speech by the patient. Some hallucinating patients even show weak muscular activity in their laryngeal muscles (e.g. Gould 1949; David 1994). Thus, the patients perceive their own inner speech as voices arising from an external source. McGuire *et al.* (1996b) examined schizophrenic patients predisposed to hallucinations (whom they called 'hallucinators'), patients with no history of hallucinations (non-hallucinators) and normal controls in tasks that entailed the monitoring of inner speech. Patients had either to think simple sentences in their mind (inner speech) or to imagine themselves hearing the same sentences spoken by an alien voice (verbal imagery). The authors verified that no vocal utterance was produced by the patients. Brain activity was measured during these tasks, using PET. The main effect of the tasks was that, when compared with controls and non-hallucinators, patients predisposed to hallucinations showed a reduction of activity in their left middle temporal gyrus during the task of imagining sentences pronounced by another person. McGuire *et al.* concluded that this reduced activity in an area specifically devoted to the processing of spoken language could interfere with the patients' recognition of their own language as self-generated. The reasoning of the authors was that regions concerned with the generation of language (e.g. in the frontal lobe) normally inform speech perception areas of imminent language output, so that the subsequently perceived speech is recognized as self-generated. This process would be dysfunctional in hallucinators, hence their vulnerability to hallucinations. Another complementary finding was obtained by Dierks *et al.* (1999) in Schneiderian patients. When these patients experienced hallucinations, their brain metabolism increased in the primary auditory cortex (Heschl gyrus) on the left side. Thus, during verbal hallucinations, the auditory temporal areas remain active, which suggests that the nervous system in these patients behaves as if it were actually processing the speech of an external speaker. On the contrary, in healthy subjects, self-generated inner speech is accompanied by a decrease in responsiveness of their primary auditory cortex.

These data speak more in favor of a defective simulation mechanism for attributing verbal thinking to the self or to another person than of a defective action monitoring mechanism. Indeed, because in verbal hallucinations there is no vocal utterance, the hypothesis of a defective simulation mechanism seems more appropriate for explaining that the sense of agency must be functioning even in the absence of comparison with external reafferences, and that actions can be monitored at the level of their representation, not only at the level of their execution. Accordingly, we would propose that the network which we normally use for attributing thoughts and intentions to their agent (be it ourselves or another person) is damaged in certain types of schizophrenic patients and therefore does not allow proper simulation of the covert operations needed for attribution. This hypothesis would be consistent with the fact that, in clinical practice, the Schneiderian symptoms concern mostly non-executed actions (see also Jeannerod *et al.* 2003).

The nature of the dysfunction responsible for misattribution of actions in pathological conditions is still an open question. It is conceivable that changes in the pattern of cortical connectivity could alter the shape of the networks corresponding to different representations, or the relative intensity of activation in the areas comprising these networks. This explanation fits with the classical observation of a defective function of prefrontal cortex in schizophrenia.

Prefrontal cortex is known to be hypoactive in many schizophrenic patients (the so-called 'hypofrontality'; see Ingvar and Franzen 1975; Weinberger and Berman 1996), and its morphological aspect has been shown to be abnormal on post-mortem examination (Goldman-Rakic and Selemon 1997). On the behavioral side, schizophrenic patients show signs of 'behavioral hypofrontality' when tested with neuropsychological tests exploring prefrontal functions (e.g. tests for working memory or for problem solving requiring the use of pre-instructed rules; see Posada *et al.* 2001; Posada and Franck 2002). Because prefrontal areas are known normally to exert an inhibitory control on other areas involved in various aspects of motor and sensorimotor processing, an alteration of this control in schizophrenic patients might result in aberrant behavior, due to the release of activity of normally inhibited parts of cortex, especially in the posterior parts of the hemispheres. Indeed, already mentioned neuroimaging studies have revealed that patients presenting verbal hallucinations show abnormal activation of primary auditory areas in their left temporal lobe, as if they were processing an external auditory stimulus. Similarly, an increased activity in the right posterior parietal lobe has been observed in patients with delusions of influence, either at rest (Franck *et al.* 2002) or during an action recognition task (Spence *et al.* 1997). In a recent paper, Farrer *et al.* (2004) submitted Schneiderian patients to the same protocol they had used in normal controls, where subjects saw a distorted feedback of their own movements. Remember that, in this condition, the activation of the right inferior parietal lobule correlated with the degree of distortion: the greater the distortion, the higher the activation (Farrer *et al.* 2003). Schizophrenic patients showed a different pattern. First, the activity of their right inferior parietal lobule in the baseline condition was already higher than in normal controls. Secondly, the increase in activity correlated poorly with the increased distortion. Thus, the patients really had no cues (as inferred from the change in activity in their parietal lobe) about whether they saw their own movements or the movements of an alien agent. It is not surprising that such patients had difficulties in correctly attributing their own movements to themselves, or in disentangling their actions from those of others.[3]

---

[3] A permanent increase in the resting activity of posterior parietal cortex has been observed in non-psychotic subjects presenting factors of vulnerability for schizophrenia (Whalley *et al.* 2004).

Chapter 5

How do we perceive and understand the actions of others

To perceive other people is to perceive their bodies and their actions. We identify others through their face, their voice, their posture and gait. In addition, even for people we do not know, their bodies and actions are the source of a special class of visual stimuli which make them appear human: faces and facial expressions, and body parts (e.g. hands) represent unique visual patterns which are clearly distinct from other visual objects, natural as well as artificial. Similarly, the motion of these body parts is distinct from the motion of objects produced by external forces. This specificity of the appearance of biological stimuli and biological motion is reflected by the existence of specialized brain mechanisms for the perception and understanding of other people. In this chapter, we describe these mechanisms separately for the perception of bodies and faces, for the perception of biological motion and for the understanding of actions. Although, arguably, only the latter mechanism pertains to motor cognition, we will meet many examples of interaction between the three. Finally, in a different chapter, we will discuss other, complementary aspects of the motor recognition of others, related to the perception of emotions and the understanding of language.

5.1 The perception of faces and bodies

The visual system is an assembly of specialized areas where specific aspects of the visual world are encoded. A number of these areas encode stimuli that relate to the human body and its different parts. They are located in the occipital and the inferotemporal cortical regions in the posterior and ventral parts of the cerebral hemispheres.

5.1.1 Face perception

Face recognition has been the subject of broad interest in psychology and neuropsychology. Faces, particularly in humans, carry the expression of affects and emotions, which are an essential aspect of social communication. Humans have a rich repertoire of facial gestures: the eyes, the eyebrows, the forehead, the lips, the tongue and the jaws can move relative to the rest of the face. Not only can lip, tongue and jaw movements serve to convey a speaker's communicative intentions, but mouth movements and lip positions can be powerful visual cues of a person's emotional states: by opening her mouth and moving her lips, a person can display a neutral face, smile, laugh or express grief. The movements and the position of the eyes in their orbits also convey information about the person's emotional state, or about the current target of her attention and/or intention. In this section, we review evidence in favor of the existence of a specialized system dedicated to the perception of human faces. The influential model of Bruce and Young (1986) predicts that the perception of invariant aspects of faces, i.e. those aspects which are common to all faces, should be distinct from the recognition of the identity of individual faces. One thing is the ability to perceive a conspecific's emotional states, the focus of her attention and her social intention by perceiving her face and facial gestures. Another thing is the ability to recognize and identify the face of an individual, whose visual appearance will change as she ages, across different facial gestures and expressions at different times.

The neural mechanism selective for face recognition was extensively studied in monkeys. Neuronal populations were identified in the inferotemporal cortex (Gross *et al.* 1972) and more specifically in the region of the superior temporal sulcus (STS), which are more responsive to the sight of faces than to any other simple or even complex stimuli of interest to the animal. David Perrett and his group (see review by Perrett *et al.* 1989; Carey *et al.* 1997) have extensively described neuronal responses to faces in the STS region. Some of these neurons are sensitive only to a single facial feature (e.g. the eyes or the mouth), while others respond to the whole face shown in a specific orientation: a given cell, for example, may prefer the front view of a face and stop responding if the face is turned to profile or is rotated upside down. Neurons can be found which respond differentially to different people or monkeys: in that case, they continue to differentiate between individuals shown from many different perspectives. Head and eye movements in specific directions are also potent stimuli for these neurons.

In humans, the neuropsychological investigation of the pathological condition known as *prosopagnosia* has revealed that patients with bilateral damage to the inferior occipito-temporal region are selectively impaired in visual face recognition, while their perception and recognition of other objects are relatively unimpaired (e.g. Farah 1996). In prosopagnosia, however, the impairment for face perception seems to be limited to the invariant aspects of faces, whereas the recognition of their familiar character is preserved. Showing a familiar face to such patients produces changes in electrodermal potentials, which are not observed for unfamiliar faces. This reveals a covert recognition of familiarity of faces which are not otherwise recognized. In contrast, in the Capgras syndrome, another pathological condition where patients fail to recognize people, the visual recognition of faces seems relatively unimpaired, but the emotional response to familiar faces may be so severely impaired that the lack of emotional response prompts these patients to assume that very close members of their family are impostors (see, for example, Ramachandran and Blakeslee 1998).

As emphasized by Haxby *et al.* (1999), face processing is mediated by a distributed neural system including three bilateral regions in the occipitotemporal extrastriate cortex: the inferior occipital gyrus, the lateral fusiform gyrus and the STS. There is growing recent evidence that the lateral fusiform gyrus might be particularly involved in processing of invariant aspects of faces (e.g. Kanwisher *et al.* 1997), while the STS region might be more involved in processing variable aspects of faces, such as facial movements which carry emotional expressions (Calvert *et al.* 1997). These data, together with the above monkey data, have led to the idea that the STS might represent a region specialized for 'social' perception from visual cues (Allison *et al.* 2000) (see Chapter 6).

5.1.2 **The perception of body parts**

In addition to visual face areas, occipital and inferotemporal cortex also include areas sensitive to the perception of stationary and moving body parts. In the monkey STS, Hietanen and Perrett (1993, 1996) have recorded neurons responsive to the perception of body parts and body motion. Neurons in this area respond to the sight of head, eyes, limbs and hands, either static or moving toward the animal or away from her. However, these neurons fail to respond when the body motion is self-produced by the animal: they are selective for limb or body movements in a particular direction when they are produced by another monkey, whereas they remain silent if these movements are the consequence of the animal's own action. In other words, these STS neurons retain the body information only to the extent that it arises from another self, i.e. they must have the additional information that the input they receive arises from external events, not from within. Also in the monkey STS, Perrett *et al.* (1989) found neurons selective to certain hand actions (e.g. reach for, retrieve, manipulate, pick, etc.), with a tendency to generalize their response to different instances of the same action. Hand–object interaction is more effective in firing the cell than object–object interaction and, in the hand–object interaction, the nature of the object itself (e.g. large or small, colored or not) seems irrelevant. Moreover, a population of cells in the anterior part of the

STS respond best to the sight of an agent reaching an object, but only when the agent is attending to the target of the reach (Jellema *et al.* 2000). We will come back later to this interesting finding which suggests that these neurons might in fact be involved in the recognition of the intentions of the agent (see Chapter 6). Thus, specific neuronal populations in the STS are involved not only in the recognition of static body postures but also in the recognition of actions (Keysers and Perrett 2004).

In humans, a distinct area responding to images of the human body has been identified by fMRI studies in the region of the lateral occipital cortex (Downing *et al.* 2001). This region, called the 'extrastriate body area' (EBA), is activated by the presentation of visual stimuli showing body parts (e.g. a hand, a foot or an arm) or whole bodies presented as photographs or even stick diagrams. Other visual stimuli, such as tools, but also stimuli representing various types of animals, are ineffective. Further studies by Astafiev *et al.* (2004), still using the fMRI activation method, revealed that the EBA responds not only to stationary images of body parts but also to the movements of one's own body. Within the area, regions responding preferentially to self-produced movements of pointing with either the hand or the foot were segregated. However, this response to body movements is only partly due to the visual perception of body motion, since it persists when sight of the moving limb is occluded and even when the subject either prepares to move or produces the action covertly by imagining it. This surprising finding indicates that the EBA is not only responsive to sensory (visual or proprioceptive) signals from the moving body part, but also to endogenous signals in relation to the action generation process. Thus, the EBA seems to fulfill the criterion for an area devoted to distinguishing the self from others: because it responds both to the visual perception of moving body parts and to the self-generation of actions with the same body parts, it can contribute to the first-person signal which refers these body parts to the agent of the action. What is new here is not that this signal exists (we already saw evidence for it in other brain areas, such as the parietal cortex), the surprise is that it is present so early in the stream of the visual processing of actions (Jeannerod 2005a).

The existence of specialized visual areas for human faces and bodies reflects the importance, in human behavior, of the distinction between the self and other individuals. Indeed, the self-other distinction is the starting point for the recognition and understanding of others, and ultimately for social interactions. In the next section, we turn to the mechanism for the perception of actions. In describing these mechanisms, we will realize that perception is only part of the problem, and that actions are also recognized and understood through an additional mechanism which involves the motor system. This will require the involvement of motor areas, i.e. areas with a motor output: the purely visual mechanisms that we have described here for encoding face and body perception are obviously not suited for this function.

5.2 The perception of biological motion

Biological movements have properties that make them unique with regard to other types of visual stimuli. First, their spatio-temporal trajectories must remain compatible with biomechanics (obviously, you cannot twist your forearm for more than 180° or so without risking pain). Secondly, biological movements usually have a goal. Goal-directed movements such as reaching for an object with your hand, for example, have distinctive kinematics that makes them look intentional: their velocity profile is asymmetrical, with a fast acceleration followed by a much longer deceleration (unlike ballistic motions of non-biological projectiles, which have a symmetrical velocity profile) Thirdly, biological movements obey distinctive kinematic rules even when they have no visible goal (e.g. expressive gestures).

5.2.1 Perceiving the distinctive features of biological movements

The point here is that not only executing, but also perceiving biological movements is influenced by these in-built features of movement generation. In other words, perception seems to obey motor rules. Perception of biological motion has been extensively studied by psychologists using the technique of point-light displays developed by Johansson (1973). In this technique, an agent is filmed in a dark room with lights attached to his main joints. When the agent moves, his body is invisible: only kinematic information is available to the perceiver. Johansson's pioneering studies showed that filmed movement patterns of walking, cycling, climbing and dancing were quickly and reliably recognized as soon as the lights were moving. Using the same experimental paradigm, other investigators further demonstrated that subjects were able to identify friends by their gait as well as identifying the gender of the walking person (Koslowsky and Cutting 1978). Data from Fox and McDaniel (1982), Dasser *et al.* (1989) and Bertenthal (1993) show that human infants as young as 3 months old are visually sensitive to the difference between the biological motion of dots produced by a walking person and the random, artificially produced, non-biological motions of similar dots. The knowledge acquired from this type of stimuli can also be exploited, not just for the recognition of action, but also for the recognition of intentions. For instance, when an agent has to lift a box, her expectation regarding the weight of the box leads her to make specific anticipatory postural adjustments; when the weight is not as expected, postural readjustments take place. Runeson and Frykholm (1983) have shown that subjects observing point-light displays of such actions are able to determine what the actor expects the weight to be and whether her expectation is correct. Furthermore, they are able to detect attempts at deception. If an actor pretends, say, that a suitcase she is carrying is heavier than it actually is, her movements will have non-natural kinematics that can be detected by observers (Grèzes *et al.* 2004).

Perception of action obeys motor rules sometimes even in spite of contradictory visual evidence. Consider for example the trick of looking at two rapidly alternating static pictures of a person. In one picture, the person has her left arm on the left side of her knee, and in the other picture her left arm is on the right of her knee. When such a pair of static images is sequentially presented and the time interval between the two displays is within 550–750 ms, then you see an apparent motion of the arm *around* the knee, i.e. a biomechanically possible apparent motion of the person's left arm. However, things change dramatically when the same pair of static images is presented with a shorter time interval of 150–350 ms: then you see the biomechanically impossible apparent motion of the person's arm *through* her knee (Shiffrar and Freyd 1990). Thus, when the time window is within a range compatible with the velocity of biological movements, subjects tend to perceive a possible arm movement around the knee, i.e. a movement that respects the biomechanical constraints of the body as it would actually be executed by the person. Let us take another example where the perception of the movements is not contaminated by the view of body parts. You are instructed to track with your own arm a light held by a robot arm moving in a random path. In doing so, you will track the light with arm movements that follow biological motor rules. One of these rules is the 'two-thirds power law' (Lacquaniti *et al*, 1983), which makes your arm decelerate when the movement path is curved. As the robot arm does not follow the two-thirds power law and keeps a constant velocity throughout, your movement will lag behind that of the robot. As a normal subject, you cannot depart from this relationship between the geometry and the kinematics of your movement. According to Paolo Viviani, the subject's movements during the attempts to track the target continue to bear the imprint of the general principle of organization for spontaneous movements, even though this is in contrast with the specifications of the target (Viviani 1990). Crucially, the same relationship between velocity and curvature is also present in a subject's perceptual estimation of the shape of the trajectory of a light. A target moving at a uniform velocity along a curved trajectory is paradoxically seen moving in a non-uniform way and, conversely, a target motion which respects the velocity–curvature relationship is perceived to be moving at a uniform velocity. Our perception is constrained by the implicit knowledge that the central nervous system has concerning the movements that it is capable of producing. In other words, there is a central representation of what a uniform movement should be, and this representation influences visual perception (Viviani and Stucchi 1992). Whether this implicit knowledge is a result of learning or an effect of some in-built property of visual perception is a matter of speculation. The fact that young infants are more interested in biologically looking movements than in mechanical ones (e.g. Dasser *et al.* 1989) is an indication in favor of the latter possibility. Another argument is the fact that the motion of objects, provided it obeys certain rules, can be given an intentional character like real biological movements. The main condition is that the object motion appears to be internally caused rather than caused by an external force. As shown by Heider and Simmel (1944), seeing the self-propelled motion of geometrical stimuli can trigger judgements of proto-social goals and intentions. A preference for self-propelled motion can be demonstrated with this type of stimuli in 6-month-old infants (Gergely *et al.* 1995; Csibra *et al.* 1999).

According to Viviani and Stucchi's (1992) view, that our perception of biological motion is biased by our implicit knowledge of the biomechanical constraints that apply to the execution of our own movements, it follows that these constraints must be represented within our motor system. Thus, in their view, the perceptual representation of biological motion delivered by the visual system is biased by representations of biomechanically possible movements stored in the motor system. This suggests the conclusion that the perception of biological motion automatically triggers in the observer the formulation of a motor plan to perform the observed movement. Perceiving and executing biological motions would thus share common representational resources. This view, of course, fits well with the contrast between the perception of biomechanically possible apparent motion and the perception of biomechanically impossible apparent motion: unlike the latter, the former triggers in the observer a motor plan to perform the perceived motion. This is what makes robotic movements look so different.

In this section, we started with the notion that the perception of body parts and biological movements is a visual mechanism in the usual sense, i.e. involving cortical areas in the occipital and infero-temporal areas. However, we progressively discovered another mechanism for the recognition of actions produced by biological systems (and specifically humans). These represent a special type of visual pattern which is not decoded in the same way as other visual stationary or moving patterns.

5.3 **The understanding of others' actions**

In this section, we discuss the arguments and the experimental data which have led to a change in perspective about the perception of actions performed by other agents. What has changed is that unlike perceptual representations, the representations we build about the actions we observe are no longer considered as originating exclusively from sensory signals. Novel findings have stressed the participation of motor mechanisms in these representations, which now come close to other types of action representations.

5.3.1 **How observed actions are represented**

As the observer of an action, we are by no means a passive spectator. We build in our own mind representations of the actions we see executed by other persons. In that sense, the observer is not merely contemplating the action of the observed agent, he is attempting to understand or predict the outcome of the action he observes. Actions of other people carry valuable information for learning skills and the use of tools, for finding solutions to technical problems or for engaging in communication. This representation of an observed action in the mind of the observer is invisible from outside, until the observer uses it to replicate the movement he has seen: it is only then that the content of the representation the observer has built is revealed. We saw in Chapter 2 that self-generated action representations can be studied by asking the subject to look inwards and to report on his own experience. In imagining an action, for example, people can determine with sufficient accuracy the moment where they begin and terminate their covert action. This is hardly possible during observation, where the parameters of the observed action are not under the control of the observer, but, rather, are imposed on him by the agent he observes.

Several methods have been used to analyze the content of action representations built from observation, in order to determine their degree of resemblance to the observed action. One of these methods is to produce interference between an action that the observer watches and an action he simultaneously executes. If the neural structures involved in the representation activated for executing an action are shared by those involved in representing the action one observes, then one should see interference between the two representations. A series of simple experiments confirms this point: Brass *et al.* (2001b), for example, noticed that the execution of pre-instructed finger movements is influenced by the observation of another person performing congruent or incongruent finger movements. If the movements performed by the observer are congruent with those performed by the other person, they are clearly facilitated (their reaction time is shorter). Conversely, incongruence of the movements of the observer with those of the other person leads to a degraded performance. Kilner *et al.* (2003) obtained similar results when subjects performed arm movements in a certain direction, while they watched another agent moving his arm in a different direction. Their movements became slower and more variable in their direction than when they observed congruent movements. Incidentally, this was not so when the observed movements were performed by a robot arm instead of the arm of a real person: no interference was found with incongruent movements of the robot arm. This interference is reminiscent of the classical effects described in psychology as 'stimulus–response compatibility': the response to a stimulus is faster when the features of the response are congruent with the corresponding features of the stimulus (e.g. it is easier to respond by pointing the right hand at a stimulus appearing in the right visual field than at a stimulus appearing in the left visual field). In the case of an interplay between observed and executed movements, it is likely that the representations of the two movements share the same neural network, and that their execution is facilitated when they are mutually congruent (Stürmer *et al.* 2000).

Another classical psychological method that can be used to reveal the content of action representations built from observation is *priming*. A classical example of priming is the situation where advanced cues are given to the subject before they perform a task. Imagine that you have to point to a visual target appearing unpredictably either to the right or to the left of a central fixation point. Your pointing movement will be facilitated if, a short time prior to the presentation of the target, an arrow is shown pointing to the side where it will appear (Posner *et al.* 1984). In the context of action perception, the motor system can also be primed by the presentation of a visual stimulus. Craighero *et al.* (2002) found that the execution of a grasping movement is facilitated when a picture of the hand in a posture that matches the planned grasping movement is shown shortly before the movement starts (see also Vogt *et al.* 2003). The facilitation effect is not obtained if the hand shown is a robotic hand instead of a human hand (Tai *et al.* 2004), which again suggests that observing the performance of another person facilitates the formation of motor representations specific for biological movements, and not global representations for the achievement of a certain goal. Günther Knoblich and his co-workers went one step further in showing that this effect is even greater if the performance one sees is self-produced. Knoblich and Prinz (2001) presented subjects with videos of an action (dart throwing) that they had previously performed, compared with videos of the same action performed by other subjects. Only the arm of the dart thrower was visible and the target itself was not shown on the video. The task consisted of predicting the accuracy of the observed action. Prediction was better when subjects observed their own dart throwing than when they observed the dart throwing of another person. Loula *et al.* (2005) similarly found that subjects who had to recognize point-light displays of movements, either self-produced or produced by one of their friends, recognized self-produced movements better. The fact that one recognizes one's own movements that one has never seen better than the visually familiar movements produced by people one has frequently observed may seem paradoxical. This becomes less surprising, however, if one considers that the mechanism activated during watching an action is the same as that activated during performing that action.

Action representations have to be formed to understand actions of others because of the inadequacy of visual perception. Conscious visual perception may give access to the spatial aspects of the observed action, e.g. the direction and the extent of the movements, the agent's body parts involved or the inter-action between the agent's body and other objects; yet, it does not give access to intrinsic aspects of the action, such as its kinematics (acceleration and velocity of the moving parts) or its dynamics (the forces involved). Those aspects which escape conscious perception are important, not only for under-standing the meaning or the goal of the observed action, but for being able to learn how to perform that action oneself. This means that aspects of the action which are beyond the capacities of conscious perception must be processed by the motor system to build the representation of that action.

In order to demonstrate this point, one has to use a different method rather than asking the subject to describe what he sees. One possibility, currently used in experimental psychology, is to place the subject in a situation of 'forced choice': the subject has to give a response to the presentation of a visual stimulus, even if he or she has not consciously perceived that stimulus. Sonia Kandel and her colleagues used this method to determine what observers can actually see from the action of handwriting. In cursorily writing a sequence of letters, the velocity of the writing movement for a given letter is influenced by the letter that follows. For example, the velocity of the descending stroke of an *l* is different if this *l* is followed by another *l* (as in the pair *ll*), or followed by an *e* (*le*) or an *n* (*ln*). In their experiment, Kandel *et al.* (2000) displayed on a screen the writing movement of the letter *l* corresponding to one of two different pairs (e.g. *ll* or *le*). The subjects had to press one of two keys (LL or LE) to indicate which letter would follow the *l*. Obviously, these strokes look the same to a naive perceiver: it is only when the subjects are forced to make a choice that their responses differ for each pair. Thus, subtle kinematic differences can be detected by observing a movement produced by another agent, and this detection is not based on the space–time co-variation of the limb position, but rather on the integration of motor rules. When these rules are artificially violated (e.g. by changing the velocity profile of the stroke such that the normal velocity–curvature co-variation is violated), the possibility of predicting the next letter disappears, and the handwriting does not look 'natural' any more. These results in fact merge with those described above by Viviani and his co-workers. They provide evidence that the rules used by the motor system of an agent to produce movements are also those which are used by an observer to perceive these movements. To paraphrase Hamilton *et al.* (2004), 'my own action influences how I perceive another person's action'. This is indeed a strong argument for the hypothesis that the actions of others have to be simulated by the motor system of the observer before being recognized, a hypothesis that will be fully developed in Chapter 6.

5.3.2 Changes in brain activity during action observation

5.3.2.1 The monkey premotor cortex and the discovery of mirror neurons

The interest of researchers in the brain mechanisms of action perception and observation began about 15 years ago, with the serendipitous discovery of a special class of neurons in monkey premotor cortex. In the early 1990s, Giacomo Rizzolatti and his colleagues were involved in mapping the activity of neurons in the motor areas. They had first provided a new topographic map of this region, based on cytochrome oxidase labeling (Matelli *et al.* 1985), and subsequently explored each of the new areas (labeled F1–F7) by recording single neuron activity. Neurons in area F1 had the typical motor properties corresponding to primary motor cortex. Areas F4 and F5, corresponding to dorsal and ventral premotor cortex (area 6), respectively, discharged in relation to the execution of certain types of movements by the monkey (Gentilucci *et al.* 1988; Rizzolatti *et al.* 1988). These neurons encode movements which involve interaction with objects, mainly during hand manipulation. According to their selectivity, they were classified as 'grasping neurons', 'holding neurons', 'tearing neurons' and 'manipulation neurons'. In Rizzolatti *et al.*'s (1995) terms, area F5 can be compared with a 'vocabulary' of object-oriented actions. Importantly, the motor properties displayed by these neurons are of a higher order than those of neurons located in primary motor cortex: first, they encode relatively complex actions, not simple one-joint movements; secondly, they encode these actions irrespective of the hand used by the animal; finally, they also respond to the presentation of visual objects shown to the monkey without an instruction to grasp them. Often, there is a close relationship between the type of prehension coded by the neuron and the size of the visual stimulus effective in triggering it. This is particularly clear for the precision grip neurons which are activated only by small visual objects. Being endowed with this dual property of being selective for a certain type of objects and for the corresponding action on these objects, premotor neurons in area F5 can play a true representational role: they do not simply describe movements or objects, they describe actions with goals. In addition, the fact that they discharge on observation of the object alone indicates that they encode a represented action, i.e. an action which remains covert according to the instructions that the monkey has received.

Area F5, which occupies the most rostral part of inferior area 6, has reciprocal connections with the parietal lobe, in particular with area AIP located at the tip of the intraparietal sulcus. Neurons in area AIP, which have been studied by Hideo Sakata and his collaborators (e.g. Taira *et al.* 1990; Murata *et al.* 2001), provide a visual analysis of the shape, orientation and size of objects. However, the analysis provided by AIP neurons differs from that provided by other visual areas. AIP does not encode the pictorial properties of objects, which are needed to access the object identification: rather, it encodes pragmatic properties of objects, those that are required but sufficient for grasping them. Arguably, neurons in AIP send the result of their visual analysis of a graspable object to neurons in F5. In turn, F5 provides AIP with the motor command signals generated for grasping the object, so that the visual analysis and the motor command are properly matched. As Rizzolatti *et al.* (1995) put it, 'AIP and F5 form a cortical circuit which transforms visual information on the intrinsic properties of objects into hand movements that allow the animal to interact appropriately with the objects. Motor information is then transferred to F1 to which F5 is directly connected'.

Besides the 'canonical' premotor neurons described above, another type of neuron was found in area F5. Those were neurons which, in addition to discharging during execution of specific object-oriented hand movements, also discharged in response to the visual observation of the same action performed by an experimenter, or by another monkey. The observed hand action has to be directed at an object (e.g. a piece of food): the neuron will not discharge if the observed movement is performed in the absence of the object, nor if the object alone is presented. The visual responsiveness of these neurons thus includes a further property, which was not present in canonical neurons: they encode an action and its goal, but irrespective of the agent who performs it. Hence the term of 'mirror neurons' that was used to designate them, and the suggestion that they could play a role in action understanding (Di Pellegrino *et al.* 1992). Over the years, striking new properties have been added to the initial description of mirror neurons. First, the direct vision of the goal does not seem to be necessary for a mirror neuron to discharge: hiding the goal and the final part of the movement behind a screen does not impair the discharge, provided the monkey 'knows' that there is a goal behind the mask (Umilta *et al.* 2001). Secondly, there are mirror neurons sensitive to actions which are not only visible but also audible (e.g. breaking a peanut), which retain their mirror property when either the noise of the action or the sight of the action is presented alone (audio-visual neurons, Keysers *et al.* 2003). Thus, because mirror neurons discharge when the action is invisible, whether it is partly hidden or it is reduced to the sound, they cannot be considered as 'perception' neurons. They relate to represented actions rather than to directly perceived actions.

More recently, a population of neurons presenting similar mirror properties was identified in the parietal lobe. These neurons are located on the convexity of the anterior part of the inferior parietal lobule, in a zone (area 7) which sends connections to area F5 in the ventral premotor cortex, and receives connections from the visual areas in the STS and the inferotemporal cortex. Like F5 premotor neurons, they are active during the execution of hand actions (e.g. grasping a piece of food to eat it). Many of them are also active when the animal watches the same action performed by an experimenter (Fogassi *et al.* 2005).

Now, let us replace premotor neurons within the framework of action understanding and action identification. Canonical neurons encode self-executed actions towards visual goals; mirror neurons also encode goal-directed actions, but irrespective of the agent who performs them. Thus, they both contribute to the representation of actions. Unlike mirror neurons, however, canonical neurons are not concerned with action identification, because their activity directly reflects the representation of the agent who executes the action. On the contrary, the mirror neuron activity is ambiguous, in the sense that it reflects the representations of two agents: that of the agent who executes the action, and that of the subject who observes it. To the extent that this activity is the same in the two conditions, the question arises of how the agent of the action can be identified. In the previous chapter about action identification and the sense of agency, we described action representations that are shared by one's own action and the action of another agent. Remember, however, that there are two properties of shared representations. First, the fact that the two representations overlap accounts for understanding the action of another agent by the observer, because the observer uses the same mechanisms to build his own action and to perceive or understand the action of the other. Secondly, the fact that the two representations overlap only partially accounts for the self-other distinction, because the two representations differ from one another. Accordingly, mirror neurons would only fulfill one of the two conditions for a shared representation, and would therefore account for one of its two functions: because they do not differentiate between the executed and the observed versions of the same action, the mirror neurons can account for action understanding, but not for disentangling a self-represented action from an action observed being performed by someone else. The process of action attribution must be effected by other neuron populations which fire only when the monkey performs the action and not when she observes it being performed by another agent, i.e. by neurons which account for the non-overlapping part of the shared representation.

Thus, the mirror neuron population in area F5 of the monkey brain can be seen as 'a cortical system that matches observation and execution of motor actions' (Gallese and Goldman 1998, p. 495). As Rizzolatti *et al.* rightly put it, 'when the monkey observes a motor action that belongs to (or resembles) its movement repertoire, this action is automatically retrieved. The retrieved action is not necessarily executed. It is only represented in the motor system. We speculate that this observation/execution mechanism plays a role in understanding the meaning of motor events' (1996a). As to the mirror neuron population in the inferior parietal lobule, it stands in a position intermediate between visual areas where actions are perceived and premotor areas where they are understood. For this reason, they may serve a more complex function than the F5 mirror neurons. This point will be discussed in Chapter 6.

5.3.2.2 Neuroimaging of the human mirror system

Soon after the discovery of monkey mirror neurons, a series of experiments confirmed the idea that a similar mechanism also existed in humans. These experiments, using neuroimagery, were aimed at comparing brain activity in normal subjects who either actively interacted with objects or watched an agent acting on the same objects in front of them. The observation of object-oriented actions was found to activate areas located in the frontal and parietal lobes. In the frontal lobe, the SMA and the lateral and ventral parts of area 6 in the precentral gyrus were involved (Grafton *et al.* 1996; Rizzolatti *et al.* 1996). The involvement of primary motor cortex, which was not apparent in the early neuroimaging studies using PET, will be dealt with below. In premotor cortex, the activation found during action observation partly overlapped with that found when the subjects actively performed actions on the objects. In later experiments, Buccino *et al.* (2001) found that the premotor areas activated during action observation are topographically organized to the same extent as those activated during action execution by the subject. Observation of actions performed with the mouth, the hand or the foot activated the respective areas which were distributed over the cortical surface according to the classical somatotopic map.

The activation of premotor cortex during action observation also extended down to the inferior frontal gyrus (Rizzolatti *et al.* 1996; Tai *et al.* 2004). This finding has raised considerable interest, for several reasons. First, the inferior frontal gyrus, which in the human brain includes Brodmann areas 44, 45 and 47, is considered as a differentiation of the monkey ventral premotor cortex where area F5 is located (von Bonin and Bailey 1947), and where mirror neurons were first found. Secondly, as we saw in Chapter 2, this very same area was also found to be involved during motor imagery, another form of action representation (Decety *et al.* 1994). Thus, in confirmation of our speculation in the preceding paragraph, representing a self-generated action and representing an action performed by another agent effectively share the same neural structures in premotor cortex. Finally, there is a third reason why activation of the inferior frontal gyrus during action observation is an important finding: it is because area 44 in the human inferior frontal gyrus on the left side correspond to Broca's area, an area known to be specialized for the executive aspects of language. This converging evidence has major implications for motor cognition. In a nutshell, the mirror neurons in monkey area F5 and their human counterpart in the inferior frontal gyrus (Broca's area) might represent a unified mechanism for representing and understanding the motor aspects of the behavior of others, including those aspects which, in humans, are carried by spoken or gestural language. Obviously, this point will be central to our discussion around the motor simulation hypothesis, in the last chapter of this book.

The frontal lobe is not the only region where activation during action observation is found. Areas located in posterior and ventral parts of the parietal lobe (e.g. area 40), more on the left side, are also found to be strongly activated. Again, the topography of these activated areas largely overlaps with that found during other forms of action representations, such as motor imagery, or even during mere observation of tools (Rumiati *et al.* 2004). In addition, the parietal lobe activation during action observation co-exists with the activation of visual areas (e.g. in the superior temporal sulcus) which are specifically responsive to biological movements (Grèzes *et al.* 2001; Grossman *et al.* 2000) or to object recognition (Shmuelof and Zohary 2005). The latter authors found an interesting dissociation between observing hand actions oriented towards objects, in two different tasks. In a task focusing on the action, not on the objects (e.g. count the fingers involved), the anterior part of the intraparietal sulcus was activated. Conversely, in a task focusing on the objects, not on the actions (name the objects), the ventral occipital areas were activated.

5.3.2.3 Changes in activity in primary motor cortex during action observation

As for motor imagery, the prototypical form of action representation, representations arising from observed actions activate the motor cortex. This contention is directly supported by recent monkey data. Monkeys were trained to observe the action of reaching and grasping objects performed by an experimenter. Their motor cortex was subsequently analyzed using a quantitative method of marking cortical metabolism with [^{14}C]deoxyglucose autoradiography. Raos *et al.* (2004) found that the metabolism in the forelimb regions of primary motor and somatosensory cortex was significantly increased following observation of actions. The same areas were activated in monkeys which had performed the reaching and grasping task themselves. However, this result may be difficult to interpret because the two conditions (observing and doing) could not be compared in the same animal, which is not possible with this technique. Human data, though obtained with more indirect methods, concur with the monkey data. TMS of motor cortex during the observation of an action demonstrates a higher excitability of those parts of the motor cortex which correspond to the observed movement. For example, when the subject watches a grasping movement, the MEPs triggered by the stimulation are larger in muscles involved in finger flexion than in other hand muscles (Fadiga *et al.* 1995; Strafella and Paus 2000; Patuzzo *et al.* 2003). As was the case for imagined movements, the change in excitability affects not only motor cortex but also the descending pathways to the spinal cord: observing finger flexion or extension produces changes in upper limb H-reflexes (Baldissera *et al.* 2001). The effects of action observation on cortical excitability are not limited to the visual aspects of the action. Luciano Fadiga and his colleagues were able to show that listening to phonemes increases the excitability of the motor cortical area corresponding to the relevant tongue muscles (Fadiga *et al.* 2002). This finding, which has obvious implications for understanding spoken language, will be discussed again in the next chapter.

Primary motor cortex activity during action observation can also be measured by recording local electromagnetic changes. Cochin *et al.* (1999) had noted changes in cortical electrical activity (EEG) in subjects who were either executing simple finger movements or watching the same movements executed by an experimenter. EEG changes were found in the two conditions at the same electrode site, corresponding to the location of motor cortex (see also van Schie *et al.* 2004). Another technique, magneto-encephalography (MEG), which allows better anatomical localization of the active sites by matching the skull location of the electrodes with anatomical brain imaging using MRI, was also used to map cortical activity during action observation.

Changes in activity measured with MEG reflect changes in the synchrony of cortical neurons: an increase in neuron synchronization can be due to a decreased inhibition and an increased excitability. Hari *et al.* (1998) showed definite activation of the precentral motor cortex during observation of another individual manipulating objects, at the same cortical site as during execution of the manipulation movements and during imagination of the same movements (see Chapter 2).[1] This is also true during observation of tool use (Järveläinen *et al.* 2004). A complementary TMS study by Clark *et al.* (2004) reached the same conclusion. The authors were able to compare MEP amplitude in the same subjects during explicitly imaging, observing and physically executing the same hand gestures. They found that observation and imagery conditions led to a similar facilitation in MEP amplitude in the relevant hand muscle. In addition, during action observation, a condition of 'active' observation (i.e. with the instruction subsequently to imitate) yielded larger MEPs than a purely passive observation. Although MEP facilitation was weaker during action representation than during physical execution of the same action, it clearly calls for a unitary mechanism for action representations in the three conditions. Taken together, these results support the view already expressed in several sections of this book that primary motor cortex is involved during different types of mental representation of actions. Motor cortex is not a purely executive area, it also has a function in motor cognition.

5.4 Functional implications of the mirror system in motor cognition

The existence of the mirror system opens up a new possibility for explaining how we understand the motor behavior of our conspecifics. The novelty is that external events can be encoded by our brain through a mechanism which departs from the classical view of afferent information processing, exclusively based on sensory systems. The recognition of motor behavior by the mirror system, although it obviously uses the resources of early stages of sensory processing, is subsequently channeled through a genuine processing line. To use the framework developed in the first chapter, the type of representations created by the mirror system does not pertain to the category of perceptual representations: rather, those are action representations, i.e. representations that include the goal and the means of a potential action.

---

[1] In a single subject with implanted subdural electrodes, Tremblay *et al.* (2004) were able to observe, on the same electrodes, changes in activity in the motor hand area during both execution and observation of finger movements.

5.4.1 The dual processing of motor events

Observed actions are in fact processed in two different ways, according to the situation in which they are seen. An action can be processed as a visual event which can be perceptually identified, verbalized and matched with previous occurrences of the same event. Alternatively, it can also be processed as a motor event that can be learned and replicated. The former mode of processing provides a pictorial description of the action; the latter provides a motor understanding of the same action. Consider, for example, yourself watching a pantomime executed by someone else, with the purpose of identifying the action that is being pantomimed in front of you. Even though no objects or tools are visible (and provided the actor is good), you will easily recognize and name actions such as writing, opening a bottle or cutting bread. Now, consider another situation where you are watching a sequence of unrecognizable movements, such as unknown symbolic gestures or signing movements, with the purpose of replicating it afterwards. In this case, although no meaning is available, and no cues for naming or categorizing the sequence can be extracted, you will still be able to learn and replicate that sequence. In a neuroimaging experiment, Decety *et al.* (1997) used this paradigm for mapping brain activity during watching either meaningful or meaningless pantomimes. In one session, subjects were instructed to watch meaningful actions with the purpose of recognizing them later on. Activation was found in areas specialized for high level visual processing, in the left middle temporal gyrus in the STS region, in the parahippocampal gyrus and in the ventral prefrontal cortex. In a different session, subjects watched meaningless movement sequences with the purpose of subsequent imitation: activated areas were located in the motor system, specifically the anterior part of the SMA and the ventral premotor cortex. The right inferior parietal cortex was also strongly activated.

Another striking illustration of this duality of the modalities of processing an action is the case of apparent motion produced by alternating static pictures of an actor. Remember that, by only changing the frequency of alternation of the pictures, one can create the impression of either biomechanically possible or impossible movements (e.g. the arm around the knee, or through the knee, as we discussed earlier in this chapter). Stevens *et al.* (2000) compared the brain activity of normal subjects during the perception of biomechanically possible and impossible movements. They found that perception of possible movements activated motor structures (the primary motor cortex and the premotor cortex) and the inferior parietal cortex, as one would expect for observing an action. In contrast, the perception of biomechanically impossible movements prompted bilateral activation of inferotemporal cortex. Thus, the type of action one observes and the task in which one is involved orient the processing in the direction of a perceptual representation or a motor representation.

The above results make a sharp distinction between perception of an action as a pure visual event and another mode of processing which considers the same action as a motor event, i.e. a set of commands that can be simulated and replicated. Clearly, only the latter mode of processing is within the realm of the mirror system. The other mechanism, that which is responsible for analyzing the visual content of an action, is mostly represented by neurons in the STS and in the inferotemporal cortex. These neurons are sensitive to a specific set of visual stimuli, such as faces and other body parts, and, in addition, have a dynamic sensitivity for the meaningful movements of these body parts: goal-oriented movements, interactions between different individuals, facial expressions, etc. What produces the difference between the processing effected by the STS neurons and that effected by mirror neurons is that, unlike mirror neurons, STS neurons have no motor output; having no motor output, they cannot match the observed action onto an executable one and, consequently, they cannot give access to the cues that are encoded in the motor system. What prompts the use of one or the other mode of processing is the context in which an external action is processed. The task requirements, as the above findings of Decety *et al.* indicate, are part of this context. The type of observed action can also be a cue for orienting its processing according to whether it belongs, or not, to the observer's repertoire: observing an action irrelevant to our human repertoire (e.g. a dog barking) activates our perceptual system rather than our mirror system (Rizzolatti and Matelli 2003). The semantic content of the movements may also orient the processing in one way or the other. Gestures which have an 'affective' content, e.g. which may express inner feelings, such as anger, and gestures which have an 'instrumental' content, with a role in communicating commands (e.g. stop!), are processed differently and activate different neural networks. Gallagher and Frith (2004) showed that the observation of gestures of the 'affective' type activated a perceptual/emotional network (the right STS, the amygdala and the anterior paracingulate cortex), whereas gestures of the 'instrumental' type activated the mirror system.

In spite of these differences, however, the two modes of processing observed actions are connected with each other. The three main anatomical sites for action recognition and understanding (the STS in the temporal lobe, area PF in the inferior parietal lobule and area F5 in premotor cortex) are reciprocally connected (for a review of these connections, see Keysers and Perrett 2004): they are part of a network where information can be exchanged between processing sites. In humans, although their activation, as we just saw, can be task specific, they can also be simultaneously activated during action observation. Thus, cues arising from the processing of the motion of body parts by STS neurons might be transferred to parietal and premotor cortices. These cues would represent the 'context' in which the action takes place. For example, the processing of the agent's head orientation or gaze direction might provide F5 neurons with indications about his intention, which can hardly be extracted from watching of the hand movement alone. Indeed, perceiving where an agent is looking while grasping an object can be a powerful indication about what the agent is intending to do after having grasped the object.

5.4.2 Learning by observation

One of the obvious functions of the mirror system is to contribute to action learning. Learning by observation is an efficient means for acquiring new skills, especially for those motor activities that cannot be described verbally and therefore cannot be learnt by reading books or listening to talks. Think of acquiring musical skills, such as playing the violin: the pupil looks at the teacher and hears the sound the teacher produces; in turn, the teacher looks at the pupil's movements and hears the result of his performance, and so on: so learning proceeds by mutual observation. Beyond informal evidence, learning by observation has also been studied experimentally. For example, Heyes and Foster (2002) found that subjects watching an experimenter performing a sequence of movements can learn the sequence as efficiently as when practic-ing the task themselves (see also Sebanz *et al.* 2003). Observing the action of another person creates in the observer a representation of that action: this representation subsequently facilitates the execution of the action by the observer. As for the action representation created during motor imagery, those which result from action observation should include sufficient information for replicating the observed action.

Another way of looking at the role of observation in learning motor skills is to compare brain activity during observation of an action in subjects who have already learned that action and in naive subjects. For example, what is the difference in brain activation of expert dancers when they watch the type of dance in which they have expertise (e.g. classical ballet), or when they watch another type of dance (e.g. the Brazilian capoeira). Expert dancers watching 'their' dance have greater activation in premotor cortex, parietal lobe and superior temporal sulcus than non-expert dancers. This result (Calvo-Merino *et al.* 2005) suggests that the mirror system is better activated by actions that one understands and that one has already learned. However, the degree of activation of this system would presumably depend on the task of the watch-ers. It is likely that a non-dancer watching either type of dance with the purpose of becoming a dancer would progressively become able to activate his mirror system, as he would become more familiar with the dance and integrate it within his own motor repertoire.

The possibility of learning new skills by mere observation suggests that observational learning, like other types of learning, can influence brain plasticity. We saw in Chapter 2 that this is the case for mental training, whereby repetitively imagining an action increases the excitability of corresponding areas of motor cortex (e.g. Pascual-Leone *et al.* 1995). This possibility of observational learning to influence brain plasticity has been exploited in the context of clinical rehabilitation, to relieve pain in patients. Patients with limb amputation or denervation frequently experience phantom limb and phantom pain in the denervated limb. This pathological phenomenon has been attributed to a progressive decay of activity of the part of motor cortex corresponding to the denervated segments (Flohr *et al.* 1995): motor cortex, in addition to its role in controlling movements, also influences the processing of sensory input arising from the effector it controls. Should it become possible to restore the deficient neural cortical activity, then the pain could be controlled. This idea was followed by Giraux and Sirigu (2003) in two such patients suffering phantom pain following a unilateral brachial plexus avulsion. The patients were submitted to a series of training sessions where the image of their good hand was visually transposed at the location of their impaired hand by way of mirrors, following a technique described by Ramachandran and Rogers Ramachandran (1996). The patients were instructed to move their good hand that they saw in the place of their impaired arm. Following a series of 24 such daily 'visuomotor' training sessions, the activity of their primary motor cortex area contralateral to their paralyzed arm, monitored by fMRI, was greatly increased. This procedure had a beneficial effect for the patients, not in improving their hand movements, which remained impaired due to the brachial plexus lesion, but in decreasing their phantom limb pain.

In all the experiments described in the present chapter, except the latter on paralyzed patients, observed actions were seen in the third-person perspective: they were detached from the observer's body and, indeed, they were actions performed by others. One may also observe one's own actions in the third-person perspective, e.g. when one's actions have been video-taped and are played back on a screen (Knoblich and Flach 2001). The situation is different, however, when one observes oneself in the first-person perspective, i.e. when I watch my writing hand, for example. Is this still action 'understanding'? Does this still activate the mirror system? If the answer is yes, that would be a prototypical example of a closed-loop system where the observer and the agent are one single person, and where the self-generated representation is matched by the self-produced action. In the above situation, the possibility for the patients to watch their own movements, or at least movements that were superimposed to their own limbs, may have provided a reinforcement of their own action representations and facilitated the reactivation of their motor cortex.

5.4.3 The pathology of action understanding

There is a pathology of action representation. In Chapter 1, we saw evidence that patients with apraxia due to lesions in the left hemisphere are impaired in representing complex actions. While they were able to perform simple visuo-motor actions, they failed to conceive and execute actions involving a sequence of movements. In addition, they had apparently lost the ability to pantomime actions in the absence of the relevant tool, and to form mental images of these actions. It is therefore not surprising that these patients were also impaired in recognizing actions either executed or pantomimed by others. Patient L.L. with a bilateral parietal lesion, described by Sirigu *et al.* (1995b), corresponded to this clinical picture: she was impaired in positioning her fingers on a spoon to grasp it for eating soup; when asked to sort out correct from incorrect visual displays of another agent's hand postures, she consistently failed. Finally, she was unable to describe verbally hand postures related to specific object uses. This clinical description confirms the idea of a common representation for conceiving an action and understanding an action performed by an external agent.

The impairment shown by apraxic patients deals with action representation, not with self-representation. This distinction is interesting to consider for comparison with other groups of patients presenting difficulties in action recognition, such as the schizophrenic patients described in Chapter 4. The substitution method previously used by Daprati *et al.* (1997) for examining schizophrenic patients was also used in apraxic patients. This method consists of instructing the subject to perform a pre-specified hand movement, while he sees on a video screen a moving hand which can either be his own hand, or the hand of another person substituted for his own. At the end of the trial, the subject is asked whether the hand he saw was his hand or not. As we saw in Chapters 3 and 4, normal subjects only make a few errors in this test, usually by misattributing the alien hand to themselves. Apraxic patients were dramatically impaired: they failed to recognize their own hand and their own movements, and made wrong attributions (Sirigu *et al.* 1999). The impairment shown by apraxic patients thus resembled that found in the schizophrenic patients tested by Daprati *et al.* who tended to misattribute their own moving hand to another agent or, conversely, to misattribute to themselves the movements executed by the other agent. This resemblance is only superficial, however. Unlike schizophrenics, apraxics do not show any evidence of self–other confusion. Their disturbance results from a defective mechanism for understanding actions, not a defective mechanism of action monitoring for disentangling the self from the other. We still badly need a more complete description of the 'social' abilities of apraxic patients. Can they learn new skills by observation? How do they communicate with other people? Have they lost the ability to understand internal states, such as intentions or desires, expressed by other people? Answering these questions would greatly contribute to the issue of the role of motor cognition in social communication (see Chapter 6).[2]

5.5 The role of the mirror system in action imitation

Here, we first meet imitation. The concept of imitation was latent in the sections dealing with action observation and, more specifically, learning by observation: the ability to perceive and understand the actions of others is obviously the first step to imitation. Yet, not all species are able to imitate the behavior of their conspecifics, which they perceive and to which they are able to react. Imitation is one step further. Its development, in non-human primates and in humans, correlates with the acquisition of high level social abilities, such as the ability to experience empathy, which are not evenly distributed across species and which are characteristics of higher primate behavior.

Imitation, however, is an ill-defined concept which includes several different (and possibly related) phenomena. These phenomena range from simply copying a movement after seeing it, to intentional off-line reproduction of an action. The degree of complexity of the imitated model and the fidelity of the copy may vary greatly from one type of imitation to the other. Here, I will make a distinction between two broad categories of imitative phenomena: one is *imitative mirroring* or *mimicry*, the ability to duplicate observed movements; the other is what I will call *true imitation*, the ability to understand the intention of another agent, or the goal of his action, and to re-enact that action to achieve the intended goal. These categories, as we will soon realize, do not have sharp boundaries: in the course of the description of these phenomena, we will find several intermediate types of behavior which can also be labeled imitation in its broad sense of action replication.

....

[2] Action understanding is also impaired in autistic children. A recent study (Zalla *et al.* 2006) shows that these children cannot order a sequence of images depicting the successive steps of an action.

In the next paragraphs, we will have, first, to specify the distinction between imitative mirroring and true imitation, and, secondly, to discuss the relevance of the different forms of imitation to motor cognition.

5.5.1 Imitative mirroring versus true imitation

One can reproduce an action one does not understand, but one must understand what an action is about to be able to imitate it. This definition states one of the major differences between imitative mirroring and true imitation. In other words, what characterizes true imitation, and makes it different from imitative mirroring, is its intentional nature. Imitative mirroring and mimicry, a widespread phenomenon in the behavior of many animal species, stands as a primitive form of imitation. Flock and herd behavior in birds and mammals, and school behavior in fishes are instances of behaviors in which different individuals, which are part of large aggregates, synchronize their movements for some adaptive reason. Seeing an individual in the collection initiate a movement triggers in others the production of a similar movement. These examples are best thought of as examples of 'resonance' behavior: upon seeing an individual behave in a certain way, others 'resonate'. Mimicry and resonance behavior are also widespread in humans. As common sense testifies, the mere detection (visual or non-visual) of some typically human behavior can cause the observer to engage in a replication of the observed behavior: yawning, laughter and emotional contagion all are examples of human resonance behavior.

Although imitative mirroring can cause the observer to engage in a replication of the observed behavior, this tendency is normally inhibited, under the pressure of social constraints. Remember the pathological cases of 'imitation' or 'utilization' behavior observed in patients with lesions in prefrontal cortex, first described by Lhermitte (1986), and detailed in Chapter 3. Patients in this condition spontaneously imitate body gestures performed by an examiner, such as scratching their head or tapping their leg with their hand. When asked the reason for doing so, the patient may reply that, because the examiner did it they felt that they had to do it too. This compulsive imitative behavior may persist even when the patient is explicitly asked not to imitate the examiner. In Chapter 3, we argued that this behavior is a consequence of a disordered or weakened volition, making the subject dependent on external events. This interpretation is supported by neuroimaging findings: when a normal subject is requested to perform a finger movement in front of another agent performing a different finger movement at the same time, a strong activation is observed in several areas of prefrontal cortex (Brass *et al.* 2001a). These areas, which are damaged in frontal patients, would serve the role of inhibiting compulsive imitative tendencies. Note that the mechanism for inhibiting imitation

Fig. 5.1 Mutual observation during communicative behavior in two chimpanzees. This type of situation emphasizes the role of action observation, observational learning and imitation. (Copyright M. Gunther/Bios).

also fulfills a critical function, that of the self–other distinction: we refrain from imitating others that we see acting because we can distinguish their intentions from our own and do not confuse their action representations with ours (Brass and Heyes 2005).

Imitative mirroring in humans starts very early in life. Meltzoff and Moore (1997) found out that newborn infants (42 min old!) are able to replicate gestures of mouth opening, tongue protrusion and lip protrusion, which they see adults perform. A question is whether neonates' replications of mouth opening and tongue protrusion are cases of true imitation or whether they are instances of mimicry. Calling this behavior mimicry would suggest the conclusion that, possibly due to the slow maturation of their prefrontal cortex, human neonates behave like patients with prefrontal lesions who cannot refrain from imitating actions they see. Later, however, infants' imitative behavior changes into a behavior which departs from the reflex nature of the early stage. As shown by Meltzoff (1995), 18-month-old children are able to 're-enact' intended actions. In one experiment, 18-month-old children saw adults engage in an action directed towards complex toys and fail to perform it: when encouraged to do the action themselves, the children did not merely reproduce the gestures seen in the adults' failed attempts to perform the action. Rather, they performed a successful version of the intended action of which they had seen an aborted version. Whether the duplication of mouth movements observed immediately after birth is a precursor of this more advanced form of imitation is indeed a matter of debate. Many reflexive behaviors observed in neonates disappear during the first months of life and are later replaced by the full-blown behavior (e.g. neonate stepping disappears long before infant walking becomes possible). These behavioral changes from neonates to infants illustrate the difference between imitative mirroring and true imitation. The advent of true imitation manifests an implicit recognition of conspecifics as 'intentional agents like me' (Meltzoff 1995). As Hauser writes, 'when humans imitate an action, they often infer the model's intention. Humans perceive actions as having goals and being guided by an actor's intention to achieve those goals. Thus, when we imitate, we are copying not only the physical action, but also the intentions underlying those actions' (Hauser 2000, p. 147–148). When we try to impersonate somebody, such as for instance copying the voice and the gestures of a famous person, we try to be accurate in copying the physical action but we also try to suggest the supposed mental content of the character we imitate. The facts that, in true imitation, the imitated action deals with the goal of the action and not only with its form, and that it can be delayed with respect to the model are key features which are not present in imitative mirroring.

Like children beyond the age of 18 months, apes can and do imitate, in the sense that they replicate complex actions by copying the result of the action, rather than merely duplicating its form (Tomasello's 'emulation', see Tomasello 2000). This behavior is clearly observed in non-enculturated animals, i.e. animals which have not been exposed to specific training procedures, and which have not learnt the action they are supposed to imitate in an unnatural social context (see Figure 5.1). Whiten and Custance (1996), for example, demonstrated to chimpanzees and to 2-to 4-year-old children the opening of a box containing food. The lid of the box was secured with bolts which could be removed in two ways (poke or twist). On each trial, one of the ways was demonstrated by the experimenter and the box was given to the chimpanzee or to the child: if the bolts were removed in the same way as was demonstrated, this was considered as an imitative response. The performance of chimpanzees was not very different from that of 2-year-old children, although 3- to 4-year-old children clearly performed better. No such evidence for imitation has ever been provided for macaque monkeys.

The reason why we are interested in imitation in non-human primates is because the above mirror neurons, which were discovered in monkey's brain, and the human mirror system, were frequently considered as a possible basis for imitation. In the next paragraph, we analyze the evidence for the involvement of the human mirror system in imitative tasks. In the next chapter, we will come back on the relationship of the mirror neurons and the mirror system with imitation in the broader framework of the simulation theory.

5.5.2 **The neural basis of imitation**

What is the best paradigm to study imitation and its neural substrate? Is it an immediate replication of the action of an experimenter? In that case, it is likely that the subjects will engage in a degraded form of imitation, by copying the experimenter. Or, is it a replication of the action after some delay? In that case, the subjects may use a motor representation built from the memory of the previously seen action, and the resulting performance will not discriminate between motor memory, motor imagery and true imitation.

In their pioneering study of brain activation during imitation, Iacoboni *et al.* (1999) used the immediate replication paradigm. They proposed a 'direct matching hypothesis' according to which the ability to copy elementary actions 'might involve a 'resonance' mechanism that directly maps a pictorial or kinematic description of the observed action onto an internal motor representation of the same action' (p. 2526). In order to fulfill this requirement, one should observe, in the involved brain structures, an added effect of imitation with respect to either merely executing the action or watching the experimenter act. Imitation should be more than simply adding together the motor execution and visual observation of an action. To demonstrate this, Iacoboni *et al.* (1999) measured brain activity with fMRI in normal subjects instructed to observe and imitate finger movements shown on videos. Stronger activation was observed in the left frontal operculum (Brodman area 44 in the inferior frontal gyrus), in a zone of the anterior parietal cortex on the right side and in the right STS region. The interesting part of this imitation network is indeed area 44, for the reasons that we discussed earlier in this chapter, mainly because human area 44 is considered the human homolog of monkey area F5 where the population of mirror neurons was found. Thus, in this study, the mirror system seems to stand as a specific system involved in imitation. Nishitani and Hari (2002) added further information about the temporal aspects of brain activation during this type of imitation. Using MEG, they were able to track the temporal progression of activation through the imitation network. They found that, following visual areas in the occipital cortex, the STS was activated, itself followed by the inferior parietal lobule, then by the region of Broca's area and finally by primary motor cortex. Incidentally, this sequence was obtained by showing the subjects pictures of lip forms that they were instructed to replicate: the imitation network was activated even though the movements to be imitated were not shown, but were only suggested by the pictures.

The question of whether changes in brain activity during action observation and imitation can discriminate true imitation from more primitive forms, such as resonance or mimicry, remains an open one. It would be interesting to know whether the representation used by the observer to replicate immediately what he has seen differs from the representation he uses off-line to achieve the same goal as the observed agent. Learning by observation may in fact involve the two modalities in succession: one first tries slavishly to copy the movements and later one becomes able to achieve the action by using one's own method (Buccino *et al.* 2004). Chaminade *et al.* (2002) showed a wide overlap of activation in the two conditions of merely copying an action or trying to achieve the goal of that action. In this study, subjects observed an agent performing the action of assembling Lego blocks. In one condition, they were shown both the actions and the final goal; in other conditions, they were shown either only the actions and not the goal or the goal and not the actions. Subjects subsequently imitated what they had seen, i.e. they either replicated the details of the actions (the means to obtain the goal) or concentrated on the goal itself by using any means. Brain activation partially overlapped in the two conditions, except that prefrontal cortex was more activated during imitation of the means, whereas premotor cortex was more activated during imitation of the goal.

This type of result raises the question of whether imitation is a natural kind, beyond phenomena such as simply copying or mimicry. We are able, by observing an action, to build a perceptual representation of that action. We are also able to reproduce what we have seen, what we call imitation. However, the delayed duplication of an action simply requires forming a representation of that action and storing it in memory. One can reproduce an action one has observed to the same extent as one can draw an object one has perceived. While perceiving an object, we build a perceptual representation of that object and subsequently produce the drawing. If the drawing is an exact and realistic reproduction of the object, then the existence of direct matching between the perceptual and the motor aspects of the task can be suspected. However, what about a creative drawing which instantiates the object's reality rather than slavishly copying it? In that case, direct matching would be of no use. This makes the difference between an imitator and an artist.[3]

....

[3] The pathology of imitation ranges from compulsive imitation to lack of imitation. We already examined cases of compulsive imitation (the so-called imitation behavior) in frontal patients, which we attributed to an impairment in volition. Another example of compulsive imitation is the pathological behavior described as 'echopraxia' in certain autistic children. On the other hand, lack of imitation, as we saw above, is typically observed in apraxic patients: they have difficulties replicating visually presented actions or pantomimes (Goldenberg and Hagman 1997; Merians *et al.* 1997). However, the deficit of imitation shown by apraxic patients reflects a broader deficit in forming action representations: they are also impaired in executing, pantomiming and imagining actions, as well as in detecting errors in actions performed by the examiner. The question is whether there is a truly specific pathology of imitation, distinct from volitional disorders or action recognition impairments.

The direct matching between observing an action and executing it is clearly an adequate mechanism for replicating and learning that action. The activation of the motor system, and specifically the mirror system, by the observed action makes possible a simulation of that action, the only way to access the intricacies of motor execution. In contrast, the more complex modalities of imitation, because they are detached from the model, require the participation of additional mechanisms, in order to understand not only the action itself but also the intention and the mental state of the agent one observes. Whether this can also be a function for the mirror system will be discussed in the next chapter.

Chapter 6

The simulation hypothesis of motor cognition

In this final chapter, we will develop the concept of simulation as a potential explanation for unifying the various aspects of motor cognition. Simulation is used here as the off-line rehearsal of neural networks involved in specific operations such as perceiving or acting. In other words, simulation is what makes it possible to activate perceptual mechanisms in the absence of a stimulus, or to activate motor mechanisms without executing an action.

To make clear what we mean by simulation, let us consider first the case of visual simulation. The concept of visual simulation had been elaborated long before that of motor simulation, to account for the content of perceptual representations. During the visual perception of an object, the output from the sensory receptors activates primary visual areas specialized for extracting the elementary features of the object (the orientation of its contours, its color, etc.). Subsequent processing dispatches this information in higher level areas, up to the point where the object can be recognized, categorized and stored in memory. The same mechanism can be used off-line, i.e. in the absence of the object, the perceiver can rehearse the representation of that object. Perceptual representations can be rehearsed consciously, e.g. by voluntarily forming a visual mental image; they can also be used non-consciously as a tool for accessing implicit knowledge about visual things. We can, for example, provide responses to questions such as: 'Do teddy bears have round or elongated ears?', not because we have a stored explicit knowledge about the shape of the ears of bears, but because we can rehearse a mental image of teddy bears we have seen, and 'inspect' this image. Ample experimental evidence shows that forming such a visual mental image involves activation of the visual system, including those areas that correspond to the early stages of information processing of the visual information. Primary visual cortex is consistently involved in visual mental imagery (Kosslyn *et al.* 1993; Le Bihan *et al.* 1993). In addition, there is a selective involvement of specialized areas for different sorts of visual imagery: visual imagery of faces activates inferotemporal cortex, whereas visual imagery of places activates occipitoparietal cortex (see Farah 1994; O'Craven and Kanwisher 2000). Why should the low level processing areas be activated during a high level cognitive activity such as mental imagery, where no sensory processing occurs? A tentative explanation is that the contribution of retinotopically organized areas, such as V1, is needed for placing the image within a retinocentric frame of reference. Higher order areas, which lack retinotopic organization, would not be able, by themselves, to achieve this task. In other words, the process of visual imagery would have to follow the same processing track as visual perception to give the image its spatial layout, a process which requires the participation of V1.

In the case of the simulation of actions, which we will refer to as 'motor simulation', the ambition is not only to understand the intrinsic functioning of action representations, but also to explore the boundaries of motor cognition. If motor cognition is based on simulation of our own actions, and if the mechanisms each individual uses to simulate his own actions is the same as that other individuals use, as we have good reason to believe, then we can develop the idea that perceiving and producing actions are the two faces of the same process. However, does this process simply tell those who observe us acting what this action is? Or, can they go beyond the mere description of the action they see and extract its deeper meaning: specifically, in observing us grasping a cup, can they simply tell 'he grasps the cup', or can they infer 'he wants to drink'? In other words, can the intention of the observed agent be deciphered through this mechanism, and how far?

The very same questions will be asked in subsequent sections of this chapter about two other domains which are directly connected to action. First, emotions should be liable to the same explanation in so far as they are expressed motorically: if I simulate the emotional expression I see, can I feel that emotion to the same extent as I can feel the emotion I express? Secondly, language also involves a strong motor component: in so far as speech is an action, it falls into the category of events which are processed by both the perceptual and the motor system. What is the outcome of the motor processing of language and to what extent does it contribute to the understanding of what my interlocutor tells me?

6.1 Motor simulation: A hypothesis for explaining action representations

Let us now consider motor simulation. If the assumption that represented actions correspond to covert, quasi-executed actions is correct, then represented actions should involve a simulation of the mechanisms that normally participate in the various stages of action generation, including motor execution. We have detailed the functional anatomy of simulation in Chapter 2 about action imagination and in Chapter 5 about action observation. In these chapters, we have accumulated data showing that this activation is highly specific to the action that is represented. Forming motor images and observing other people act both involve motor cortex, premotor cortex, SMA, the basal ganglia and the cerebellum, i.e. the main neural structures which are needed for action execution. Now, the question raised about the involvement of primary visual cortex in visual imagery arises again: if motor images are non-executed actions, why should they involve the activation of executive neural structures? This question is at the core of the concept of motor simulation. Because primary motor cortex is the final link to the motoneuron level, its activity reflects the content of the motor commands. The activation of motor areas (including primary motor cortex) in representing an action is thus required to provide the represented action with a 'motor' format, to the same extent as the involvement of primary visual cortex in visual mental imagery is required to restore the topographical layout of the image. In other words, in order for a represented action to be felt as a real action, it needs to be framed in the constraints which are those of a real action (Jeannerod 2001).

This is not to say that activation of the motor system is the same during execution and various forms of simulation: simulating is not doing, and substantial differences are observed between simulation and execution. First, the activation of most of the areas of the motor system during action representation is consistently weaker than during execution. Secondly, it is coupled with an additional mechanism for suppressing motor output, a prerequisite for the off-line functioning of the representation. Thirdly, because the muscles do not contract and the limbs do not move, the sensory reafferences normally produced by a movement are lacking. These differences are sufficient to disentangle simulating from doing. In addition, however, as we saw previously, the representations for executing and simulating do not completely overlap, which may allow this distinction to be made even in the absence of sensory reafferences. Remember that the deafferented patient G.L., in spite of being deprived of all sensory reafferences, was still able to self-attribute her movements. This is also the way by which an agent is able to disentangle his own intended actions from the actions he observes from other agents.

6.1.1 Motor simulation as a rule-based process

Motor simulation can thus be proposed as an explanation for the embodiment of action representations and their grounding in the neural substrate. The core of the explanation is that the simulation mechanism is comprised of a set of 'rules' which are embedded in the neural substrate of the action representations.[1] Every normally developed human subject is endowed with a set of motor rules which become progressively installed as maturation of the nervous system progresses, and which are activated whenever an action has to be performed, for building, assembling and coordinating the movements needed to achieve the goal. They apply to all skillful actions human agents can produce when they act with their hands or their face, manipulate and use tools, speak, sing, write, etc. The motor rules which are used in the motor simulation process closely correspond to the regularities described for biological movements in general. As from the data reviewed in Chapters 2 and 5, they account for the description of movement kinematics (e.g. the asymmetric velocity profile of reaching, the velocity–curvature relationship), visuomotor transformation (e.g. the speed/accuracy trade-off as expressed in Fitts' law, the scaling of maximum grip aperture to object size during grasping), optimization of postures (e.g. the selection of overhand versus underhand grasps, according to the notion of posture-based planning), etc. At a still lower level, the biomechanical limitations of the joint rotations, the initial position of the limb, the coordination of the joints involved in the action, the optimization of the trajectory dynamics and the muscular force to be applied, must also be represented. An important feature of the present simulation hypothesis is that because they are embedded in the representation of the action, these rules operate not only in shaping the executed actions but also in shaping covert actions: as we saw, they can be detected at a purely cognitive level, as in mental motor imagery or in perceptual accounts. Recall that represented actions follow Fitts' law, and that the perception of dots moving along curved trajectories follows the velocity–curvature relationship to the same extent as real actions, to give only those two examples.

The motor rules as conceived here are assumed to be stable over time, once they have developed during the phase of maturation. They are presumably not dependent on learning; rather, they are part of a basic motor repertoire which pertains to all human agents, and possibly to agents from many other species as well. This stability over time and this regularity across species make them highly reliable for anticipating the unfolding of an action and predicting its outcome (see page 135). As we have seen in several places in this book, motor behavior looks ahead in time: the outcome of an action is anticipated in its

---

[1] The term *rule* should be understood here as more or less equivalent to the terms *law* or *principle* which have frequently been used by motor physiologists to describe regularities observed in motor behavior. The term *rule* is also connected with, but does not overlap, other terms that we used in Chapter 1 in a historical context, such as *movement formula* or *engram*, or in the context of theories of action, such as *schema*.

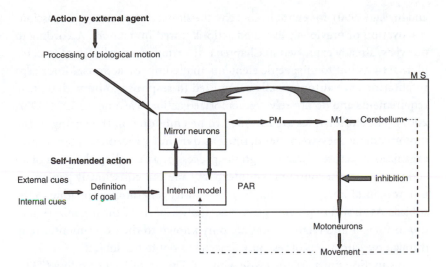

Fig. 6.1 A schematic diagram of the motor simulation process. For two modalities of action representations, i.e. built from observing action of an external agent or generated from a self-produced intention, the common motor simulation network is depicted inside a large box labeled MS. The network includes first a recipient part where the premotor mirror neurons and the posterior parietal cortex (PAR) interact to establish an internal model of the represented action. The network also includes a more executive part where premotor cortex (PM), primary motor cortex (M1) and possibly the cerebellum intervene to specify the detailed kinematic parameters of the representation. Finally, execution itself can be blocked by an inhibitory process. If executed, the movement generates reafferent information for updating the various parts of the representation. Rearranged from Jeannerod (2004b).

representation, and its results can be checked against this anticipation. This stresses the fact that the motor rules are of a dynamic nature: motor simulation is an ongoing process which requires an orderly activation of the motor system. The information contained in the motor commands at the level of the primary motor cortex or upstream of it propagates to many other structures: the output from the motor cortex, on its way to the spinal cord, is distributed through collateral fibers to other cortical areas. These collateral pathways represent the neural substrate for efference copies, which, as we saw, play a critical role in the feedforward models of action representation. The cerebellum is likely to participate in this process: it receives central information about the motor commands through its connections with motor cortical areas, as well as feedback information generated by the movements through its connections with the spinal cord; in turn, it sends information back to the motor cortex (Figure 6.1).

The present motor simulation hypothesis is distinct from other theories of action representation which have also used the concept of simulation. Decety and Ingvar (1990), for example, conceive the simulation process as a conscious reactivation of previously executed actions stored in memory. According to our view, already expressed in Chapter 1, the simulation relates not to complete actions but to unspecific elements that comprise actions. Motor representations are automatically assembled in response to immediate task requirements and do not rely on memorized actions (Jeannerod 1994, 1997, 2001). The motor rules are assumed to be embodied in the wiring of the motor system: they are better defined as dynamic procedures than as pre-organized structures. Even though the process of assembling elements of an action may have a conscious counterpart (one can consciously generate a motor mental image, for example), most of its generation is opaque to the subject. As shown in previous sections, many aspects of the organization of motor images and related states are only known to the experimenter (e.g. through measurements of response times), but not to the subject.

A distinction must also be made with the Theory of Event Coding (TEC) proposed by Wolfgang Prinz and his colleagues. This theory posits that the 'late' processes of perceptual coding share the same code as the 'early' antecedents of action. Thus, cognitive perceptual representations, that are the end-product of perception, would be indistinguishable from cognitive action representations. In other words, 'Perceiving a stimulus object and action planning are functionally equivalent, inasmuch as they are alternative ways of doing the same thing: internally representing external events' (Hommel *et al.* 2001, p. 860). The TEC shares a number of features with our present view, notably the fact that action representations are available prior to the action itself and consequently can anticipate the intended action effects. We do agree that actions are represented in terms of their goal: but we assume that the goal is only part of the content of the action representation. By representing the goal, we can answer the question of 'What the action is about', but not the question of 'How to do it'. The latter question requires motor simulation to be answered (and we saw how important it may be to answer it for mentally rehearsing an action or learning it by observation). Another point of disagreement between our view and the TEC is that our view is not limited to object-oriented actions. Object-oriented actions have a definite goal, such that the action to be performed on an object shares features with the object itself: for example, the intended grip to grasp the object reflects the perceived size of that object. However, as recognized by Hommel *et al.* (2001), there is no way in which the sensory code representing the object size would be similar to the muscular innervation pattern forming the appropriate grip. The sensory and the motor codes can only be shared at an abstract level where object properties and action plans become sufficiently vague to be matched. In the motor simulation hypothesis, we do assume that not only object properties but also the movements themselves that comprise the action on that object have to be represented and simulated in action plans. This is the way in which the feasibility of an action can be estimated; this is also the way in which an observed action can be understood and replicated, and not only perceived.

6.1.2 Motor simulation and the detection of intentions

Rule-based simulation is ubiquitous in normal behavior, whenever we think about an action, evaluate its feasibility, anticipate its consequences or prepare to execute it. We fully discussed its role in mental training or in decision making, as well as its potential applications in motor rehabilitation or neuroprosthesis. In addition, beyond the solipsist context, where an agent is rehearsing his own actions for himself, motor simulation also pertains to representations originating from the observation of other agents. In that case, the simulation provides a frame for the recognition of the action: the observer understands the action he sees to the extent he can simulate it. In order for the observed action to be real, however, the simulation must be complete, i.e. it must involve all the aspects of the action, including its motor aspects. As we emphasized in Chapter 5, mere visual perception of the moving agent without involvement of the motor system would provide an incomplete description of the movements of the agent, and would not give access to the intrinsic structure of the observed movements, which is critical for understanding what the action is about, what is its goal and how to reproduce it.

Human actions are understandable (and replicable) by external observers because they are composed according to the motor rules of a common repertoire. Even though the rules used in motor simulation are basic rules which pertain to biological motion in general, their integration into meaningful actions is a species-specific process. This specificity represents an obvious limitation for understanding and imitating actions performed by animals with a different repertoire. Thus, observation of an action performed by another agent of the same species as the observer automatically activates the motor system of the observer (see below for a discussion of the automatic nature of this activation). By way of motor simulation, an observed action becomes immediately transferable into a potentially executed one, which makes the observer able, among other things, to replicate and learn actions of the other agent. Incidentally, it would be interesting to check how people with motor disabilities of a central origin (e.g. with cerebellar ataxia) represent and understand actions they observe being performed by other agents. Given the fact that their motor system is damaged and their motor function is disorganized, they might not be able to retrieve the motor rules normally used for simulating an action. In other words, their perception of others' actions might be impaired to the same extent as their capacity to carry out their own actions correctly is impaired[2].

Mirror neurons are part of this mechanism of action understanding and prediction through motor simulation. Because they are activated during both execution and observation of the same action, mirror neurons use the same code for signaling the action of the agent and that of the observer: what an observer perceives from the other, he can do, and vice versa. Mirror neurons owe this property to their position in the perception–action circuit. First, during action observation, they receive visual information, through the ventral posterior parietal cortex in the inferior parietal lobule, and from STS areas specialized in the processing of body parts, body motion and biological movements (Jellema *et al.* 2000). As we saw earlier, they are not activated by actions that do not fulfill the above motor rules, such as robotic actions (although they may have the capacity to acquire new rules). Their somato-topic organization allows them to differentiate between action information arising from the movements of different body parts. They also receive information from motor areas, including higher order premotor structures respons-ible for action planning, and motor cortex itself, where the basic motor rules are represented. In turn, when the observer becomes the agent, the same mir-ror neurons are activated by premotor and primary motor cortex neurons in parallel with execution. This symmetrical activation in the two conditions accounts for the matching between the rules of the perceived and the executed action. Finally, although there is as yet no clear empirical evidence for this, mirror neurons may also be active during covert actions (e.g. intended, planned or imagined actions). If that were actually the case, motor simula-tion would clearly fulfill the criterion for a unifying mechanism operating at different stages of motor cognition. In Chapter 1, we described the motor cognitive behavior of apraxic patients: they are as much impaired in

---

[2] An indirect confirmation of this suggestion is provided by Bosbach *et al.* (2005). They examined the ability of two deafferented patients (including patient G.L. already described in Chapter 3) to understand the actions of other agents. To this aim, they showed the patients videos of people lifting boxes of different weights: these people had received either correct or incorrect information about the weights of the boxes they had to lift. In the case of incorrect information, there was a mismatch between the lifter's expectation (as from his posture and movements before the lift) and his actual movement during the box lifting. The patients were asked to determine whether the motor preparation of the lifter matched the weight of the box. They were both unable to make correct judgements. This result indicates that peripheral sensation from one's own body contributes to building and updating the mental motor representations that one uses to simulate the actions of others.

generating representations for their own actions (e.g. they are poor in using tools or in forming motor images) as in understanding actions performed by others (many of them cannot imitate actions they see, neither can they detect errors in actions made by another agent). We had concluded, based on both the lesion localization in these patients and the activation data from normal subjects during tasks involving action representations, that the posterior parietal lobe is a critical site for action representations. In the context of the motor simulation hypothesis, the mirror neurons system, which is distributed through posterior parietal and premotor cortices, obviously represents one of the links of the simulation network which accounts for the functioning of action representations (see Figure 6.1).

One of the consequences of the fact that actions are built from a set of rules common to the agent and the observer is that the observer can predict the outcome of the actions of the observed agent. As we said earlier, the motor rules reflect regularities, or invariant properties, of motor behavior across different conditions of planning and execution; and, because motor behavior has invariant properties, it is predictable. Prediction is an essential aspect of human social behavior: by observing our conspecifics, we try to anticipate the outcome of their actions, to decipher their intentions and, ultimately, to read their minds. The problem at this point is, first, to determine the role of the motor simulation process in predicting the behavior of others; and, secondly, to examine whether motor simulation can give access to more than a simple prima facie description of an action, i.e. to action properties that are part of the representation of the agent, but have not yet become visible to the observer.

With regard to the first question, it has been argued that the activity of mirror neurons, which are part of the motor simulation network, might signal the intention underlying the action of the observed agent. This is indeed a strong statement, because many intentions are not readily transferred into executed action: if mirror neurons are to detect intentions, they will only be able to detect intentions that are already being expressed by an action, i.e. those that we earlier called 'motor intentions', but not intentions that are still covertly represented (the 'prior intentions'; see Chapter 1). This is exactly what is revealed by a recent experiment with monkeys by Fogassi et al. (2005). They recorded neurons in the parietal lobe with mirror properties quite similar to those initially found in the ventral premotor cortex, to which they are connected (see Chapter 5). The animal was trained to either execute or watch an action involving a sequence of two steps. During execution, the animal first reached for and grasped a small object on a table, then brought this object to a different place. However, although the first step was invariant throughout the trials, the second step differed from trial to trial: the animal was trained either to bring the object to the mouth or to bring it to a container placed close to her face. During watching, the animal observed an experimenter performing the same two-step actions. The question was the following: can the monkey, by watching only the first, invariant movement of grasping the object, predict what will be the second step? According to Fogassi *et al.*'s data, the parietal mirror neurons were found to code the same act of grasping in a different way, according to the goal of the action in which it was embedded. The important point here is that this differential coding held not only when the animal was the agent (i.e. executed the action) but also when it was the observer: the neuron activity related to the observation of the first step of the action differed according to the content of the second step.[3]

These findings remind us that representations of actions include the goal of the action, in addition to the kinematics of each individual step. It is therefore not surprising that a given single step of a complex action can reflect its final goal. The only question is about how far back the final goal can 'penetrate' the early components of the action so as to affect their kinematics. If I see someone rising from her chair and leaving the room, can my motor simulation apparatus by itself (in the absence of contextual information) tell me why this person left the room? Was she intending to make a phone call or to prepare tea? In other words, was the end result of her action already influencing her first move? Keeping this obvious limitation in mind (more on this in the next section), motor simulation does account for some of the data supporting the idea of a minimal understanding of intentions. Watching somebody writing the letter *l* can tell me whether the next letter he intends to write is an *e* or an *n* (Kandel *et al.* 2000); looking at an agent grasping a cup can tell me whether he intends to clean the cup or to drink from it (Iacoboni *et al.* 2004). I can also detect, by looking at somebody preparing to lift a weight, whether he thinks that the weight is light or heavy. The weight lifter and I can even both be deceived if the weight looks heavy while it is actually very light. This is indeed a classical trick used by clowns: the clown pretends that the huge cardboard

---

[3] The obvious explanation for this finding is that the first step of the action differs kinematically in the two conditions, and that this difference can be detected by the observer. Some years ago, Ron Marteniuk and his colleagues had shown that apparently identical movements (reaching to grasp an object) embedded in two different actions (either fit the object in a small container or throw it into a large container) were kinematically different. The grasping movement preceding the action of fitting had a smaller velocity peak than the same movement preceding the action of throwing (Marteniuk *et al.* 1987). This should be the function of the motor simulation mechanism to detect such subtle differences in kinematics, which would otherwise be undetectable by a purely visual perceptual mechanism.

box is very heavy, prepares his effort for lifting it and falls on his back. Everybody laughs at the clown because, as Sigmund Freud suggested in his book on Jokes (Freud 1905/1960), the spectators were simulating an effortful action, and the outcome did not match their anticipation. Discrepancies of that sort are powerful factors for generating emotions, such as surprise, or comic effects. In this type of situation, one clearly sees how motor simulation can carry information for predicting different outcomes for observed movements with different kinematics: the observer simulates the movement of the agent by applying the same motor rules as if he were actually himself executing it. In addition, because the movements are part of a natural repertoire, this information is immediately available to the observer and does not require learning. It is therefore not surprising that subjects involved in deciphering the 'intentions' of agents writing letters or grasping cups were found to activate their motor simulation system (Chaminade *et al.* 2001; Iacoboni *et al.* 2004).

Note that, in this section, we implicitly assumed that the simulation system possibly involved in deciphering motor intentions is only looking at the effector that is performing the action: most monkey experiments, where isolated hand movements directed at objects are shown to the animal, are built on this assumption; this is also true for human experiments where 'actions' shown to the subject (on videos or otherwise) are isolated from their context most of the time. In normal life outside laboratories, however, other cues are available to decipher intentions, especially in an interactive, or social, context: for example, the direction of the gaze of the observed agent seems to be a critical indicator for anticipating the next step of his action. In addition, the mechanism for detecting the direction where the eyes are looking (the 'eye direction detector'; EDD) is considered by cognitive psychologists as one of the early components of the ability of young infants to detect social intentions (see Baron-Cohen 1995). This type of information is likely to be processed by STS neurons, not by parietal or premotor mirror neurons, and the way in which mirror neurons could use it to simulate intentions beyond motor intentions remains an unanswered question.

6.1.3 Simulation and action planning

The prediction of the outcome of an action based on motor simulation differs from another mode of prediction, based on the recognition of sequential patterns. We constantly make predictions about ongoing temporal sequences, with the purpose of anticipating sensory events or preparing motor responses. Goal-directed actions are one example of such events that can be predicted.

Consider, for example, the situation described by Flanagan and Johansson (2003). In their experiment, they monitored the eye movements of subjects involved in a task of either assembling wooden blocks by hand or watching another agent performing the same task. When the subjects performed the task themselves, their eye movements anticipated their hand actions on the blocks. When the subjects observed the same task performed by an experimenter, they also made eye movements in advance with respect to the experimenter's hands movements toward the blocks: in other words, the subjects anticipated the next step, as if they were mentally simulating the task to predict future events, instead of following the events as they occurred. This was possible because the subjects had acquired some knowledge about what the final outcome of the action should be. In this case, however, the information for predicting the outcome does not arise from detecting the kinematics of the agent's movements; rather, it is provided by the temporal structure of the event watched by the observer. Kilner *et al.* (2004) recently reported that the mere observation of a grasping movement is sufficient to generate, in the observer's brain, an activation of the motor system: they showed that readiness potentials, which are normally recorded during the preparation of a movement by an agent, can be recorded from an observer before the (predicted) movement starts, as if the observer was himself the agent of that movement. This fact that the motor system of an observer can anticipate or predict the execution of an action by another agent has indeed been exploited in many situations where people actively interact with each other: in a soccer game, for example, the trick of the shooter during a penalty shot is to make the goalkeeper prepare to respond to an action different from that which will be executed.

This type of anticipation of events is part of action planning. Action planning corresponds to the rehearsal of steps (once compared with the scripts of a movie scenario, see Grafman 1989) which concur with the achievement of a goal. Whether this rehearsal corresponds to neural simulation to the same extent as the above motor simulation is a completely open question. In contradistinction to motor simulation, which rehearses the short-term, fast and automatic unfolding of a movement, however, action planning deals with the long-term and largely explicit unfolding of a complex action. However, although one can easily conceive what sort of neural operations occur during motor simulation, this is hardly the case during action planning. Several studies have provided a description of the neural structures involved in action planning, but have left unanswered the question of what exactly is simulated. In a neuroimaging study by Ricarda Schubotz and Yves von Cramon, subjects were shown sequences of still images displaying hand actions on objects or a series of non-biological objects (Schubotz and von Cramon 2004). Subjects were instructed to determine whether the hand actions they were shown would yield a successful result or would fail (a response based on action observation). In another run where the images also represented hand actions on objects, the question was whether the object would be deformed by the action or not (a response based on motor imagery). Finally, with the series of non-biological objects (visual stimuli of different shapes and colors), the subjects had to determine whether the sequences were orderly or not (a response based on visual working memory). In all three conditions, an activation was found in the area of the inferior frontal gyrus next to the ventral premotor cortex. Interestingly, however, although the activated areas partially overlapped in the three conditions, condition-specific activation could be found. In the two conditions involving hand actions, the activation predominated in the left inferior frontal gyrus, whereas activation during the inspection of object sequences was restricted to the right inferior frontal gyrus. (This latter finding with still sequences of objects replicates previous work by the same authors: Schubotz and von Cramon 2002.) Motor activation during the observation of motor sequences also occurs when the sequence is violated and 'errors' are detected by the observer (van Schie *et al.* 2004). Again, the observer was anticipating the correct action, and the mismatch between what was anticipated and what is observed resulted in an increased activity in motor areas.

A closely related experiment, also involving the representation of a temporal sequence, and performed in behaving monkeys by Cisek and Kalaska (2004), sheds some light on the neural process underlying prediction. In this experiment, monkeys learned to make reaching movements to a target designated by an arbitrary color cue. The sequence of events was the following: the animals first saw for a few seconds two color-coded potential targets on a computer screen; then, they saw a color cue indicating which target they had to reach for; finally, they performed the reaching movement, usually after having made an ocular saccade in the direction of the target. After the monkeys were trained, they were shown the same sequence of events unfolding on the screen, while the task was performed by an unseen party. In this action observation task, the monkeys were able to anticipate the unfolding of the sequence, as demonstrated by the fact that they made an ocular saccade in the direction of the correct target before they saw the reaching movement. Single neurons were recorded in the dorsal premotor cortex during the action execution and the action observation tasks: a number of these neurons exhibited similar discharge patterns whenever the animals performed the task themselves or observed its unfolding when it was performed by the other party.

These studies reveal, both at the single neuron level and at the level of large neuronal assemblies, that mental rehearsal of a temporally organized action (whether one is preparing or observing it) involves activation of motor areas with 'mirror' properties. In the human experiment, Broca's area and its homolog in the opposite hemisphere are activated. In the monkey experiment, typical mirror neurons located in the dorsal premotor cortex (PMd) symmetrically encode the same action sequence during both execution and observation. Note that the latter finding departs from the current description of mirror neurons in the usual sense, which have been located in interconnected areas of the ventral premotor and posterior parietal cortices. Cisek and Kalaska consider that the two sets of neurons might have complementary functions: 'This covert simulation or mental rehearsal of motor acts may contribute to nominally "cognitive" functions underlying the assessment and understanding of observed events. For ventral premotor neurons, those events are natural and familiar, whereas for the PMd neurons, they include sensory events whose relation to motor behavior is acquired through learned stimulus–response associations' (2004, p. 996). This suggestion fits the distinction we made earlier in this section between different modalities of prediction of motor events using the motor simulation or the action planning mechanisms, respectively.

The explanation may not be so simple, however. The problem raised by the results of Schubotz and von Cramon is that premotor cortex and Broca's area are involved not only in representing sequential actions but also in monitoring sequential perceptual events. One possibility suggested by Schubotz and von Cramon (2002) is that the perception of sequences activates motor mechanisms because they induce potential movements in relation to the attended stimuli: hand movements for visual stimuli, speech articulatory movements for auditory sequences, etc. This idea can hardly be followed for the type of visual stimuli (colored circles and diamonds of the same size) the same authors used in their 2004 study. Another possibility is that premotor mirror neurons involved in these studies fulfill a higher level function for processing sequential events in general, including motor sequences. Planning ahead sequences, detecting regularities in a sequence and learning it, and anticipating the next step of a sequence, are cognitive operations that require working memory. This applies to motor sequences, and particularly to language production and comprehension. The role of ventral premotor cortex and of areas overlapping with Broca's area could be that of a specialized working memory for action. This function would clearly separate out the role of motor mechanisms used in motor simulation for understanding actions and possibly motor intentions from a more cognitive function for the organization of motor behavior.

In this section about the role of motor simulation, we have adopted the framework of a Motor Theory of Action Representation[4], by showing how motor simulation can be an effective mode for action representations: we can represent to ourselves our own actions, with the purpose of preparing them, evaluating their feasibility and their consequences. We can also represent to ourselves the actions of others with the purpose of understanding or replicating them. By monitoring the difference between representing one's own actions and representing the actions of others, we can derive the sense of agency as a cue for attributing actions to their authors.

6.2 Motor simulation and social cognition

The point in this section is to determine how far one can extend the concept of simulation as a generalized explanation of behavior. Is it possible to envisage a theory of social cognition where simulation would operate in a similar way to how it does in motor cognition? In other words, when we speak of simulation in the context of social cognition, do we mean the same thing as when we speak of simulation in the context of motor cognition?

The notion of simulation has been extensively used in cognitive psychology within the framework of the Theory of Mind. The Theory of Mind is said to be an attribute of normal human subjects aged >3–4 years, which they use to understand each other's minds. This mind-reading ability has been conceptualized in two different ways. A first conception is the 'theory–theory' version of the Theory of Mind, which postulates that a subject uses a set of implicit cognitive mechanisms to identify the mental states of others. Alternatively, the 'simulation' version of the Theory of Mind postulates that a subject *simulates* within his own mind the mental states he deciphers from others and experiences these mental states himself: by experiencing them, he becomes able to understand them. This simulation version of the Theory of Mind is distinct from the idea of motor simulation, in the sense that it has a much broader scope: it is thought to account for the understanding of others' intentions, emotions, desires, expectations and beliefs, i.e. a large spectrum of mental states that are not necessarily related to action *per se* and which are, for many of them, very remote from any observable behavior. Yet, there is a trend among theoreticians and even some experimentalists to assume that motor simulation could represent the basis for a simulation theory of mind-reading. Here, we discuss this hypothesis which tends to derive social cognition from motor cognition.

---

[4] I use this expression in analogy to the well-known Motor Theory of Speech Perception that we will discuss in the final section of this chapter.

6.2.1 **The simulation of emotions**

Let us start our discussion with the understanding of emotions. Emotions are both a good and a bad case for the role of simulation in mind-reading. They are a good case because emotions involve a number of observable components, such as facial expressions, which are part of a motor repertoire and are liable to motor simulation. They are also a bad case, however, because human facial expressions are visual patterns shaped by evolution and which are likely to be directly understandable by human beings without an obvious need for simulation.

Take the bad case first. Perceiving an emotion activates several brain areas. An emotion expressed by a face, for example, activates occipitotemporal areas selective for social stimuli, especially in the region of the STS (Allison *et al.* 2000, see Chapter 5). Very young babies (at around 5 months of age) are able to recognize that a person is expressing an emotion, although they do not seem to experience this emotion themselves. It is only later (at 2 years of age) that they begin to respond to the emotions expressed by other people (e.g. Nelson 1987). In other words, it is possible to recognize an emotion without having it. This is not to say, however, that perceived emotions are solely processed in the visual cortex: emotions carried by facial expressions are also processed in subcortical areas, such as the amygdala, which, in turn, influence the visual cortex. Patients with intact visual cortex but damaged amygdala on both sides can recognize faces, but fail to recognize emotional expressions of fear. Adolphs *et al.* (1998) found that patients with bilateral damage to the amygdala were impaired in their social judgement, in that they judged to be trustworthy faces that normal subjects would judge untrustworthy and unreliable. Conversely, one patient with extensive damage in his striate cortex on one side was still able to recognize emotional expressions of faces presented in the blind area of his visual field, in spite of not being aware of the presentation of visual stimuli (an example of 'affective blindsight', de Gelder *et al.* 1999). In this patient, a neuroimaging study revealed that the presentation of fearful faces in the blind area activated the amygdala (presumably via an extrageniculostriate pathway, Morris *et al.* 2001). Finally, Vuilleumier *et al.* (2004) found that patients with bilateral amygdala damage fail to show the normal activation of their visual cortex during emotional face processing, suggesting that the activation of the amygdala by an emotional stimulus normally potentiates the role of visual cortex in emotion recognition. Thus studies using brain imaging in normal subjects, as well as the observation of patients with damage to the amygdala, provide evidence that this region participates in extracting the emotional significance of facial expressions. This is also true for other brain regions as well, including the ventromedial prefrontal cortex and the insular cortex. A complete set of data has been accumulated concerning the role of the anterior insula in a specific emotion, disgust. This cortical region has a particular anatomical status: it receives connections from olfactory and gustatory receptors, as well as from the STS areas coding for facial expressions. It also receives abundant input from visceral afferents through the spinal cord and the solitary tract. Finally, its stimulation produces motor reactions accompanied by autonomic and visceromotor responses. On the functional side, brain imaging studies have shown activation of the anterior insula by olfactory and gustatory stimuli, selective for the disgusting nature of these stimuli. In addition to disgusting stimuli, activation can also be obtained with the sight of faces displaying disgusted expressions: the sector in the insula activated by a disgusting stimulus exactly superimposes on the sector activated by disgusted faces (Krolak-Salmon *et al.* 2003; see review in Gallese *et al.* 2004).[5]

The role of localized brain areas in both perceiving an emotion and reacting to it is consistent with a 'simulationist' view of emotion understanding. Indeed, what is common to areas such as the amygdala and insular cortex is that they are connected to visceral effectors. Their activation by an emotional stimulus modifies the state of the autonomic system of the perceiver: changes in heart rate, respiration, cutaneous blood flow and motility of the digestive tract are among the somatic markers which contribute to the representation and the identification of an emotional state. If emotions perceived in another person are represented in the same way as when they are self-experienced, this suggests that, in addition to the perceptual mechanism based on sensory processing, emotions can also be understood through a simulation mechanism similar to that which we described for understanding actions. The notion that changes in the autonomic system can be simulated is illustrated by a simple experiment which may actually bridge the gap between emotion and action. In this experiment, the subjects equipped for their respiration rate to be recorded sit in front of a large screen on which they see an actor performing an effortful action. The actor stands on a treadmill that is either motionless or

---

[5] A closely similar result was recently reported by Krolak-Salmon *et al.* (2005) in a patient with an electrode placed in the left pre-SMA. When the electrode was used to *stimulate* the pre-SMA, the patient smiled and laughed, experiencing a real feeling of happiness for which she could not find a plausible reason (see also Fried *et al.* 1998). The electrode could also be used to *record* the electrical activity within this same region: the presentation to the patient of stimuli representing happy faces triggered ample responses, distinct from those triggered by neutral stimuli. The co-existence, at the same site, of mechanisms for triggering, recognizing and experiencing an emotion clearly speaks in favor of a mirror activity in the pre-SMA.

moves at a constant velocity, or progressively accelerates from 0 to 10 km/h over 1 min. Paccalin and Jeannerod (2000) observed that the observer's respiration rate increased during the observation of the actor walking or running at an increasing speed. Typically, the average increase during observation of the actor running at 10 km/h was about 25 per cent above the resting level. Further, the increase in respiration frequency positively correlated with running velocity. Watching an action is thus different from watching a visual scene with moving objects. During watching an action, as we said in the previous section, the observer is not only seeing visual motion, he is also internally simulating the action he sees. In so doing, the observer rehearses his motor system, including those mechanisms that contribute to adaptation to effort (see an explanation of this mechanism in Chapter 2). Now consider the same experiment where the actor, instead of performing an effortful action such as running, displays an emotional state such as joy. Joy would be expressed on the actor's face with different degrees of intensity by a set of mimics ranging from a subtle smile up to being excited and laughing. What would be the conclusion to be drawn from that experiment if, say, the respiration rate or the heart rate of the observer increased as a function of the degree of joy expressed on the face of the actor? According to the conclusion drawn from the action observation experiment, the conclusion here should be that the observer is simulating the emotion displayed by the actor, and that this simulated emotion activates his own autonomic system to the same extent as it occurs in actually experiencing emotions. Although this particular experiment may not have been performed, the speculation proposed here seems highly plausible (see Zajonc 1985; de Gelder *et al.* 2004). Other experimental findings in the domain of mental imagery support this view. According to Lang and colleagues (Lang 1979; Lang *et al.* 1980) and Levenson *et al.* (1990), imagining or mimicking an emotional state induces in the subject the appearance of physiological reactions specific for the imagined or mimicked emotion, to the same extent as it does during motor imagery (see also Jeannerod 2004a).

If we assume that experiencing and watching an emotion are the two faces of the same phenomenon, we come close to the idea of simulation as it was used in the action understanding section. This is exactly what is assumed by Gallese *et al.*: 'When we witness someone else's action, we activate a network of premotor and parietal areas, which is also active while we perform similar actions. When we witness the disgusted facial expressions of someone else, we activate part of our insula, which is also active while we experience disgust' (2004, p. 400). Not surprisingly, Gallese *et al.* claim that their interpretation is compatible with the role of mirror neurons in this process of understanding emotions. We will come back to this point.

6.2.2 Simulation and social communication

Emotions are part of the mental content of people with whom we interact and communicate. The purpose of social communication is to exchange mental states, i.e. to decipher the mental content of others and to make one's own mental states accessible to them. What seems relatively simple to conceive for emotions, for which there are identifiable stimuli and recognizable facial expressions, may be more difficult for other mental states which remain covert, such as desires or beliefs.

There are several situations where simulation could be an explanation of how mental states can be exchanged between individuals. Let us consider first the situation of *emotional contagion*. Emotional contagion is the automatic replication of a behavior or an emotion displayed by another individual, as in contagious laughing or crying, for example. As such, it stands close to other imitative behaviors that we have already discussed, such as mirroring or mimicry. In other words, contagion is another example of the type 'I see, I do', which is clearly relevant to the role of mirror neurons and to the simulation hypothesis. Yet, emotional contagion can only provide the observer with the information that the person he sees is producing a certain type of behavior or is experiencing a certain type of emotion; but, because it does not tell the observer what the emotion is about, it cannot be a useful means for reacting to the emotion of that person, and would not yield an appropriate response in a social interaction. Imagine facing somebody who expresses anger and threat: the adaptive response in that case seems to be avoidance rather than imitation, i.e. not to experience anger oneself, but to experience fear and eventually to run away. Emotional contagion thus represents a primitive form of understanding the experience of another person. As it is widespread throughout animal life, it has been classically assigned an adaptive function for the development of early social abilities, e.g. for shaping the ability to recognize the behavior of others, or facilitating the mother–infant bond (Darwin 1872). Like compulsive imitation, however, it tends to be controlled and inhibited in human adults.

Another, more elaborate and controlled situation where individuals exchange their mental states is *empathy* (for a review, see Preston and de Waal 2002). The concept of empathy implies that two individuals involved in a communicative interaction share the same feelings, such that whatever affects one of them will also affect the other (see Goldie 1999). Originally, the term empathy was translated by Titchener (1908) from the German term *Einfühlung*. German philosophers and psychologists of the last century, such as Theodor Lipps (e.g. Lipps 1903), used the term *Einfühlung* to designate an implicit process of knowledge, different from the rational mode of knowledge, which gave access to the esthetical or the emotional content of a situation. In listening to a piece of music, for example, I may share some of the impressions and emotions that the composer felt when he created the piece of music, not through an act of perception, but rather through a modification of my own emotional state. Lipps considered empathy as the source of knowledge about other individuals, to the same extent as sensory perception is the source of knowledge about objects. His idea was that we understand, for example, facial expressions displayed by other persons not because we compare them with our own expressions, that we cannot see, but because the vision of an expression on the face of someone else 'awakens [in the observer] impulses to such movements that are suited to call just this expression into existence' (Lipps 1903). Beyond this 'sensory motor' version, empathy can also operate at more cognitive levels: think, for example, of the contagion of suicides which spread over Europe following the publication of Wolfgang Goethe's *Werther* in 1774!

The concept of empathy, and its consequences on behavior, is taken by the simulation theorists as a form of mind-reading, because it contributes to understanding the mind and predicting the behavior of others. Vittorio Gallese and Alvin Goldman have proceeded one step further in proposing an explanation of mind-reading in terms of brain mechanisms, in what they called the 'simulation theory of mind-reading'. Along with the sensory motor concept of Lipps, they proposed that the observed behavior would activate, in the observer's brain, the same mechanisms that would be activated were that behavior intended or imagined by the observer. They express the idea that 'when one is observing the action of another, one undergoes a neural event that is qualitatively the same as [the] event that triggers actual movement in the observed agent'. Thus 'a mind-reader represents an actor's behavior by recreating in himself the plans or movement intentions of the actor' (Gallese and Goldman 1998, p. 498). In a more recent paper, Gallese (2003) proposes to extend the concept of simulation beyond the realm of action. His argument is that 'simulation is not a prerogative of the motor system, it is not just confined to the executive control strategies presiding over our functioning in the world, but a basic functional mechanism, used by vast parts of the brain'. The function of this mechanism, he says, is the 'representation of reality' through 'an interactive model of what cannot be known by itself'. Its mode of operation is unconscious, automatic and pre-reflexive: Gallese's simulation is thus an embodied simulation, different, he insists, from the deliberate and voluntary mode postulated by the proponents of the simulation version of the Theory of Mind.

The Gallese's theory (Gallese and Goldman 1998; Gallese 2003; Gallese *et al.* 2004) is a synthesis of several ideas. First, it is inspired by the notion of motor simulation in its strong sense. As for motor simulation and for emotional contagion, the ability to mind-read is assumed to rely on mirror neurons, primarily those described in the motor system, but also possibly in other brain areas. Gallese *et al.* (2004) propose the insular mechanism of disgust as an example of a system with mirror properties outside the motor system. Secondly, the simulation theory of mind-reading is inspired by the idea of shared representations. According to Gallese, the representations of actions or emotions that are shared by two persons rely on a vast shared manifold encompassing all the neural systems involved in simulating their actions and emotions. Note, however, that shared representations as defined in Chapter 4 have two components. One component is the overlapping part of the representations built by the agent and the observer, respectively; this component enables the observer to experience (and understand) the agent's action by simulating it. The other component is the non-overlapping part, specific to each representation, by which the observer can identify himself as different from the agent. This notion of a self–other differentiation, which is so critical in social communication, is not specifically addressed in the simulation theory of mind-reading.

Extending the concept of simulation to a unifying explanation of social cognition raises several problems. The central argument for assuming that motor cognition could be a gateway to social cognition is that the mechanism of motor simulation can reveal the intentions at the origin of an action, including an action with social significance. However, as we saw earlier, although motor simulation can clearly give access to motor intentions (those that account for elementary actions), it cannot give access to the intention of a more complex action that requires several steps to be completed. One of the reasons for this impossibility is that there is no univocal relationship between a motor intention and the more complex intention that governs the more complex action in which it is embedded: the same motor intention can be embedded in several different complex intentions or actions; furthermore, the same complex intention can take many different paths to achieve its goal (this property has been referred to by motor theorists as 'motor equivalence'). Decoding a motor intention is thus of no help in understanding the higher level intention and *a fortiori* its possible social meaning, except in highly predictable situations which are rarely found in everyday life. Jacob and Jeannerod (2005) have illustrated this point by the striking story of Dr Jekyll and Mr Hyde from the classical R.L. Stevenson novel written in 1886. Dr Jekyll is a renowned surgeon who performs operations on his anesthetized patients. Mr Hyde is a dangerous sadist who performs exactly the same hand movements on his unanesthetized victims. As it turns out, Mr Hyde is Dr Jekyll and Dr Jekyll's motor intention is the same as Mr Hyde's. However, Dr Jekyll's social intention clearly differs from Mr Hyde's. Deciphering a complex intention requires prior knowledge about the agent and, most of all, knowledge about the context in which the intention is formed and the action is undertaken. This type of knowledge cannot be made available through motor simulation. The question is whether it can be made available through simulation at all: how could one model in one's brain a neural process corresponding to a mental state one does not know, unless one uses cognitive processes such as judgement and inferences? As Rebecca Saxe (2005) remarks, subjects tend to make systematic errors in attributing mental properties (e.g. rationality) to others, which suggests that the direct understanding of others provided by simulation of their minds would fail to make the correct attribution if it were not complemented by other mechanisms.

Another problem raised by the simulation explanation of social cognition is that of the self–other differentiation. The prerequisite for social relationships is that the two communicating selves can preserve their individuality. The purpose of communication is not so much to be 'in' the other, as illustrated by the expression 'putting oneself in another's shoes', it is to be 'with' the other. Etymologically, the 'in' and the 'with' attitudes are each assigned a different terminology: to be 'in' is the definition of empathy, whereas to be 'with' is defined as sympathy. Empathy and sympathy, however, are not scientifically defined terms, and have often been considered as equivalent (for a review, see Decety and Chaminade 2003). The point is that simulation, which puts me 'in' the other, is not communication. If communication between two individuals consists of exchanging information about their respective mental states, how could I communicate with an individual whose mental state I simulate, so as to reproduce in my brain the same neural representation as that which he has formed in his own brain? On the contrary, what I would need is to create in my brain a neural representation of his mental state, different from my own. Social cognition is about recognition of differences rather than similarities between individuals. This can be achieved by representations which only partially overlap, i.e. by a mechanism which aims at minimizing the influence of simulation. Simulation is an automatic process which can be controlled or inhibited in the social context. The persistence of uncontrolled contagion, mimicry, mirroring and other forms of resonance beyond early developmental stages, or their reappearance in adult life, would be deleterious to social relationships and would generate maladaptive responses. As asked by Jacob and Jeannerod in the conclusion of their paper, 'Would a male monkey respond to the perception of a female's behavioral response to his own courting behavior by matching her observed movements? We predict that it would not' (2005, p. 24). Thus, the permanent need for a clear self–other differentiation is a *de facto* limitation for the role of simulation in understanding the mental states of others and establishing communication with them. Psychiatrists and psychotherapists are aware that they have to stay 'with', and not try to get 'in', their patient if they want to establish an efficient therapeutic relationship.

6.3 Motor simulation and language understanding

Like actions and emotions, language has a strong sensory motor component. Whether it is expressed through articulatory movements of the vocal tract or other types of movement (e.g. hand movements in sign language), language production is a member of the broad category of actions: it results from sequences of motor commands which are assembled according to certain rules to reach a given goal. Human actions can be directed at visible or invisible goals. Expressive gestures, for example, have the goal of rendering manifest a feeling or an intention; pantomimes are actions where the goal is virtual but is revealed by the spatio-temporal structure of the movements. So is language: a sentence can be said to have the goal of conveying a certain meaning, and possibly influencing the course of external events. The question we ask now is whether the sensory motor aspects of language can carry meaningful information about the content of language utterances

In this section, we first examine the motor features of language production and comprehension which are common to other types of goal-directed actions. Secondly, we describe the anatomical and functional properties of the neural system responsible for these features. Thirdly, we discuss the possible role of the simulation of the rules of language utterance in giving access to the meaning of this utterance.

6.3.1 Language as goal-directed action

Language is characterized by the plurality of the motor systems that can be used to convey the same meaning. The two main forms of human language, spoken and sign language, fulfill the same function by articulating sounds or gesturing signs, respectively. Comparative studies of spoken and sign languages have revealed both differences and similarities. The form of signs, unlike the form of words, is not entirely arbitrarily related to their meaning. Many signs retain a degree of iconicity in the sense that their configuration evokes the object or the action to which they refer. Unlike words, signs are not built from sequences of units, they are built from the simultaneous occurrence of spatial and postural elements. Sign language, unlike spoken language, expresses verbal modifications by modifying the form of the sign (e.g. a verb sign) rather than by modifying the sequence of the elements. Aside from these differences, however, there is considerable evidence that spoken and sign languages pertain to the same language faculty. There is evidence that children mobilize the same resources in acquiring sign language as they do for acquiring spoken language. For example, deaf children whose parents do not know a sign language have been observed to improvise a gestural communication system which displays rudiments of grammatical structure, such as consistent word order and incipient morphological marking (Senghas *et al.* 2004). Thus, there are characteristics in sign language which appear to be common to the acquisition of other forms of language, presumably because there are universal perceptual and cognitive constraints on the acquisition system. Another important argument in favor of motor equivalence between modalities of language production is the fact that both spoken language and sign language involve the same brain areas, as we will see below.

The gestural language used by deaf signers is distinct, but related to, the commonly observed spontaneous gestures accompanying speech in normally speaking subjects. Some of those movements obviously serve a communicative purpose, although they do not share the hierarchical structure characteristic for spoken and sign language: they are single emblems, which are not combined into gesture strings and do not form a linguistic system. This is the case for gestures that convey information that can hardly be transmitted by speech alone (e.g. about shape, size and spatial relationships), as well as for gestures children use at the pre-linguistic stage to convey thoughts for which they have no words. In contradistinction to sign language, however, communication is not the sole function of spontaneous gestures during speech: they are observed in congenitally blind children, even when they speak to another blind person! (Iverson and Goldin-Meadow 1998). We also gesture when we speak on the telephone and the interlocutor is absent from view. These remarks suggest that gestures, in addition to their role in communication, might also reflect thought processes that take place during spoken language.

There is a controversy about whether spontaneous gestures accompanying speech are controlled by the same neural structures as the other motor aspects of language. These gestures are usually performed with the right hand, hence corresponding to the left hemisphere lateralization for language structures. However, they are dissociated from spoken language in Broca's aphasia, where they are increased (an effect which is not found in other types of aphasia), and where they might substitute for the defective spoken language. The aphasic patient described by Broca in 1861, although he could barely pronounce one single syllable (tan) usually uttered twice (tan-tan), used a great variety of gestures to express his ideas (Broca 1861). This dissociation suggests that spontaneous gestures and speech might share common mechanisms at the conceptual level, but become dissociated at the output level (McNeill 1992; see also Feyereisen 1987). This discussion about the relationship between spontaneous gestures and speech is important because of the evolutionary role attributed to gestures in the appearance of language. It is true that in children, gestures anticipate speech, although, as we saw, these gestures are not concatenated into 'linguistic' strings: they have a deictic and sometimes an iconic function, and soon become associated with words to form speech–gesture messages (see review in Goldin-Meadow 1999). In contrast, non-human primates, although they also use gestures to communicate, do not use this means of communication in the way children do: unlike children who use gestures not only to request things but also to comment on distant events, chimpanzees in the wild apparently use gestures only to request immediate action from conspecifics.

As a motor process, the production and comprehension of language and the matching of the two should proceed from an action representation. As we emphasized in Chapters 1 and 2, one of the distinctive features of action representations is that they may remain covert, i.e. invisible (and inaudible) to an external observer. Like the production of goal-directed movements, language production should therefore also include a covert stage where language is produced, but not uttered. This stage, commonly known as 'inner speech' or 'thinking in words', has been investigated in ways very similar to motor images, i.e. by looking at their behavioral correlates. Inner speech has frequently been found to be accompanied by tiny muscular contractions of vocal tract muscles. EMG activity of vocal muscles increases during thinking, imagining speaking or silent reading (e.g. McGuigan 1966; McGuigan 1978). This muscular activity is specific to the mentally rehearsed material, e.g. the lip EMG is stronger than the tongue EMG when the subject processes words with labial phonemes, whereas the reverse is true for words containing lingual phonemes. These findings are consistent with the fact that inner speech is associated with activation of Broca's area, in the inferior frontal gyrus, as detected by an fMRI mapping study (Hinke *et al.* 1993).[6,7]

---

[6] Subvocal speech was first interpreted as a source of peripheral kinesthetic information which, when projected to central nervous structures, generated auditory images of the corresponding words. The same interpretation was given to the low intensity EMG recorded during mental motor imagery of limb actions, which was thought to be the origin of the feelings experienced by the subject during mental rehearsal (Jacobson 1930), or to the eye movements recorded during mental visual imagery (e.g. Brandt and Stark, 1997). However, this interpretation of mental processes as consequences of peripheral feedback is now disproved by recent experiments showing complete absence of muscular activity in many subjects during motor imagery. When present, this activity is rather assumed to be a consequence of incomplete inhibition of motor output during mental states involving motor simulation. This same interpretation might also hold for inner speech.

[7] Subvocal speech has been found to correlate with verbal hallucinations (voices) in schizophrenic patients. Maneuvers which interfere with subvocal speech (e.g. mouth opening)

6.3.2 The functional anatomy of the language production–comprehension interface. The role of Broca's area

Action production, as we know, is only one facet of motor cognition. Action representations also operate for understanding actions of others. As we saw in Chapter 5, the observation of an action performed by an external agent induces, in the observer's brain, changes which testify to the activation of the representation they have formed of the action they are observing. These changes are reflected in an increased excitability of the motor pathways corresponding to the observed action. This is also the case with language. Luciano Fadiga and his colleagues showed that hearing speech sounds produces in the listener an activation of muscles of the vocal tract. Applying TMS at the level of the face representation of motor cortex, they found that listening to words involving tongue muscles automatically activated these muscles (Fadiga *et al.* 2002). The same effect was also independently reported by Watkins *et al.* (2003), who found, in addition, that the excitability of vocal muscles was also enhanced by viewing speech-related movements (e.g. lip movements). A few years earlier, Kerzel and Bekkering (2000) had conjectured that, if motor structures participate in analyzing visible speech, then looking at the speaker's mouth should activate these motor structures. For example, if an observer pronounces the same utterance as the speaker he observes, this utterance should be facilitated; conversely, pronouncing a different vocal utterance should render the performance more difficult. Kerzel and Bekkering found that subjects uttering, for example, the phoneme /ba/ while watching a mouth articulating /da/ took a significantly longer time to respond than when the two phonemes were the same. Note that we reported the same effects with watching/performing compatible or incompatible hand movements in Chapter 5 (e.g. Brass *et al.* 2001b; Kilner *et al.* 2003). These results, which demonstrate that speech perception, either by listening to speech or by observing speech movements, activates motor structures involved in speech

----

tend to interrupt voices in hallucinating patients (Bick and Kinsbourne 1987). The idea is that subvocal speech, which tends to be inhibited in normal subjects, is increased in patients. This suggests that auditory hallucinations are associated with abnormal activity in the areas of the frontal and temporal lobes concerned with speech, with a frontal lobe activity too low to exert its inhibitory role on posterior areas (see Chapter 4). Assuming that the pathological model represents an exaggeration of the normal process, the above results show that covert speech production is a mental motor process, similar to motor imagery for limb movements. Verbal thinking may also rely on the same mechanism. If correct, this would support the hypothesis that motor processes are already present at an early stage of language production.

production, fall within the framework of the Motor Theory of Speech Perception. This theory holds that 'the objects of speech perception are the intended phonetic gestures of the speaker, represented in the brain as invariant motor commands that call for movements of the articulators through certain linguistically significant configurations' (Liberman and Mattingly 1985, p. 2). Obviously, we will have to keep in mind this definition when we discuss the role of motor simulation in understanding language.

We will now examine the arguments supporting the existence of a production–comprehension matching system for language, similar to the execution–observation matching system that we found for actions and emotions. Indeed, this hypothesis was amply developed in the previous chapter: it is based on the existence of neurons in monkey ventral premotor cortex which are activated during both execution and observation of compatible hand movements (the mirror neurons). In man, the cortical region thought to include these neurons is part of the premotor cortex (dorsal and ventral Brodman area 6) in the precentral gyrus, and a set of areas (Brodman areas 44, 45 and 47), located more ventrally and rostrally, in the inferior frontal gyrus. The inferior frontal gyrus areas are not evenly distributed in both hemispheres: they are larger on the left side, where they roughly correspond to Broca's area, than in the homologous region on the right side. In addition, as is well known from both neuroimagery studies and clinical observations, this anatomical asymmetry has a clear functional counterpart (see below). Broca's area is a heterogeneous cortical zone, corresponding to several entities as defined by both cytoarchitectonic and functional mapping. Brodman areas 44, in the *pars opercularis* of inferior frontal gyrus, and 45 in the *pars triangularis* have an intermediate cytoarchitectonic structure: like area 4 (primary motor area), they have a layer III densely provided with pyramidal cells; but, like prefrontal areas, they have the laminated pattern characteristic of granular cortex (Galaburda and Pandya 1982). Recent studies using receptor labeling similarly conclude that Brodman areas 44 and 45 show a 'fingerprint' very similar to that of the primary motor area (area 4), whereas area 47, in the *pars orbitalis* of inferior frontal gyrus, has a 'fingerprint' close to that of the classical granular prefrontal areas (Amunts *et al.* 1999). Area 44, which is frequently considered as the 'true' Broca's area (e.g. Petrides *et al.* 2005), is thus a transitional zone between agranular cortex (areas 4 and ventral area 6) and prefrontal granular cortex. Finally, another partition can also be made on the basis of anatomical connections of the left inferior frontal gyrus: it is connected to superior temporal and inferior parietal cortex by two main anatomical projection streams. The ventral inferior frontal gyrus (*pars triangularis* and *pars orbitalis*) is connected with the rostral and ventral part of the auditory association cortex via the uncinate fasciculus, whereas the dorsal inferior frontal gyrus (*pars opercularis*) is connected with the caudal and dorsal part of the auditory association cortex and the inferior parietal cortex via the arcuate fasciculus.

The heterogeneity of the left inferior frontal gyrus is also reflected in functional neuroimagery studies, using both linguistic and non-linguistic tasks. Most activation studies with linguistic tasks have identified the left inferior frontal gyrus region and the adjacent areas as the neural substrates of syntax processing either for comprehension or for production. Ni *et al.* (2000), for example, found specific activation in the left inferior frontal gyrus during presentation of sentences featuring grammatical errors. Several attempts have been made to segregate areas activated in relation to semantic processing from those activated by syntactic processing. Using verbal fluency tasks, Paulesu *et al.* (1997) found that the anterior part is activated during a semantic fluency task whereas the posterior part is more activated by a phonemic fluency task. Dapretto and Bookheimer, in experiments manipulating semantic and syntactic complexity independently, found that the activity of area 47 is associated with semantic judgement whereas area 44 is associated with syntactic judgment. Thus, there are indications that Broca's area generally shows a ventral to dorsal gradient, with semantic processing activating more ventral areas (area 47), syntactic processing activating areas 45 and 44, and phonological processing activating areas 44 and ventral area 6 (Bookheimer 2002; see Hagoort 2004). The production of sentences has not been studied as widely as comprehension. Indefrey *et al.* (2001) described a graded activation of the left inferior frontal gyrus when subjects produced word sequences, noun phrases or full sentences.

As expected from the common features of speaking and signing reported above, Broca's area also participates in the production of sign language. This is illustrated by an observation in a deaf signer who underwent a cortical stimulation procedure for medical purposes. During electrical stimulation of his Broca's area, the subject was asked to name by signing objects presented as line drawings, and to replicate signing presented on a video. The stimulation affected the articulatory pattern of the signs and resulted in imperfect formation of the signs (Corina *et al.* 1999) Interestingly, these effects were obtained during stimulation of the posterior part of Broca's area, which is consistent with the above findings showing the involvement of this region in the phonemic aspects of word production. In addition, area 44 has been shown to be activated in bilingual subjects (i.e. speaking English and using sign language) when they produce complex articulatory movements either by speaking or by gesturing (Horwitz *et al.* 2003).

Finally, a major argument as to the role of Broca's area in matching language production and comprehension can be found in the observation of clinical cases of aphasic patients. There is a tradition, in clinical neurology, to consider Broca's aphasia (the language disorder created by a lesion affecting Broca's area) as a 'motor' aphasia, specifically impairing language production, as opposed to a 'sensory' aphasia due to a more posterior lesion and affecting language comprehension. This classical view, which may have some utility for diagnostic purposes, has been questioned by neurolinguistic studies. Caramazza and Zurif (1976), for example, tested aphasic subjects in a sentence–picture matching task for passive sentences. Broca's aphasics could make the correct matching for semantically constrained sentences (i.e. sentences that could not be reversed without violating semantics, such as 'the man was bitten by the dog'), but failed for sentences where the meaning was equally plausible when the sentence was reversed, e.g. 'the horse was followed by the dog'. From these data, they conclude that brain damage in Broca's aphasics 'affects a general language processing mechanism that subserves the syntactic component of both comprehension and production. The implication that follows is that the anterior language area of the brain is necessary for syntactic-like cognitive operations' (1976, p. 581). Because these patients are still able to use semantic heuristics to understand simple language superficially, their syntactic impairment may escape gross clinical examination (for a review of precise syntactic deficits in Broca's aphasics, see Grodzinsky 2000).

So far, we have reviewed a number of arguments which call for a motor simulation process in producing and understanding language, similar to that we described for executing/understanding hand actions and expressing/understanding emotions. It is thus tempting to reconstruct for language the same logic as we did for the other two domains. Thus, the first step is to look, in the monkey brain, for an area which would bear some analogy with the human system that contributes to the language comprehension–production matching, i.e. Broca's area. As a matter of fact, monkey ventral area 6 includes neurons with mirror properties not only for hand movements but also for mouth movements: these neurons respond while the monkey executes or watches an experimenter producing 'communicative' mouth movements (e.g. lip protrusion or lip smacking, Ferrari *et al.* 2003). Interestingly, in a recent paper, Petrides *et al.* (2005) reported a combined anatomical and neurophysiological study showing that monkeys do possess an area with cytoarchitectural characteristics similar to the human area 44, topographically close to but distinct from the ventral area 6 where the hand mirror neurons were found. Electrical stimuli applied to this monkey area 44 were found to elicit orofacial movements[8]. The fact that a region in monkey premotor cortex shows characteristics close to those of the human Broca's area raises key questions about the evolution of language. These questions, however, are beyond the scope of this book (reviewed in Arbib 2005).

At this point, the problem that remains is to determine what, among the various motor aspects of language, is actually being simulated, and to what extent this simulation would contribute to the understanding of language. Few attempts have been made in this direction. Rather, discussions have focused on evolutionary aspects of language, and hypotheses have been proposed on how speech might have evolved from manual gestures (see Corballis 2003). Rizzolatti and Arbib (1998) have conjectured that the primitive method of communication in primates using the orofacial musculature was complemented by the appearance of a more advanced system using the arm and the hand. Using the hand for communicating has an obvious advantage over using the face, in allowing deictic movements (e.g. showing or pointing at an object) and transitive actions on objects. In a further step, vocalization could have developed for potentiating and supplementing the gestural system. According to this hypothesis, the mirror system for matching understanding and executing hand actions, located in the monkey ventral premotor cortex, could have evolved into a speech comprehension–production matching system in the human Broca's area. Although this hypothesis opens up interesting perspectives, it does not propose a direct explanation of what one can obtain by observing a speaking face or listening to a voice. This would require a full analysis of the linguistic features that can be predominantly accessed through motor mechanisms, i.e. independently from the perception of the words and of their sequential arrangement. By analogy with other actions, motor simulation of speech could provide the listener with the meaning embedded in the 'kinematics' of speech, i.e. the inflections of the voice and the prosody of the discourse. It could also possibly contribute to the perception of phonemes.

The perception of phonemes, at first sight, seems a relatively simple process: we identify them as elementary auditory patterns, because they have been processed by our auditory system. Other arguments, however, reveal the complexity of phonemic perception. Consider the effect described by McGurk and MacDonald in 1976 (the so-called McGurk effect). A subject is presented synchronously with a speech sound (e.g. a voice uttering the phoneme /ba/)

---

[8] This study was performed in anesthetized animals, which limits the significance of its results. Specifically, the fact that the authors report only orofacial movements as an effect of electrical stimulation of this area is in disagreement with studies in behaving animals reporting many neurons related to hand movements in this area.

and a video of a face articulating another phoneme (e.g. /da/). The resulting percept is something in between the two (e.g. /ga/), which shows that the two sensory inputs are 'read' as a single speech gesture. This is indeed a unique feature of speech movements to result in a single percept in spite of being processed by different sensory channels: this is because they are integrated with each other by a speech-specific mechanism which operates beyond the level of sensory processing and participates in the motor execution of the corresponding speech movement. Thus, the McGurk effect reveals the existence of a comprehension–production matching system for the understanding of simple speech sounds. Whether this system includes Broca's area still remains to be demonstrated.

The usefulness of such a system at the phonemic level is clearly apparent during language development in children. It should also be useful to adults who learn a new language. In language learning, the problem is not only to identify a speech sound, it is to transfer it into a corresponding vocal movement: the simulation of the phoneme by the matching system then becomes critical, particularly during the babbling stage in infants. Mirror neurons responding to acoustic speech stimuli and engaged in vocal movements ('echo-neurons', as suggested by Pulvermüller) could play this role. As we saw earlier, this idea of matching the perceived sound and the corresponding vocal gesture was already present in the Motor Theory of Speech Perception (Liberman and Mattingly 1985), or even earlier (Fry 1966). A deficient matching between perception and action has been proposed as an explanation for the difficulties encountered by autistic children in learning language (Williams *et al.* 2001).

6.3.3 The role of Broca's area in action representation

The contribution of Broca's area to motor cognition, however, may not be limited to processing the motor aspects of language. Neuroimaging experiments conducted over the last 10 years have extended its role to the representation of actions, self-generated as well as performed by others. We saw in Chapter 2 that the posterior part of the left inferior frontal gyrus (Brodman area 44) is activated in subjects imagining themselves performing or observing grasping hand movements (Decety *et al.* 1994; Grafton *et al.* 1996). This is also true in situations related to language for action, such as generating action words (Martin *et al.*, 1995; Hamzei *et al.* 2003; Tettamenti *et al.* 2005), naming man-made tools (Martin *et al.* 1996) or observing man-made tools (Perani *et al.* 1995). Thus, Broca's area could be part of a network where actions are represented and ultimately understood, but in a way distinct from the processing of language utterances (speech, mouth movements and gestures) themselves.

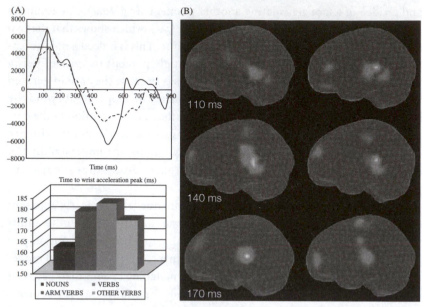

Fig. 6.2 Co-processing of limb movements and action-related language in motor cortical areas. (A) The Boulenger *et al.* experiment. A subject is instructed to make a hand pointing movement at a target in front of him. At the exact time where the movement starts a word is projected on a screen near the target. The kinematics of the arm are measured. If the word is an action verb (e.g. reach), the early kinematics of the movement are perturbed. The curve at the upper left shows the acceleration profile of the arm in a control condition (non-action word presented, solid curve) and in the action verb condition (broken curve): note that the acceleration peak is delayed and reduced in amplitude in the action verb condition. Lower left: from left to right, latency of the acceleration peak in the control conditions (non-action words) and in different conditions with action verbs. From Boulenger *et al.* (2006). (B) Brain activity recorded with the magneto-encephalographic (MEG) technique during presentation of action verbs referring to arm or face actions (left) or leg actions (right). MEG recording is triggered by the onset of the second syllable of the word. Note that activation of the language recipient area in the left temporal lobe occurs and is shortly followed by propagation of activity in the motor regions. From Pulvermüller *et al.* (2005b), with kind permission of the first author.

What suggests the existence of this additional mechanism is that it involves not only Broca's area but also the ensemble of the motor system that participates in the represented action. Not surprisingly, language would stand as one of the gateways giving access to motor representations, to the same extent as action observation. Pioneering work by Gentilucci and Gangitano (1998) had shown that the action of reaching for an object can be influenced by the simultaneous presentation of a word: participants were requested to reach for a rod on which a single word (*lungo* or *corto*, i.e. long or short) was printed. Gerntilucci and Gangitano found that the kinematics of the initial phase of the reach (peak acceleration and velocity) were affected by the word, such that the subjects automatically associated the meaning of the word with the distance to be covered. When the subjects saw, for example, the word *corto*, they activated a motor program for a nearer object position. Thus, a word related to the metrics of a movement influences the representation of the goal of that movement, and interferes with its execution (see also Glover *et al.* 2004).

More recently, a host of new data has confirmed this intuition at both the behavioral and the neural levels. Boulenger *et al.* (2006) instructed subjects to reach a visual target by hand. At the time of departure of the hand movement, they presented the subjects with a word appearing on a screen. This presentation created an interference which could be detected at the level of the hand kinematics: when the presented word was an action verb, the acceleration of the ongoing hand movement was decreased. This effect was not found with words unrelated to action, such as concrete nouns (see Figure 6.2). Thus, processing an action word affected the visuomotor processing of another action executed with the hand. Note that this interference between the two processes occurred within a very short time after the presentation of the action word. Indeed, the hand acceleration peaked at around 150 ms after movement onset: as the word was shown precisely at movement onset, its processing interfered with motor cortex activity at the end of the dynamic phase where corticospinal neurons are recruited for accelerating the hand. This is an important finding, because it suggests that the processing of language related to action shares the same resources as the corresponding motor actions. Supporting this suggestion, in the experiment of Boulenger *et al.*, verbs referring to hand actions were even more effective in affecting the kinematics of the hand than verbs referring to leg actions. Other findings also show that the motor system is influenced by verbal cues. The visual presentation of action words related to face, arm or leg actions (e.g. *lick*, *pick* or *kick*, respectively) specifically activates regions in the primary motor cortex. According to the fMRI experiment of Hauk *et al.* (2004), the area activated by the presentation of an action verb referring to the hand (e.g. *pick*) overlaps with that activated during execution of a hand movement (see Figure 6.2). Similarly, the excitability of motor cortex (tested with TMS) is increased when participants listen to action-related sentences. Again, this effect is somatotopically selective: hand action-related sentences influence more the excitability of the hand motor area than foot action-related sentences, and vice versa (Floël *et al.* 2003; Buccino *et al.* 2005). When arm muscle contractions are elicited by TMS pulses applied to the arm motor area, the processing of arm-related action words is facilitated relative to leg-related action words (Pulvermüller *et al.* 2005a).

The fact that processing action words and processing the corresponding action share the same resources can be interpreted in different ways. One possibility is that hearing or seeing an action word or sentence activates the motor centers because it elicits a motor image of the verbally presented action. We have described in Chapter 2 situations where a motor image is formed implicitly when an action is prepared or a decision has to be made about its feasibility. This hypothesis implies that the action words are understood prior to eliciting the motor image, i.e. that the activation of the motor system occurs at a post-lexical stage. According to this suggestion, action words would not have a special status with respect to other words: they would affect the motor system because of their relationship to executable actions, but the resulting activation would not in itself contribute to their understanding. Motor simulation, as in other types of motor images, would provide a pragmatic knowledge of the action, distinct from the semantic identification of the related action words. The fact that the motor system activation is topographically related to the action evoked by the words is an argument in this direction. This suggestion is in line with the idea that motor imagery is a central phenomenon in motor cognition, which can account for many of the situations we have encountered. An example is the sight of action-related objects, such as tools, where, as we saw earlier, the motor system is also activated (Chao and Martin 2000). In that case, the motor simulation of the tool action not only contributes to the identification of the tool, but it also provides the pragmatic information of how to use it.

A different interpretation of the motor activation induced by action words has been proposed by Friedemann Pulvermüller. In his view, this activation is not a consequence of the relationship of the words to a potential action: rather, it is intrinsically linked to the processing of their meaning (e.g. Pulvermüller 2005). One of the main arguments to this hypothesis is that the motor system activation occurs rapidly during the presentation of the words. The result of Boulenger *et al.* cited above shows that an action word can influence an ongoing movement during its acceleration, i.e. within 150 ms or so. Such a short delay is compatible with the intervention of the motor system in the lexico-semantic processing of the words: studies using event-related potentials (a technique with a high temporal resolution) show that lexico-semantic processes (e.g. reflecting the difference between word categories) occur within 100–200 ms after presentation of the words (e.g. Sereno *et al.* 1998). Rapid as it is, the 'motor' processing of action words is likely to be entirely automatic, which is compatible with the typical feature of language processing to be effortless and compulsory. This view introduces semantics in the motor network in a way distinct from that held by the tenets of motor simulation as a source of language understanding. According to Pulvermüller, somatotopic motor activation occurs during action processing because of the links between an action and the corresponding words that are actively created during the language learning period. In the cortex, the motor program and the neural representation of the word are therefore activated almost simultaneously, so that synaptic connections between neurons in specific motor and premotor areas and those in the language areas become stronger (Pulvermüller *et al.* 2005b). This hypothesis proposes a change in perspective on the mutual influence of language and action, where language understanding is seen as the result of a learning process which associates a word and an action within a specific network, and not as a process which simulates the action it sees or hears about.

Although it has been proposed for action-related language, Pulvermüller's idea could be expanded to other linguistic categories. Assuming that associations between a word and the reality it represents can be created by learning, it would not be surprising that words that depict, for example, the visual features of objects are associated with a specific activation of those visual areas where these features are processed. If that were the case, then action words would be one category among others and not a special case. As a matter of fact, the notion of category-specific knowledge is currently used in neuropsychology to account for deficits in recognizing and naming objects of a given category, following localized lesions of the visual system (e.g. Shallice 1988). In normal subjects, as we saw above, Martin *et al.* (1996) found that naming visually presented objects of different types activated different brain areas. For example, naming living objects (e.g. animals) activated an area in the medial occipital region, whereas naming tools activated premotor cortex and an area in the middle temporal gyrus. Thus, the perception of a word would automatically activate the mechanism for recognizing and identifying the corresponding reality: action words would activate the motor system to the same extent as visual words would activate the visual system, etc. Whether these considerations represent a possible basis for a generalized simulation theory of understanding language and storing knowledge is a matter of discussion.

The precise role of Broca's area in this action representation network is still an open question. We know from the neuropsychological literature that deficits in Broca's aphasics are not limited to language production and comprehension. These patients also recognize gestures and pantomimes poorly (e.g. Goodglass and Kaplan 1963). In a recent study, Saygin *et al.* (2005) showed that aphasics are impaired in an action–picture matching task, and that this deficit in non-linguistic action comprehension is associated with lesions in the inferior frontal gyrus, in the precentral and postcentral gyri and in the head of the caudate nucleus. This result fits with the contribution of Broca's area, in association with the motor network, to the action representations, whether they are built from internal or external cues.

Concluding remarks

In this book, we have identified a number of critical cognitive functions which involve the activity of the motor system. These functions comprise the field of motor cognition. In this conclusion section, we summarize the results of our investigation of motor cognition, by recalling what motor cognition is and what it is not, and propose some free speculations about its possible biological function.

1 The core of motor cognition is the concept of action representation, the covert counterpart of any goal-directed action, executed or not. Assuming that action representations are the core of motor cognition means that the objective of a study of motor cognition is to understand the content of these representations. This has been (and still is) one of the most challenging enterprises in cognitive science. The main property disclosed in action representations is that they exist as dynamic covert states: as experimentally demonstrated, they take time to unfold, to the same extent as overt actions; they can be described in terms of mental kinematics which follow the same rules as in real actions. Whenever an action is represented, the motor system is rehearsed, and the mechanisms which prepare the forthcoming action are activated. Action representations thus simulate the actions they represent.

The material for building action representations, however, originates from both within and outside the agent. Action representations built from within are about actions that are planned, intended or imagined by the agent. We posited that, in this case, the activity of the motor system corresponds to a motor simulation in the first-person perspective. The role of this mechanism is to 'evaluate' the feasibility of the action, its potential consequences and its adequacy with respect to the anticipated goal. Action representations arising from outside are about actions performed by other agents, and perceived and simulated by an observer in a third-person perspective. These two modalities of action representations share common neural mechanisms, in the sense that the same subject can either be the agent or the observer of the same action, and that his motor system will become activated in both cases. Further mechanisms come into play for blocking the transfer of the representation into an overt action, i.e. for preventing the intention from being executed or the observed action being imitated. This fact that action representations can be shared by two or more individuals is central to motor cognition. It implies that the two representations, although they partially overlap, should remain distinguishable from one another. The parts of the representations that differ between actions in the first- and in the third-person perspectives provide information about *attributing* the action to its proper agent; the parts of the representations that are common in the two conditions provide information for *understanding* actions one observes others performing.

2 The co-existence, within the same brain, of the two modalities of action representations thus raises the problem of identifying the author of these representations. Because actions are so closely linked to the self who produces them, this problem is in fact that of distinguishing oneself from other selves. Mechanisms for solving this problem operate at several levels. On the one hand, overt actions represent a relatively simple case: the fact that they are executed provides the agent with cues for disentangling those that are self-produced from those that are externally produced. The correlation (both in time and in body space) between central command signals and sensory signals that result from execution can be monitored by specific brain areas. This process is the source of the sense of being the agent of that action (the sense of agency), itself being a necessary and sufficient condition for self-attributing it. On the other hand, the attribution of covert actions is more difficult to account for, because the observable signals generated by execution are lacking. In this case, the sense of agency must arise from the activity of brain areas that are specific to self-generated representations (the above non-overlapping parts of shared representations). This is a fragile process: pathological conditions reveal that one can be misled about the origin of one's own intended actions or one's own inner speech (as in schizophrenia) or even that one can fail to realize the existence of intentions or action representations in other people (as in autism).

3 Realizing that actions performed by others are directed towards goals and that they have a meaning is the other dimension of motor cognition, that which considers not only actions and their representations but also interactions between subjects. Human actions have a distinctive pattern that makes them understandable. It is the role of motor simulation in the third-person perspective to give access to the understanding of actions performed by other humans. Because the observer uses the motor rules which are embedded in his motor system to simulate the action he observes, the representation he builds from that action is immediately understandable and potentially transferable into an action. This

mechanism is the basis for replicating and imitating the actions of others, and for learning new skills.

Can motor simulation give access to covert stages of action representations, beyond what can be directly observed? The cautious answer to that question, based on classical sensory motor physiology, tends to be negative: the nervous system needs stimuli to perceive external reality. It is hard to believe that one can infer the final goal of an action which extends over time from the mere observation of one of its early components. Even a very precise motor simulation of the kinematics of this component would not allow anticipation of its final goal, unless there are other indications derived from previous observation and learning, or from the context in which the action is performed. In addition, other cognitive systems exist for efficiently guessing, reasoning, judging and making inferences which do not depend on simulation mechanisms.

Another, less cautious answer to the above question is that intentions may be perceivable through additional behavioral cues such as gaze direction, facial expressions, gait or postures. These cues, which are common to both action representations and emotions, and can indeed bridge the gap between the two, are encoded by specific neural systems distinct for those responsible for motor simulation. It is conceivable that these cues could provide the motor simulation system with a 'context' sufficient for accessing the global intention at the origin of the action. It would be important to demonstrate that neurons that are active during the observation of a hand action, for example, are also influenced by the direction of the gaze of the agent during the hand action. The evidence for an integration, in the same neurons, of cues for action and intention is still lacking.

4 Attributing an action to its agent and understanding others' actions are distinct but connected functions. They both refer to the existence of two acting selves, if not of two interacting selves. Attributing refers to the self–other differentiation: it can be seen as a relatively simple default process, whereby perceived events that do not fulfill the conditions for being attributed to me (existence of central commands and correlation between movement-generated signals) must belong to someone else. The sense of agency and the related sense of self would be a further step, although still oriented towards the self and not towards others. Understanding, on the other hand, takes for granted that the person one observes is distinct from the self. As a matter of fact, one of its basic mechanisms (the mirror neurons) is not suited for the self–other differentiation, as it encodes the action in the same way irrespective of who is executing it. Pathological conditions may even dissociate the two functions from one

another: schizophrenic patients may misattribute actions (to themselves or to others) without showing any evidence of misunderstanding the content of these actions.

It would probably be a mistake to consider the function of understanding as a primarily social function, in the sense of an active intersubjective communication between two people. An observer can very well understand an action performed outside of any social context, i.e. an action which is not directed at him and is not part of a communicative exchange with him. Motor cognition tells more to the self about the action than about its agent. It can tell what the action is about, how to do it and to some extent who does it, but not why it is being done here and now by this particular agent.

5 Philosophical theories of action have primarily insisted on the role of the self as the cause of actions, and much less on the consequences of these actions for the self who caused them. An action, as we said in the Introduction, is at the transition between the process which caused that action to appear and the changes that its occurrence will produce. Among these changes are those that affect the agent himself. Action execution is the ultimate test of whether the represented anticipation of its goal was adequate or not. If the goal has been reached, the representation can be validated; if not, it must be re-evaluated and modified. This circular process, from self-representing an action to experiencing its effects and to adapting the representation according to these effects, is a metaphor which has been widely used in biology for explaining certain aspects of the development of the nervous system and in psychology for understanding the development of cognition.

Generally speaking, a motor representation can be conceived as a structure that anticipates interactions with the environment: it directs movements and exploratory activities to the external world, thus making more information available. This information arising from the interaction with the environment, if congruent with the anticipation, will stabilize the representation and set its parameters for more and more successful interaction. This process results in selecting, possibly among a larger repertoire, those representations which conform best with the available information about the external world. The postulate inherent to these theories is that actions are driven from within and that the interaction with the external world is caused by the subject, and not by external factors. Thus, organisms are not thought of as purely reactive systems: rather, they exhibit spontaneous behavior which testifies to pre-existing endogenous activity. In other words, they are thought to be endowed with prior 'knowledge' about themselves and the external world, which makes them able to anticipate the effects of interacting with the environment. This mechanism seems to operate from the very beginning, including during fetal life. In mammalian fetuses, the ventral aspect of the spinal cord matures far in advance with respect to its dorsal aspect. Yet, fetuses exhibit spontaneous movements which closely resemble those from the normal repertoire observed after birth (De Vries *et al.* 1982) before the time where the dorsal roots are functional, i.e. before these movements could be triggered or influenced by any external stimulus. These early movements could represent an epigenetic factor for the stabilization of synaptic connections during maturation of the nervous system (e.g. Changeux and Danchin 1976).

What is true for biological development also seems to be the case for the emergence of psychological functions. In psychology, the idea that action contributes to the construction of cognitive functions was indeed the core of the Piagetian theory of intelligence. The child, in what Piaget calls his sensory motor period, makes systematic attempts at interacting with the external world, guided by inborn elementary structures (or 'schemes'). The results of this guided search are integrated with the pre-existing structures, so that the external reality becomes more and more familiar and predictable, and the subsequent interactions are facilitated (see Piaget 1936; Neisser 1976). More recent theories of cognitive development have insisted on the importance of the initial state of the newborn. Very soon after birth, naive children show evidence of knowledge about elementary physical laws, temporal regularities, causal relationships, etc. (e.g. Spelke *et al.* 1992). The competency of newborns also extends to establishing communication with other individuals (e.g. Trevarthen, 1993) or to parsing the acoustic flow of natural languages. All these data testify to the existence of a biological and psychological initial state which owes little to perception and which can serve as a guide for initiating the interaction with the environment.

Finally, the role of action in acquiring new knowledge is not limited to the development period, it continues throughout life. This role of action has been emphasized by many experiments comparing active and passive exposure during various forms of learning: for example, adaptation to visuomotor conflicts (e.g. produced by laterally displacing prisms) is rapidly obtained when the subjects actively move their arm during exposure to the conflict. No such adaptation can be obtained if they see their arm passively displaced (Held 1961). At a more cognitive level, action facilitates the encoding in memory of verbal material. Vocally presented sentences describing simple actions are better recalled if the described actions are additionally acted out by the subjects, as compared with vocal presentation alone (the enactment effect, Engelkamp 1998). This notion of an action-dependent cognition is best expressed by the various forward models which have been around in the literature since the 1950s and even much earlier if one considers antecedents such as Helmhotz's account of the correction of the effects of eye movements on visual perception (Helmholtz 1860) or Freud's explanation of the consequences of the satisfaction or dissatisfaction of desires (Pribram and Gill 1976).

6 The role of motor cognition, however, is not limited to the contribution of action to the acquisition or stabilization of new capacities: this is what the self can gain from his own actions in a 'selfish' version of motor cognition. Motor cognition also expands its scope to the intersubjective context, that of an interaction between selves. This dimension of motor cognition involves reciprocity between two selves: unlike in the selfish version, where the self drives his actions on the external world according to his needs or desires, in the intersubjective version the self may stand at either end of the interaction process: he may be the initiator as well as the receiver of the interaction, if it has been initiated by the other self. The contribution of motor cognition studies has been to show that such interactions cannot be 'perceived' in the usual sense, and that actions of others have to be 'experienced' in order to be understood: the motor system has to substitute for perceptual systems, for generating within the observer an internal experience of what he observes from the other. Modern neuroscience adds new arguments in this direction by showing the existence of mechanisms which can account for this notion of understanding by doing (or by simulating). At present, although we have at our disposal an ample demonstration of the existence of these mechanisms, we still need additional data on the function that would be missing if they were impaired or dysfunctional. Closer observation of pathological groups showing specific deficits in action understanding and in action imitation might provide this missing link.

7 The nature of the simulation mechanisms, which are central to motor cognition, can be interpreted in several different ways. One view, that of an embodied cognition, emphasizes the rapid and automatic mode of operation of motor simulation, supported by the impression that goal-directed actions most of the time are executed outside conscious awareness and that the mirror system of the observer of an action seems to be activated without delay and in a mandatory fashion. This view insists on the non-conceptual side of action representations and assumes that bodily

mechanisms, primarily involving the motor system, could mediate the understanding of the external world, physical as well as social: accordingly, external cues, especially those arising from conspecifics, would directly feed into a simulation machine (the mirror system) and generate the appropriate reactions without going through a conscious control. This non-conceptual view easily accounts for several of the critical functions attributed to motor cognition, such as learning, imitating, copying, empathizing or mimicking. Motor cognition, however, includes other domains, which require a control of bodily mechanisms by a more detached cognitive system. We know that compulsive imitation normally leaves place to more elaborate imitation, or that emotional reactions can be hidden, or pretended. Thus, the basic mechanisms of automatic simulation are supervened by controlled processes with a conceptual content. The fact that the functioning of action representations and the end-products of this functioning are frequently outside conscious awareness does not mean that motor cognition is in essence an ensemble of non-conscious and non-conceptual processes. It is true that motor cognitive mechanisms have to follow strong constraints, mainly when they come to execution, which require automaticity and rapidity. However, the activated representations can become explicit and their conceptual content can be retrieved by way of appropriate methods, as the existence of conscious motor images testifies.

The conceptual content of action representations does in fact spontaneously become manifest when time is allowed for this content to appear, or when the information load exceeds the capacities of the automatic mode. In such cases, there is an observable transition between automatic functioning and conscious monitoring. The conditions for this transition to appear consistently show that action representations are always close to the edge of consciousness: the sense of agency, the self–other distinction or the ability to understand and imitate others testify to the existence of an explicit, controlled mode of functioning of motor cognition. The very fact that action representations can have a conceptual content, like representations in other domains of cognition, thus suggests that a direct interaction between the body and the external and social milieu may not represent the only framework for motor cognition.

References

Adams, L., Guz, A., Innes, J. A. and Murphy, K. (1987). The early circulatory and ventilatory response to voluntary and electrically induced exercise in man. *Journal of Physiology*, **383**, 19–30.

Adolphs, R., Tranel, D. and Damasio, A.R. (1998). The human amygdala in social judgment. *Nature*, **393**, 470–4.

Allison, T., Puce, A. and McCarthy, G. (2000). Social perception from visual cues: role of the STS region. *Trends in Cognitive Science*, **4**, 267–78.

Amunts, K., Schleicher, A., Bürgel, U., Mohlberg, H., Uylings, H. B.M. and Zilles, K. (1999). Broca's region revisited: cytoarchitecture and intersubject variability. *Journal of Comparative Neurology*, **412**, 319–41.

Arbib, M. A. (1981). Perceptual structures and distributed motor control. In *Handbook of physiology, section I: the nervous system, vol. 2: motor control* (ed. V. B. Brooks), pp. 1449–80. Williams and Wilkins, Baltimore.

Arbib, M. A. (2005). From monkey-like action recognition to human language: an evolutionary framework for neurolinguistics. *Behavioral and Brain Sciences*, **28**, 105–67.

Astafiev, S. V., Stanley, C. M., Shulman, G. L. and Corbetta, M. (2004) Extrastriate body area in human occipital cortex responds to the performance of motor actions. *Nature Neuroscience*, **7**, 542–48

Bahrick, L. E. (1995). Intermodal origins of self-perception. In *The self in infancy. Theory and research* (ed. P. Rochat), pp. 349–73. Elsevier, Amsterdam.

Bahrick, L. E. and Watson, J. S. (1985). Detection of intermodal proprioceptive-visual contingency as a potential basis of self-perception in infancy. *Developmental Psychology*, **21**, 963–73.

Baldissera, F., Cavallari, P., Craighero, L. and Fadiga, L. (2001). Modulation of spinal excitability during observation of hand action in humans. *European Journal of Neuroscience*, **13**, 190–4.

Baron-Cohen, S. (1995). *Mindblindness. An essay on autism and theory of mind*. MIT Press, Cambridge, MA.

Bartlett, F. C. (1926). Review of aphasia and kindred disorders of speech, by Henry Head. *Brain*, **49**, 581–7.

Bastian, C. (1897). The 'muscular sense', its nature and cortical localization. *Brain*, **10**, 1–137.

Bekkering, H., Brass, M., Woschina, S. and Jacobs, A. M. (2005). Goal-directed imitation in patients with ideomotor apraxia. *Cognitive Neuropsychology*, **22**, 419–32.

Bellugi, U., Poizner, H. and Klima, E. S. (1989). Language, modality, and the brain. *Trends in Neuroscience*, **12**, 380–8.

Berlucchi, G. and Agliotti, S. (1997). The body in the brain: neural bases of corporeal awareness. *Trends in Neuroscience*, **20**, 560–4.

Bernstein, N. (1967). *The coordination and regulation of movements*. Pergamon Press, Oxford.

Berrios, G. E. and Gili, M. (1995). Will and its disorders: a conceptual history. *History of Psychiatry*, **6**, 87–104.

Bertenthal, B. I. (1993). Perception of biomechanical motion in infants: intrinsic image and knowledge-based constraint. In *Carnegie Symposium on Cognition: visual perception and cognition in infancy* (ed. C. Granrud), Erlbaum Hillside, NJ.

Berti, A., Bottini, G., Gandola, M., Pia, L., Smania, M., Stracciari, A., *et al.* (2005). Shared cortical anatomy for motor awareness and motor control. *Science*, **309**, 488–91.

Beyer, L., Weiss, T., Hansen, E., Wolf, A. and Siebel, A. (1990). Dynamics of central nervous activation during motor imagination. *International Journal of Psychophysiology*, **9**, 75–80.

Bick, P. A. and Kinsbourne, M. (1987). Auditory hallucinations and subvocal speech in schizophrenic patients. *American Journal of Psychiatry*, **144**, 222–5.

Binet, A. (1886). *La psychologie du raisonnement. Recherches expérimentales par l'hypnotisme.* Alcan, Paris.

Binkofski, F., Dohle, C., Posse, S., Stephan, K.M., Hefter, H., Seitz, R. J., and Freund, H. J. (1998). Human anterior intraparietal area subserves prehension. A combined lesion and functional MRI activation study. *Neurology*, **50**, 1253–59.

Bisiach, E. and Berti, A. (1987). Dyschiria. An attempt at its systemic explanation. In *Neurophysiological and neuropsychological aspects of spatial neglect* (ed. M. Jeannerod), pp. 183–201. Elsevier North Holland, Amsterdam.

Bizzi, E., Kalil, R. E. and Tagliasco, V. (1971). Eye–head coordination in monkeys. Evidence for centrally patterned organization. *Science*, **173**, 452–4.

Blakemore, S. J., Wolpert, D. and Frith, C. D. (1998). Central cancellation of self-produced tickle sensation. *Nature Neuroscience*, **1**, 635–40.

Blakemore, S. J., Frith, C. and Wolpert, D. (1999). Spatio-temporal prediction modulates the perception of self-produced stimuli. *Journal of Cognitive Neuroscience*, **11**, 551–559.

Blakemore, S. J., Smith, J., Steel, R., Johnstone, E.C. and Frith, C. D. (2000). The perception of self-produced sensory stimuli in patients with auditory hallucinations and passivity experiences: evidence for a breakdown in self-monitoring. *Psychological Medicine*, **30**, 1131–9.

Blakemore, S. J., Frith, C. D. and Wolpert, D. (2002) Abnormalities in the awareness of action. *Trends in Cognitive Science*, **6**, 237–42.

Blanke, O., Ortigue, S., Landis, T. and Seeck, M. (2002). Stimulating illusory own-body perceptions. The part of the brain that can induce out-of-body experiences has been located. *Nature*, **419**, 269.

Bonnet, M., Decety, J., Requin, J. and Jeannerod, M. (1997). Mental simulation of an action modulates the excitability of spinal reflex pathways in man. *Cognitive Brain Research*, **5**, 221–8.

Bookheimer, S. Y. (2002) Functional MRI of language. New approaches to understanding the cortical organization of semantic processing. *Annual review of Neuroscience*, **25**, 151–188.

Bosbach, S., Cole, J., Prinz, W. and Knoblich, G. (2005). Inferring another's expectation from action: the role of peripheral sensation. *Nature Neuroscience*, **8**, 1295–7.

Botvinick, M. and Cohen, J. (1998). Rubber hands 'feel' touch that eyes see. *Nature*, **391**, 756.

Boulenger, V., Roy, A. C., Paulignan, Y., Deprez, V., Jeannerod, M. and Nazir, T. A. (2006) Cross-talk between language processes and overt motor behavior in the first 200 ms of processing. *Journal of Cognitive Neuroscience* (in press).

Brandt, S. A. and Stark, L. W. (1997). Spontaneous eye movements during visual imagery reflect the content of the visual scene. *Jounal of Cognitive Neuroscience*, **9**, 27–38.

Brass, M. and Heyes, C. (2005). Imitation: is cognitive neuroscience solving the correspondence problem. *Trends in Cognitive Science*, **9**, 489–95.

Brass, M., Zysset, S. and von Cramon, Y. (2001a). The inhibition of imitative response tendencies. *Neuroimage*, 14, 1416–23.

Brass, M., Bekkering, H. and Prinz, W. (2001b). Movement observation affects movement execution in a simple response task. *Acta Psychologica*, 106, 3–22.

Bridgeman, B., Kirsch, M. and Sperling, A. (1981). Segregation of cognitive and motor aspects of visual function using induced motion. *Perception and Psychophysics*, **29**, 336–42.

Broca, P. (1861). Remarques sur le siège de la faculté du langage articulé, suivies d'une observation d'aphémie (perte de la parole). *Bulletin de la Société d'Anthropologie*, **6**, 330–57.

Brodal, A. (1973). Self-observations and neuroanatomical considerations after a stroke. *Brain*, **96**, 675–94.

Bruce, V. and Young, A. (1986). Understanding face recognition. *British Journal of Psychology*, **77**, 305–27.

Buccino, G., Binkofski, F., Fink, G. R., Fadiga, L., Fogassi, L., Gallese, V., *et al.* (2001). Action observation activates premotor and parietal areas in a somatotopic manner: an fMRI study. *European Journal of Neuroscience*, **13**, 400–4.

Buccino, G., Vogt, S., Ritzi, A., Fink, G. R., Zilles, K., Freund, H. J., and Rizzolatti, G. (2004). Neural circuits underlying imitation learning of hand actions: an event-related fMRI study. *Neuron*, **42**, 323–34.

Buccino, G., Riggio, L., Melli, G., Binkofski, F., Gallese, V. and Rizzolatti, G. (2005). Listening to action-related sentences modulates the activity of the motor system: a combined TMS and behavioral study. *Cognitive Brain Research*, **24**, 355–63.

Buxbaum, L. J., Johnson-Frey, S. H. and Bartlett-Williams, M. (2005). Deficient internal models for planning hand-object interactions in apraxia. *Neuropsychologia*, **43**, 917–29.

Calvert, G. A., Bullmore, E. T., Brammer, M. J., Campbell, R., Williams, S. C. R. and McGuire, P. K. (1997). Activation of auditory cortex during silent lipreading. *Science*, **276**, 593–595.

Calvo-Merino, B., Glaser, D. E., Grèzes, J., Passingham, R. E. and Haggard, P. (2005). Action observation and acquired motor skills: an fMRI study with expert dancers. *Cerebral Cortex*, **15**, 1243–49.

Caramazza, A. and Zurif, E. (1976). Dissociation of algorithmic and heuristic processes in language comprehension: evidence from aphasia. *Brain and Language*, **3**, 572–82.

Carey, D. P., Perrett, D. I. and Oram, M. W. (1997). Recognizing, understanding and reproducing action. In *Handbook of neuropsychology. Vol. 11. Action and cognition* (ed. M. Jeannerod), pp. 111–29. Elsevier, Amsterdam.

Carter, C. S., Braver, T. S., Barch, D. M., Botwinick, M. M., Noll, D. and Cohen, J. D. (1998). Anterior cingulate cortex, error detection and the online monitoring of performance. *Science*, **280**, 747–9.

Castiello, U., Paulignan, Y. and Jeannerod. M. (1991). Temporal dissociation of motor responses and subjective awareness. A study in normal subjects. *Brain*, **114**, 2639–55.

Cerritelli, B., Maruff, P., Wilson, P. and Currie, J. (2000). The effect of an external load on the force and timing components of mentally represented actions. *Behavioral Brain Research*, **18**, 91–6.

Chadwick, P. and Birchwood, M. (1994). The omnipotence of voices. A cognitive approach to auditory hallucinations. *British Journal of Psychiatry*, **164**, 190–201.

Chaminade, T., Meary, D., Orliaguet, J. P. and Decety, J. (2001). Is perceptual anticipation a motor simulation? A PET study. *Neuroreport*, **12**, 3669–74.

Chaminade, T., Meltzoff, A. N. and Decety, J. (2002). Does the end justify the means. A PET exploration of the mechanisms involved in human imitation. *Neuroimage*, **15**, 318–28.

Changeux, J. P. and Danchin, A. (1976) Selective stabilization of developing synapses as a mechanism for the specification of neuronal networks. *Nature*, **264**, 705–12.

Chao, L. L. and Martin, A. (2000). Representation of manipulable man-made objects in the dorsal stream. *Neuroimage*, **12**, 478–94.

Cincotti, F., Mattia, D., Babiloni, C., Carducci, F., Salinari, S., Bianchi, L., *et al.* (2003). The use of EEG modifications due to motor imagery for brain–computer interfaces. *IEEE Transactions in Neural Systems and Rehabilitation Engineering*, **11**, 131–133.

Cisek, P. and Kalaska, J. F. (2004). Neural correlates of mental rehearsal in dorsal premotor cortex. *Nature*, **431**, 993–6.

Clark, M. A., Merians, A. S., Kothari, A., Poizner, H., Macauley, B., Rothi, L. J. G., *et al.* (1994). Spatial planning deficits in limb apraxia. *Brain*, **117**, 1093–106.

Clark, S., Tremblay, F. and Ste-Marie, D. (2004). Differential modulation of corticospinal excitability during observation, mental imagery and imitation of hand actions. *Neuropsychologia*, **42**, 993–96

Cochin, S., Barthelemy, C., Roux, S. and Martineau, J. (1999). Observation and execution of movement: similarities demonstrated by quantified electroencephalography. *European Journal of Neuroscience*, **11**, 1839–1842.

Cole, J. and Paillard J. (1995). Living without touch and peripheral information about body position and movement: studies with deafferented subjects, pp 245–66. In *The Body and the Self* (ed. J. L. Bermudez, A. Marcel and N. Eilan). MIT Press, Cambridge, MA.

Corballis, M. C. (2003). From mouth to hand: gesture, speech, and the evolution of right-handedness. Laterality and human speciation. *Behavioral and Brain Sciences*, **26**, 199–260.

Corina, D. P., McBurney, S. L., Dodrill, C., Hinshaw, K., Brinklry, J. and Ojeman, G. (1999). Functional roles of Broca's area and SMG: evidence from cortical stimulation mapping in a deaf signer. *Neuroimage*, **10**, 570–81.

Craighero, L., Fadiga, L., Umilta, C. A. and Rizzolatti, G. (1996). Evidence for visuomotor priming effect. *Neuroreport*, **8**, 347–9.

Craighero, L., Bello, A., Fadiga, L. and Rizzolatti, G. (2002). Hand action preparation influences the responses to hand pictures. *Neuropsychologia*, **40**, 492–502.

Craik, K. J. W. (1947). Theory of the human operator in control system. I: the operator as an engineering system. *British Journal of Psychology*, **38**, 56–61.

Csibra, G., Gergely, G., Biro, S., Koos, O. and Brockbank, M. (1999). Goal attribution without agency cues: the perception of 'pure reason' in infancy. *Cognition*, **72**, 237–67.

Daprati, E., Franck, N., Georgieff, N., Proust, J., Pacherie, E., Dalery, J., and Jeannerod, M. (1997). Looking for the agent. An investigation into consciousness of action and self-consciousness in schizophrenic patients. *Cognition*, **65**, 71–86.

Daprati, E., Sirigu, A., Pradat-Diehl, P., Franck, N. and Jeannerod, M. (2000). Recognition of self produced movement in a case of severe neglect. *Neurocase*, **6**, 477–86.

Darwin, C. (1872). *The expression of emotions in man and animals*, New Edition, University of Chicago Press, Chicago, 1965.

Dasser, V., Ulbaek, I. and Premack, D. (1989). The perception of intention. *Science*, **243**, 365–7.

David, A. S. (1994). The neuropsychological origin of auditory hallucinations. In *The neuropsychology of schizophrenia* (ed. A. S. David and J. C. Cutting), pp. 269–313. Lawrence Erlbaum, Hove, UK.

Decety, J. and Boisson, D. (1990) Effect of brain and spinal cord injuries on motor imagery. *European Archives of Psychiatry and Neurological Sciences*, **240**, 39–43.

Decety, J. and Chaminade, T. (2003). Neural correlates of feeling sympathy. *Neuropsychologia*, **41**, 127–38.

Decety, J. and Ingvar, D. H. (1990). Brain structures participating in mental simulation of motor behavior: a neuropsychological interpretation. *Acta Psychologica*, 73, 13–24.

Decety, J. and Jeannerod, M. (1996). Fitts' law in mentally simulated movements. *Behavioral Brain Research*, **72**, 127–34.

Decety, J., Jeannerod, M. and Prablanc, C. (1989). The timing of mentally represented actions. *Behavioural Brain Research*, **34**, 35–42.

Decety, J., Jeannerod, M., Germain, M. and Pastene, J. (1991). Vegetative response during imagined movement is proportional to mental effort. *Behavioural Brain Research*, **42**, 1–5.

Decety, J., Jeannerod, M., Durozard, D. and Baverel, G. (1993). Central activation of autonomic effectors during mental simulation of motor actions in man. *Journal of Physiology*, **461**, 549–63.

Decety, J., Perani, D., Jeannerod, M., Bettinardi, V., Tadary, B., Woods, R., et al. (1994). Mapping motor representations with PET. *Nature*, **371**, 600–2.

Decety, J., Grezes, J., Costes, N., Perani, D., Jeannerod, M., Procyk, E., et al. (1997). Brain activity during observation of action. Influence of action content and subject's strategy. *Brain*, **120**, 1763–77.

DeCharms, R. C., Christoff, K., Glover, G. H., Pauly, J. M., Whitfield, S. and Gabrieli, J. D. E. (2004). Learned regulation of spatially localized brain activation during real-time fMRI. *Neuroimage*, **21**, 436–43.

Dechent, P., Merboldt, K. D. and Frahm, J. (2004). Is the human primary motor cortex involved in motor imagery? *Cognitive Brain Research*, **19**, 138–44.

De Gelder, B., Vroomen, J., Pourtois, G. and Weiskrantz, L. (1999) Non-conscious recognition of affect in the absence of striate cortex. *Neuroreport*, **10**, 3759–63.

De Gelder, B., Snyder, J., Greve, D., Gerard, G. and Hadjikhani, N. (2004). Fear fosters flight: a mechanism for fear contagion when perceiving emotion expressed by a whole body. *Proceedings of the National Academy of Sciences of the USA*, **101**, 16701–6.

De Lange, F., Hagoort, P. and Toni, I. (2005). Neural topography and content of movement representations. *Journal of Cognitive Neuroscience*, **17**, 97–112.

De Lange, F. P., Kalkman, J. S., Bleijenberg, G., Hagoort, P., van der Wert, S. B., van der Meer, J. W. M., et al. (2004). Neural correlates of the chronic fatigue syndrome. An fMRI study. *Brain*, **127**, 1948–57.

De Sperati, C. and Stucchi, N. (1997). Recognizing the motion of a graspable object is guided by handedness. *Neuroreport*, **8**, 2761–2765.

de Vignemont, F. and Fourneret, P. (2004). The sense of agency: a philosophical and empirical review of the 'Who' system. *Consciousness and Cognition*, **13**, 1–19.

De Vries, J. I. P., Visser, G. H. A. and Prechtl, H. F. R. (1982). The emergence of fetal behavior. I Quantitative aspects. *Early Human Develoment*, **7**, 301–322.

Dierks, T., Linden, D. E. J., Jandl, M., Formisano, E., Goebel, R., Lanferman, H., and Singer, W. (1999). Activation of the Heschl's gyrus during auditory hallucniations. *Neuron*, **22**, 615–21.

Di Pellegrino, G., Fadiga, L., Fogassi, L., Gallese, V. and Rizzolatti, G. (1992). Understanding motor events: a neurophysiological study. *Experimental Brain Research*, **91**, 176–82.

Donoghue, J. P. and Sanes, J. N. (1987). Peripheral nerve injury in developing rats reorganizes representation pattern in motor cortex. *Proceedings of the National Academy of Sciences of the USA*, **84**, 1123–6.

Downing, P. E., Jiang, Y., Shuman, M. and Kanwisher, N. (2001). A cortical area selective for visual processing of the human body. *Science*, **293**, 2470–3.

Driskell, J. E., Cooper, C. and Moran, A. (1994). Does mental practice enhance performance? *Journal of Applied Psychology*, **79**, 481–92.

Ehrsson, H., Geyer, S. and Naito, E. (2003). Imagery of voluntary movements of fingers, toes and tongue activates corresponding body-part specific motor representations. *Journal of Neurophysiology*, **90**, 3304–16.

Ehrsson, H. H., Spence, C. and Passingham, R. E. (2004). That's my hand! Activity in premotor cortex reflects feeling of ownership of a limb. *Science*, **305**, 875–7.

Engelkamp, J. (1998). *Memory for actions*. Psychology Press, Hove, UK.

Ersland, L., Rosen, G., Lundervold, A., Smievoll, A.I., Tillung, T., Sundberg, H., and Hugdahl, K. (1996). Phantom limb imaginary fingertapping causes primary motor cortex activation: an fMRI study. *Neuroreport*, **8**, 207–10.

Fadiga, L., Fogassi, L., Pavesi, G. and Rizzolatti, G. (1995). Motor facilitation during action observation. A magnetic stimulation study. *Journal of Neurophysiology*, **73**, 2608–11.

Fadiga, L., Buccino, G., Craighero, L., Fogassi, L., Gallese, V. and Pavesi, G. (1999). Corticospinal excitability is specifically modulated by motor imagery: a magnetic stimulation study. *Neuropsychologia*, **37**, 147–58.

Fadiga, L., Craighero, L., Buccino, G. and Rizzolatti, G. (2002). Speech listening specifically modulates the excitability of tongue muscles: a TMS study. *European Journal of Neuroscience*, **15**, 399–402.

Farah, M. (1994). The neurological basis of mental imagery. A componential approach. *Cognition*, **18**, 245–72.

Farné, A., Pavani, F., Meneghello, F. and Ladavas, E. (2000). Left tactile extinction following visual stimulation of a rubber hand. *Brain*, 123, 2350–60.

Farné, A., Roy, A. C., Paulignan, Y., Rode, G., Rossetti, Y. and Jeannerod, M. (2003) Right hemisphere visuomotor control of the ipsilateral hand. Evidence from right brain damaged patients. *Neuropsychologia*, **41**, 739–757.

Farrer, C. and Frith, C. D. (2002). Experiencing oneself vs another person as being the cause of an action: the neural correlates of the experience of agency. *Neuroimage*

Farrer, C., Franck, N., d'Amato, T., and Jeannerod, M. (2004). Neural correlates of action attribution in schizophrenia. *Psychiatry Research: Neuroimaging*, **131**, 31–44.

Farrer, C., Franck, N., Georgieff, N., Frith, C. D., Decety, J. and Jeannerod, M. (2003). Modulating the experience of agency: a PET study. *Neuroimage*, **18**, 324–33.

Feinberg, I. (1978). Efference copy and corollary discharge. Implications for thinking and its disorders. *Schizophrenia Bulletin*, **4**, 636–40.

Feldman, A. G. (1966). Functional tuning of the nervous system during control of movement or maintenance of a steady posture. II. Controllable parameters of the muscle. *Biophysics*, **11**, 565–78.

Feltz, D. L. and Landers, D. M. (1983). The effects of mental practice on motor skill learning and performance: a meta-analysis. *Journal of Sport Psychology*, **5**, 25–57.

Ferrari, P.F., Gallese, V., Rizzolatti, G. and Fogassi, L. (2003). Mirror neurons responding to the observation of ingestive and communicative mouth actions in the monkey ventral premotor cortex. *European Journal of Neuroscience*, **17**, 1703–14.

Feyereisen, P. (1987). Gestures and speech, interactions and separations. A reply to MacNeill (1985). *Psychological Review*, **94**, 493–8.

Fink, G. R., Marshall, J. C., Halligan, P. W., Frith, C. D., Driver, J., Frackowiack, R. S. J. and Dolan. R J. (1999). The neural consequences of conflict between intention and the senses. *Brain*, **122**, 497–512.

Fitts, P. M. (1954). The information capacity of the human motor system in controlling the amplitude of movement. *Journal of Experimental Psychology*, **47**, 381–91.

Flanagan, J. R. and Johansson, R. S. (2003). Action plans used in action observation. *Nature*, **424**, 769–71.

Flöel, A., Ellger, T., Breitenstein, C. and Knecht, S. (2003). Language perception activates the hand motor cortex: implications for motor theories of speech perception. *European Journal of Neuroscience*, **18**, 704–8.

Flohr, H., Elbert, T., Knecht, S., Wienbruch, C., Pantev, C., Birbaumer, N., *et al.* (1995). Phantom limb pain as a perceptual correlate of cortical reorganization following arm amputation. *Nature*, **375**, 482–4.

Fogassi, L., Gallese, V., Buccino, G., Craighero, L. and Rizzolatti, G. (2001). Cortical mechanisms for the visual guidance of hand grasping movements in the monkey: a reversible inactivation study. *Brain*, **124**, 571–86.

Fogassi, L., Ferrari, P. F., Gesierich, B., Rozzi, S., Chersi, F. and Rizzolatti, G. (2005). Parietal lobe: from action organization to intention understanding. *Science*, **308**, 662–6.

Fourneret, P. and Jeannerod, M. (1998). Limited conscious monitoring of motor performance in normal subjects. *Neuropsychologia*, **36**, 1133–40.

Fourneret, P., Franck, N., Slachevsky, A. and Jeannerod, M. (2001). Self-monitoring in schizophrenia revisited. *Neuroreport*, **12**, 1203–8.

Fourneret, P., Paillard, J., Lamarre, Y., Cole, J. and Jeannerod, M. (2002). Lack of conscious recognition of one's own actions in a haptically deafferented patient. *Neuroreport*, **13**, 541–7.

Fox, R. and McDaniel, C. (1982). The perception of biological motion by human infants. *Science*, **218**, 468–78.

Franck, N., Farrer, C., Georgieff, N., Marie-Cardine, M., Daléry, J., D'Amato, T., and Jeannerod, M. (2001). Defective recognition of one's own actions in schizophrenic patients. *American Journal of Psychiatry*, **158**, 454–9.

Franck, N., O'Leary, D. S., Flaum, M., Hichwa, R. D. and Andreasen, N. C. (2002). Cerebral blood flow changes associated with schneiderian first-rank symptoms in schizophrenia. *Journal of Psychiatry and Clinical Neuroscience*, **14**, 277–82.

Frak, V. G., Paulignan, Y. and Jeannerod, M. (2001). Orientation of the opposition axis in mentally simulated grasping. *Experimental Brain Research*, **136**, 120–7.

Freud, S. (1905). *Der Wite uns seine Beziehung zum Unbewussten*, Deuticke, Leipzig.

Fried, I., Katz, A., McCarthy, G., Sass, K. J., Williamson, P., Spencer, S. S., *et al.* (1991). Functional organization of human supplementary motor cortex studied by electrical stimulation. *Journal of Neuroscience*, **11**, 3656–66.

Fried, I., Wilson, C. L., MacDonald, K. A. and Behnke, E.J. (1998). Electric current stimulates laughter. *Nature*, **391**, 650.

Frith, C. D. (1992). *The cognitive neuropsychology of schizophrenia*. Lawrence Erlbaum Associates, Hove, UK.

Frith, C. D. and Done, D. J. (1989). Experiences of alien control in schizophrenia reflect a disorder in the central monitoring of action. *Psychological Medicine*, **19**, 359–63.

Frith, C. D., Friston, K. Liddle, P. F. and Frackowiak, R. S. J. (1991). Willed action and the prefrontal cortex in man. A study with PET. *Proceedings of the Royal Society B: Biological Sciences*, **244**, 241–6.

Frith, C. D., Blakemore, S. J. and Wolpert, D. M. (2000). Abnormalities in the awareness and control of action. *Philosophical Transactions of the Royal Society B: Biological Sciences* **355**, 1771–88.

Fry, D. B. (1966). The development of the phonological system in the normal and deaf child. In *The genesis of language* (ed. F. Smith and G. A. Miller), pp. 187–206. MIT Press, Cambridge, MA.

Galaburda, A. M. and Pandya, D. (1982). Role of architectonics and connections in the study of primate brain evolution. In *Primate brain evolution: methods and concepts* (ed. E. Armstrong and B. Falk). Plenum, New York.

Gallagher, H. L. and Frith, C. D. (2004). Dissociable neural pathways for perception and recognition of expressive and instrumental gestures. *Neuropsychologia*, **42**, 1725–36.

Gallagher, S. (1995). Body schema and intentionality. In *The body and the self* (ed. J. L. Bermudez, A. Marcel and N. Eilan), pp. 225–44. MIT Press, Cambridge, MA.

Gallagher, S. (2000). Philosophical conceptions of the self: implications for cognitive science. *Trends in Cognitive Sciences*, **4**, 14–21.

Gallagher, S. and Jeannerod, M. (2002). From action to interaction. *Journal of Consciousness Studies*, **9**, 3–26.

Gallese, V. (2003). The manifold nature of interpersonal relations: the quest for a common mechanism. *Philosophical Transactions of the Royal Society B: Biological Sciences*, **358**, 517–28.

Gallese, V. and Goldman, A. (1998). Mirror neurons and the simulation theory of mind reading. *Trends in Cognitive Science*, **2**, 493–501.

Gallese, V., Fadiga, L., Fogassi, L. and Rizzolatti, G. (2002). Action representation and the inferior parietal lobule. In *Common mechanisms in perception and action. Attention and performance XIX* (ed. W. Prinz and B. Hommel), pp. 334–55.

Gallese, V., Keysers, C. and Rizzolatti, G. (2004). A unifying view of the basis of social cognition. *Trends in Cognitive Science*, 8, 396–403.

Gandevia, S. G. and McCloskey, D. I. (1977). Changes in motor comands, as shown by changes in perceived heaviness, during partial curarization and peripheral anaesthesia in man. *Journal of Physiology*, **272**, 673–89.

Gandevia, S. C., Killian, K., McKenzie, D. K., Crawford, M., Allen, G. M., Gorman, R.B., *et al.* (1993). Respiratory sensations, cardiovascular control, kinesthesia and transcranial stimulation during paralysis in humans. *Journal of Physiology*, **470**, 85–107.

Gandevia, S. C., Wilson, L. R., Inglis, J. T. and Burke, D. (1997). Mental rehearsal of motor tasks recruits alpha motoneurons but fails to recruit human fusimotor neurones selectively. *Journal of Physiology*, **505**, 259–66.

Gentilucci, M. and Gangitano, M. (1998). Influence of automatic word reading on motor control. *European Journal of Neuroscience*, **10**, 752–6.

Gentilucci, M., Fogassi, L., Luppino, G., Matelli, M. Camarda, R. and Rizzolatti, G. (1988). Functional organization of inferior area 6 in the macaque monkey. 1. Somatotopy and the control of proximal movements. *Experimental Brain Research*, **71**, 475–90.

Georgieff, N. and Jeannerod, M. (1998). Beyond consciousness of external reality. A 'Who' system for consciousness of action and self-consciousness. *Consciousness and Cognition*, **7**, 465–77.

Georgopoulos, A. P. (2000) Neural aspects of cognitive motor control. *Current Opinions in Neurobiology*, **10**, 238–41.

Georgopoulos, A. P. and Massey, J. T. (1987). Cognitive spatial-motor processes. *Experimental Brain Research*, **65**, 361–70.

Georgopoulos, A. P., Lurito, J. T., Petrides, M., Schwartz, A. B. and Massey, J. T. (1989). Mental rotation of the neuronal population vector. *Science*, **243**, 234–6.

Gérardin, E., Sirigu, A., Lehéricy, S., Poline, J.-B., Gaymard, B., Marsault, C., *et al.* (2000). Partially overlapping neural networks for real and imagined hand movements. *Cerebral Cortex*, **10**, 1093–104.

Gergely, G., Nadasdy, Z., Czibra, G. and Biro, S. (1995). Taking the intentional stance at 12 months of age. *Cognition*, **56**, 165–93.

Gibson, J. J. (1979). *The ecological approach to visual perception*. Houghton-Mifflin, Boston.

Gillihan, S. J. and Farah, M. J. (2005). Is self special? A critical review of evidence from experimental psychology and cognitive neuroscience. *Psychological Review*, **131**, 76–97.

Giraux, P., Sirigu, A., Schneider, F. and Dubernard, J. M. (2001). Cortical reorganization in motor cortex after graft of both hands. *Nature Neuroscience*, **4**, 691–2.

Giraux, P. and Sirigu, A. (2003). Illusory movements of the paralyzed limb restore motor cortex activity. *Neuroimage*, **20**, 107–11.

Glover, S. (2004). Separate visual representations in the planning and control of action. *Behavioral and Brain Sciences*, **27**, 3–78.

Glover, S., Rosenbaum, D.A., Graham, J. and Dixon, P. (2004). Grasping the meaning of words. *Experimental Brain Research*, **154**, 103–8.

Goldenberg, G. and Hagman, S. (1997). A study of visuo-imitative apraxia. *Neuropsychologia*, **35**, 333–41.

Goldie, P. (1999). How we think of others' emotions. *Mind and Language*, **14**, 394–423

Goldin-Meadow, S. (1999). The role of gesture in communication and thinking. *Trends in Cognitive Science*, **3**, 419–29.

Goldman-Rakic, P. S. and Selemon, L. D. (1997). Functional and anatomical aspects of prefrontal pathology in schizophrenia. *Schizophrenia Bulletin*, **23**, 437–58.

Gomi, H. and Kawato, M. (1996) Equilibrium-point control hypothesis examined by measured arm stiffness during multijoint movement. *Science*, **272**, 117–120.

Goodale, M. A., Pélisson, D. and Prablanc, C. (1986). Large adjustments invisually guided reaching do not depend on vision of the hand or perception of target displacement. *Nature*, **320**, 748–50.

Goodale, M. A., Milner, A. D., Jakobson, L. S. and Carey, D. P. (1991). Perceiving the world and grasping it. A neurological dissociation. *Nature*, **349**, 154–6.

Goodglass, H. and Kaplan, E. (1963). Disturbance of gestures and pantomime in aphasia. *Brain*, **86**, 703–20.

Goodwin, G. M., McCloskey, D. I. and Mitchell, J. H. (1972). Cardiovascular and respiratory responses to changes in central command during isometric exercise at constant muscle tension. *Journal of Physiology*, **226**, 173–90.

Gottlieb, G. L., Corcos, D. M. and Argawal, G. C. (1989). Strategies for the control of voluntary movements with one mechanical degree of freedom. *Behavioral and Brain Sciences*, **12**, 189–250.

Gould, L.N. (1949) Auditory hallucinations in subvocal speech: objective study in a case of schizophrenia. *Journal of Nervous and Mental Diseases*, **109**, 418–27.

Grafman, J. (1989). Plans, actions and mental sets. Managerial knowledge units in the frontal lobes. In *Integrative theory and practice in clinical neuropsychology* (ed. E. Perecman). Erlbaum, Hillsdale, NJ.

Grafton, S. T., Arbib, M. A., Fadiga, L. and Rizzolatti, G. (1996). Localization of grasp representations in humans by positron emission tomography. 2. Observation compared with imagination. *Experimental Brain Research*, **112**, 103–11.

Grèzes, J. and Decety, J. (2001). Functional anatomy of execution, mental simulation, observation and verb generation of actions: a meta-analysis. *Human Brain Mapping*, **12**, 1–19.

Grèzes, J., Fonlupt, P., Bertenthal, B., Delon-Martin, C., Segebarth, C. and Decety, J. (2001). Does perception of biological motion rely on specific brain regions? *Neuroimage*, **13**, 775–85.

Grézes, J., Frith, C. D. and Passingham, R. E. (2004) Inferring false beliefs from the actions of oneself and others. *Neuroimage*, **21**, 744–50.

Grillner, S. (1985) Locomotion in vertebrates: central mechanisms and reflex interactions. *Science*, **228**, 143–49.

Grodzinsky, Y. (2000). The neurology of syntax: language use without Broca's area. *Behavioral and Brain Sciences*, **23**, 1–71.

Gross, C. G., Rocha-Miranda, C. E. and Bender, D. B. (1972). Visual properties of neurons in inferotemporal cortex of the macaque. *Journal of Neurophysiology*, **35**, 96–111.

Grossman, E., Donnelly, M., Price, R., Pickens, D., Morgan, V., Neighbor, G., *et al.* (2000). Brain areas involved in perception of biological motion. *Journal of Cognitive Neuroscience*, **12**, 711–20.

Grush, R. (2004). The emulation theory of representation: motor control, imagery and perception. *Behavioral and Brain Sciences*, **27**, 377–425.

Haaland, K. Y., Harrington, D. L. and Knight, R. T. (2000). Neural representations of skilled movements. *Brain*, **123**, 2306–13.

Habib, M. and Poncet, M. (1988). Loss of vitality, of interest and of the affect (athymhormia syndrome) in lacunar lesions of the corpus striatum. *Revue Neurologique*, **144**, 571–577 (in French).

Haggard, P. and Eimer, M. (1999). On the relation between brain potentials and the awareness of voluntary movements. *Experimental Brain Research*, **126**, 128–33.

Haggard, P., Clark, S. and Kalogeras, J. (2002). Voluntary action and conscious awareness. *Nature Neuroscience*, **5**, 282–5.

Haggard, P., Martin, F., Taylor-Clarke, M. Jeannerod, M. and Franck, N. (2003). Awareness of action in schizophrenia. *Neuroreport*, **14**, 1081–5.

Hagoort, P. (2004) Broca's complex as the unification space for language. In *Twenty-first century psycholinguistics. Four cornerstones* (ed. A. Cutler). Erlbaum, Hillsdale, NJ.

Hales, J. P. (1993). Respiratory sensations, cardiovascular control, kinesthesia and transcranial stimulation during paralysis in humans. *Journal of Physiology*, **470**, 85–107.

Hamilton, F., Wolpert, D. and Frith, C. D. (2004) Your own action influences how you perceive another person's action. *Current Biology*, **14**, 493–98.

Hamzei, F., Rijntjes, M., Dettmers, C., Glauche, V., Weiller, C. and Büchel, C. (2003). The human action recognition system and its relationship to Broca's area: an fMRI study. *Neruroimage*, **19**, 637–44.

Hanakawa, T., Immisch, I., Toma, K., Dimyan, M.A., Van Gelderen, P. and Hallett, M. (2003). Functional properties of brain areas associated with motor execution and imagery. *Journal of Neurophysiology*, **89**, 989–1002.

Hari, R., Forss, N., Avikainen, S., Kirveskari, E., Salenius, S. and Rizzolatti, G. (1998). Activation of human primary motor cortex during action observation: a neuromagnetic study. *Proceedings of the National Academy of Sciences of the USA*, **95**, 15061–5.

Harris, C. S. (1965). Perceptual adaptation to inverted, reversed and displaced vision. *Psychological Review*, **72**, 419–44.

Hashimoto, R. and Rothwell, J. C. (1999). Dynamic changes in corticospinal excitability during motor imagery. *Experimental Brain Research*, **125**, 75–81.

Haueisen, J. and Knosche, T. R. (2001). Involuntary motor activity in pianists evoked by music perception. *Journal of Cognitive Neuroscience*, **13**, 786–92.

Hauk, O., Johnsrude, I. and Pulvermüller, F. (2004). Somatotopic representation of action words in human motor and premotor cortex. *Neuron*, **41**, 301–7.

Hauser, M. (2000). *Wild minds*. Penguin Books, New York.

Haxby, J. V., Grady, C. L., Horwitz, B., Ungerleider, L. G., Mishkin, M., *et al.* (1991) Dissociation of object and spatial visual processing pathways in human extrastriate cortex. *Proceedings of the National Academy of Sciences of the USA*, **88**, 1621–1625.

Haxby, J. V., Horwitz, B., Ungerleider, L. G., Maisog, J. M., Pietrini, P. and Grady, C. L. (1994). The functional organization of human extrastriate cortex. A PET-rCBF study of selective attention to faces and locations. *Journal of Neuroscience*, **14**, 6336–53.

Haxby, J. V., Ungerleider, L. G., Clark, V. P., Schouten, J. L., Hoffman, E. A. and Martin, A. (1999). The effect of face inversion on activity in human neural systems for face and object perception. *Neuron*, **22**, 189–99.

Head, H. (1920). *Studies in neurology*. Hodder and Stoughton, London.

Heider, F. and Simmel, M. (1944). An experimental study of apparent behavior. *American Journal of Psychology*, **57**, 243–59.

Heilman, K. (1979). The neuropsychological basis of skilled movements in man. In *Handbook of behavioral neurobiology, II neuropsychology* (ed. M. S. Gazzaniga), pp. 447–460. Plenum, New York.

Heilman, K., Rothi, L. J. G. and Valenstein, E. (1982). Two forms of ideomotor apraxia. *Neurology*, **32**, 342–6.

Held, R. (1961). Exposure-history as a factor in maintaining stability of perception and coordination. *Journal of Nervous and Mental Diseases*, **132**, 26–32.

Helmholtz, H. (1860). *Handbuch der physiologischen Optik*. Voss, Hamburg. English translation: Handbook of physiological optics. Dover, New York, 1924–1925.

Hesslow, G. (2002). Conscious thought as simulation of behavior and perception. *Trends in Cognitive Science*, **6**, 242–7.

Heyes, C. M. and Foster, C. L. (2002). Motor learning by observation: evidence from a serial reaction time task. *Quarterly Journal of Experimental Psychology*, **55A**, 593–607.

Hietanen, J. K. and Perrett, D. I. (1993). Motion sensitive cells in the macaque superior temporal polysensory area. I. Lack of response to the sight of the monkey's own hand. *Experimental Brain Research*, **93**, 117–28.

Hietanen, J. K. and Perrett, D. I. (1996). A comparison of visual response to object motion and ego-motion in the macaque superior temporal polysensory area. *Experimental Brain Research*, **108**, 341–5.

Hinke, R. M., Hu, X., Stillman, A. E., Kim, S. G., Merkle, H., Salmi, R. and Ugurbil, K. (1993). Functional magnetic resonance imaging of Broca's area during internal speech. *Neuroreport*, **4**, 675–8.

Hommel, B., Müsseler, J., Aschersleben, G. and Prinz, W. (2001). The theory of event coding: a framework for perception and action planning. *Behavioral and Brain Sciences*, **24**, 849–937.

Horwitz, B., Amunts, K., Battacharyya, R., Patkin, B., Jeffries, K., Zilles, K., *et al.* (2003). Activation of Broca's area during the production of spoken and signed language: a combined cytoarchitectonic mapping and PET analysis. *Neuropsychologia*, **41**, 1868–76.

Hunter, M. D., Farrow, T. F. D., Papadakis, N. G., Wilkinson, I. D., Woodruff, P. W. R. and Spence, A. A. (2003). Approaching an ecologically valid functional anatomy of sponta-neous 'willed' action. *Neuroimage*, **20**, 1264–9.

Iacoboni, M., Woods, R. P., Brass, M., Bekkering, H., Mazziotta, J. C. and Rizzolatti, G. (1999). Cortical mechanisms of human imitation. *Science*, **286**, 2526–8.

Iacoboni, M., Molnar-Skakacs, I., Gallese, V., Buccino, G., Mazziotta, J. C. and Rizzolatti, G. (2004) Grasping the intentions of others with one's mirror neuron system. *PLoS Biology*, **3**, 529–35.

Indefrey, P., Hagoort, P., Herzog, H., Seitz, R. J. and Brown, R. J. (2001) Syntactic processing in left prefrontal cortex is independent of lexical meaning. *Neuroimage*, **14**, 546–55.

Ingvar, D. H. and Franzen, G. (1975) Distribution of cerebral activity in chronic schizophrenia. *Lancet*, **21**, 1484.

Ingvar, D. and Philipsson, L. (1977). Distribution of the cerebral blood flow in the dominant hemisphere during motor ideation and motor performance. *Annals of Neurology*, **2**, 230–237.

Iverson, J. M. and Goldin-Meadow, S. (1998). Why people gesture when they speak. *Nature*, **396**, 228.

Jackson, P. L., Doyon, J., Richards, C. L. and Malouin, F. (2004). The efficacy of combined physical and mental practice in the learning of a foot sequence after stroke. A case report. *Neurorehabilitation and Neural Repair*, **18**, 106–11.

Jacob, P. and Jeannerod, M. (2003). *Ways of seeing. The scope and limits of visual cognition*. Oxford University Press, Oxford.

Jacob, P. and Jeannerod, M. (2005). The motor theory of social cognition: a critique. *Trends in Cognitive Science*, **9**, 21–5.

Jacobson, E. (1930). Electrical measurements of neuro-muscular states during mental activities. III. Visual imagination and recollection. *American Journal of Physiology*, **95**, 694–702.

Jakobson, L. S. and **Goodale, M. A.** (1991). Factors affecting higher-order movement planning: a kinematic analysis of human prehension. *Experimental Brain Research*, **86**, 199–208.

Jancke, L., **Shah, N. J.** and **Peters, M.** (2000). Cortical activation in primary and secondary motor areas for complex bimanual movements in professional pianists. *Cognitive Brain Research*, **10**, 177–183.

Janet, P. (1937). Les troubles de la personnalité sociale. *Annales Médico-Psychologiques*, **II**, 149–200.

Järveläinen, J., **Schürmann, M.** and **Hari, R.** (2004). Activation of the human primary motor cortex during observation of tool use. *Neuroimage*, **23**, 187–92.

James, W. (1890). *Principles of psychology*. MacMillan, London. New Edition, Dover, New York, 1950.

Jeannerod, M. (1981). Intersegmental coordination during reaching at natural visual objects. In *Attention and performance IX* (ed. J. Long and A. Baddeey), pp. 153–168. Erlbaum, Hillsdale, NJ.

Jeannerod, M. (1983). *Le cerveau-machine. Physiologie de la volonté*. Fayard, Paris. English translation: *The brain-machine. The development of neurophysiological thought*. Harvard University Press, Cambridge, MA, 1985.

Jeannerod, M. (1988). *The neural and behavioural organization of goal-directed movements*. Oxford University Press, Oxford.

Jeannerod, M. (1994). The representing brain. Neural correlates of motor intention and imagery. *Behavioral and Brain Sciences*, **17**, 187–245.

Jeannerod, M. (1995). Mental imagery in the motor context. *Neuropsychologia*, **33**, 1419–32.

Jeannerod, M. (1997). *The cognitive neuroscience of action*. Blackwell, Oxford.

Jeannerod, M. (1999). To act or not to act: perspectives on the representation of actions. *Quarterly Journal of Experimental Psychology*, **52A**, 1–29.

Jeannerod, M. (2001). Neural simulation of action: a unifying mechanism for motor cognition. *Neuroimage*, **14**, 103–9.

Jeannerod, M. (2003a). The mechanisms of self-recognition in humans. *Behavioral Brain Research*, **142**, 1–15.

Jeannerod, M. (2003b). Consciousness of action and self-consciousness. A cognitive neuroscience approach. In *Agency and self-awareness. Issues in philosophy and psychology* (ed. J. Roessler and N. Eilan), pp. 128–49. Oxford University Press, New York.

Jeannerod, M. (2004a). How do we decipher others' minds. In *Who needs emotions ? The brain meets the robot* (ed. J. M. Fellous and M. A. Arbib), pp. 147–69. Oxford University Press, Oxford.

Jeannerod, M. (2004b). Actions from within. *International Journal of Sport and Exercise Psychology*, **2**, 376–402.

Jeannerod, M. (2004c). Visual and action cues both contribute to the self-other distinction. *Nature Neuroscience*, **7**, 422–3.

Jeannerod, M. and **Frak, V. G.** (1999). Mental simulation of action in human subjects. *Current Opinions in Neurobiology*, **9**, 735–9.

Jeannerod, M. and **Jacob, P.** (2005). Visual cognition. A new look at the two visual systems model. *Neuropsychologia*, **43**, 301–12.

Jeannerod, M. and **Pacherie, E.** (2004). Agency, simulation and self-identification. *Mind and Language*, **19**, 113–46.

Jeannerod, M., Farrer, C., Franck, N., Fourneret, P., Daprati, E. and Georgieff, N. (2003). Recognition of action in normal and schizophrenic subjects. In *The self in neuroscience and psychiatry*, (ed. T. Kircher and A. David), pp. 380–406. Cambridge University Press, Cambridge.

Jellema, T., Baker, C.I., Wicker, B. and Perrett, D. I. (2000). Neural representation for the perception of the intentionality of actions. *Brain and Cognition*, **44**, 280–302.

Ji, H., Ploux, S. and Wehrli, E. (2003). Lexical knowledge representation with contexonyms. In *Proceedings of the 9th MT Summit*. pp. 194–201.

Johansson, G. (1973) Visual perception of biological motion and a model for its analysis. *Perception and Psychophysics*, **14**, 201–11.

Johnson, H. and Haggard, P. (2005) Motor awareness without perceptual awareness. *Neuropsychologia*, **43**, 227–237.

Johnson, P. (1982). The functional equivalence of imagery and movement. *Quarterly Journal of Experimental Psychology*, **34A**, 349–365.

Johnson, S. H. (2000). Thinking ahead: the case for motor imagery in prospective judgements of prehension. *Cognition*, **74**, 33–70.

Johnson, S. H., Rotte, M., Gafton, S. T., Hinrichs, H., Gazzaniga, M. S. and Heinze, H. J. (2002). Selective activation of a parietofrontal circuit during implicitly imagined prehension. *Neuroimage*, **17**, 1693–704.

Johnson-Frey, S. H. (2004). The neural bases of complex tool use in humans. *Trends in Cognitive Science*, **8**, 71–8.

Kandel, S., Orliaguet, J. P. and Boë, J. L. (2000). Detecting anticipatory events in handwriting movements. *Perception*, **29**, 953–64.

Kanwisher, N. (2000). Domain specificity in face perception. *Nature Neuroscience*, **3**, 759–63.

Kanwisher, N., McDermott, J. and Chun, M. M. (1997). The fusiform face area: a module in human extrastriate cortex specialized for face perception. *Journal of Neuroscience*, **17**, 4302–11.

Karni, A., Myer, G., Jezzard, P., Adams, M. M., Turner, R. and Ungerleider, L. G. (1995). Functional MRI evidence for adult motor cortex plasticity during motor skill learning. *Nature*, **377**, 155–8.

Keele, S. W. (1968). Movement control in skilled motor performance. *Psychological Bulletin*, **70**, 387–404.

Keller, I. and Heckenhausen, H. (1990). Readiness potentials preceeding spontaneous motor acts: voluntary vs. involuntary control. *Electroencephalography and Clinical Neurophysiology*, **76**, 351–61.

Kerzel, D. and Bekkering, H. (2000) Motor activation from visible speech: evidence from stimulus–response compatibility. *Journal of Experimental Psychology. Human Perception and Performance*, **26**, 634–47.

Keysers, C. and Perrett, D. I. (2004). Demistifying social cognition: a Hebbian perspective. *Trends in Cognitive Science*, **8**, 501–7.

Keysers, C., Kohler, E., Umilta, M.A., Fogassi, L., Nanetti, L. and Gallese, V. (2003). Audio-visual mirror neurones and action recognition. *Experimental Brain Research*, **153**, 628–36.

Kilner, J. M., Paulignan, Y. and Blakemore, S. J. (2003). An interference effect of observed biological movement on action. *Current Biology*, 13, 522–5.

Kilner, J. M., Vargas, C., Duval, S., Blakemore, S. J. and Sirigu, A. (2004). Motor activation prior to observation of a predicted movement. *Nature Neuroscience*, 7, 1299–1301.

Kim, S.-G., Jennings, J. E., Strupp, J. P., Andersen, P. and Ugurbil, K. (1995). Functional MRI of human motor cortices during overt and imagined finger movements. *International Journal of Imaging Systems and Technology*, **6**, 271–9.

Kimble G. A. and Perlemuter, C. C. (1970) The problem of volition. *Psychological Reviews*, **77**, 361–84.

Kircher, T. T. J., Senior, C., Phillips, M. L., Rabe-Hesketh, S., Benson, P. J., Bullmore, E. T., *et al.* (2001). Recognizing one's own face. *Cognition*, **78**, B1–15.

Kleist, K. (1934). *Gehirnpathologie*. Leipzig, Barth.

Knoblich, G. (2002). Self recognition: body and action. *Trends in Cognitive Science*, **6**, 447–9.

Knoblich, G. and Flach, R. (2001). Predicting the effects of action: interactions of perception and action. *Psychological Science*, **12**, 467–72.

Knoblich, G. and Prinz, W. (2001). Recognition of self-generated actions from kinematic displays of drawing. *Journal of Experimental Psychology. Human Perception and Performance*, **27**, 456–65.

Knoblich, G. and Kircher, T. T. J. (2004). Deceiving oneself about being in control: conscious detection of changes in visuomotor coupling. *Journal of Experimental Psychology. Human Perception and Performance*, **30**, 657–66.

Knuf, L., Aschersleben, G. and Prinz, W. (2001). An analysis of ideomotor action. *Journal of Experimental Psychology. General*, **130**, 779–98.

Kornhuber, H. H. and Deecke, L. (1965). Hirnpotentialänderungen bei Wilkürbewegungen und passiven Bewegungen des Menschen: Bereitschaftspotential und reafferente potentiale. *Pflügers Archiv für Gesamte Physiologie*, **284**, 1–17.

Koslowski, L. T. and Cutting, J. E. (1978). Recognizing the sex of a walker from point-lights mounted on ankles: some second thoughts. *Perception and Psychophysics*, **23**, 459.

Kosslyn, S. M., Alpert, N. M., Thompson, W. L., Maljkovic, V., Weise, S. B., Chabris, C. F., *et al.* (1993). Visual mental imagery activates topographically organized visual cortex: PET investigations. *Journal of Cognitive Neuroscience*, **5**, 263–87.

Kosslyn, S. M., Digirolomo, G. J., Thompson, W. L. and Alpert, N. M. (1998). Mental rotation of objects versus hands: neural mechanisms revealed by positron emission tomography. *Psychophysiology*, **35**, 151–61.

Krogh, A. and Lindhard, J. (1913). The regulation of respiration and circulation during the initial stages of muscular work. *Journal of Physiology*, **47**, 112–36.

Krolak-Salmon, P., Henaff, M. A., Isnard, J., *et al.* (2003). An attention modulated response to disgust in human ventral anterior insula. *Annals of Neurology*, **53**, 446–53.

Krolak-Salmon, P., Henaff, M.A., Vighetto, A., Bauchet, F., Bertrand, O., Mauguière, F., *et al.* (2005). Experiencing and detecting happiness in humans: the role of the supplementary motor area. *Annals of Neurology*, **58**, 196–99.

Lacourse, M. G., Orr, E. L. R., Cramer, S. C. and Cohen, M. J. (2005). Brain activation during execution and motor imagery of novel and skilled sequential hand movements. *Neuroimage*, **27**, 505–19.

Lacquaniti, F., Terzuolo, C. and Viviani, P. (1983). The law relating kinematic and figural aspects of drawing movements. *Acta Psychologica*, **54**, 115–30.

Lafargue, G., Paillard, J., Lamarre, Y. and Sirigu, A. (2003). Production and perception of grip force without proprioception: is there a sense of effort in deafferented subjects. *European Journal of Neuroscience*, **17**, 2741–9.

Lafleur, M. F., Jackson, P. L., Malouin, F., Richards, C. L., Evans, A. C. and Doyon, J. (2002). Motor learning produces parallel dynamic functional changes during the execution and imagination of sequential foot movements. *Neuroimage*, **16**, 142–57.

Landauer, T. K. (1962). Rate of implicit speech. *Perceptual and Motor Skills*, **15**, 646.

Lang, P. J. (1979) A bioinformational theory of emotional imagery. *Psychophysiology*, **16**, 495–512.

Lang, P.J., Kozak, M.J., Miller, G.A., Levin, D.N. and McLean, A. (1980). Emotional imagery: conceptual structure and pattern of somato-visceral response. *Psychophysiology*, **17**, 179–92.

Lang, W., Zilch, O., Koska, C., Lindinger, G. and Deecke, L. (1989). Negative cortical DC shifts preceding and accompanying simple and complex sequential movements. *Experimental Brain Research*, **74**, 99–104.

Lashley, K. S. (1917). The accuracy of movement in the absence of excitation from the moving organ. *American Journal of Physiology*, **43**, 169–94.

Lashley, K. S. (1951). The problem of serial order in behavior. In *Cerebral mechanisms and behavior* (ed. L. A. Jeffress), pp. 112–36. Wiley, New York.

Lau, H. C., Rogers, R. D., Haggard, P. and Passingham, R. E. (2004a). Attention to intention. *Science*, **303**, 1208–10.

Lau, H.C., Rogers, R.D., Ramnani, N. and Passingham, R.E. (2004b). Willed action and attention to the selection of action. *Neuroimage*, **21**, 1407–15.

Le Bihan, D., Turner, R., Zeffiro, T. A., Cuénod, C. A., Jezzard, P. and Bonnerot, V. (1993). Activation of human primary visual cortex during visual recall: a magnetic resonance imaging study. *Proceedings of the National Academy of Sciences of the USA*, **90**, 11802–5.

Leonardo, M., Fieldman, J., Sadato, N., Campbell, G., Ibanez, V., Cohen, L., *et al.* (1995). A functional magnetic resonance imaging study of cortical regions associated with motor task execution and motor ideation in humans. *Human Brain Mapping*, **3**, 83–92.

Leube, D. T., Knoblich, G., Erb, M. and Kircher, T. J. (2003). Observing one's hand become anarchic. An fMRI study of action identification. *Consciousness and Cognition*, **12**, 597–608.

Levenson, R. W., Ekman, P. and Friesen, W. V. (1990). Voluntary facial action generates emotion-specific autonomic nervous system activity. *Psychophysiology*, **27**, 363–84.

Lhermitte, F. (1983). Utilisation behaviour and its relation to lesions of the frontal lobes. *Brain*, **106**, 237–255.

Lhermitte, F. (1986). Human autonomy and the frontal lobes. Part II: patient behavior in complex and social situations: the 'environmental dependency syndrome'. *Annals of Neurology*, **19**, 326–334.

Liberman, A. M. and Mattingly, H. G. (1985). The motor theory of speech perception revised. *Cognition*, **21**, 1–36.

Libet, B. (1985). Unconscious cerebral initiative and the role of conscious will in voluntary action. *Behavioral Brain Science*, **6**, 529–66.

Libet, B. (1991) Conscious or unconscious? *Nature*, **351**, 195.

Libet, B. (1992). The neural time-factor in perception, volition and free will. *Revue de Métaphysique et de Morale*, 255–72.

Libet, B., Gleason, C. A., Wright, E. W. and Pearl, D. K. (1983). Time of conscious intention to act in relation to onset of cerebral activity (readiness-potential). The unconscious initiation of a freely voluntary act. *Brain*, **106**, 623–42.

Liepmann, H. (1900). Das Krankheitsbild die Apraxie (motorischen Asymbolie). *Monatschrift für Psychiatrie und Neurologie*, **8**, 15–44, 102–32, 182–97.

Liepmann, H. (1905). *Ueber Störungen des Handelns bei gehirnkrankin*. S. Kargen, Berlin.

Lipps, T. (1903). *Aesthetik: Psychologie des Schönen und der Kunst*. Voss, Hamburg.

Lotze, M., Montoya, P., Erb, M., Hülsmann, E., Flor, H., Klose, U., *et al.* (1999). Activation of cortical and cerebellar motor areas during executed and imagined hand movements: an fMRI study. *Journal of Cognitive Neuroscience*, 11, 491–501.

Lotze, M., Flor, H., Grodd, W., Larbig, W. and Birbaumer, N. (2001). Phantom movement and pain. An fMRI study in upper limb amputees. *Brain*, **124**, 2268–77.

Loula, F., Prasad, S., Harber, K. and Shiffrar, M. (2005). Recognizing people from their movement. *Journal of Experimental Psychology. Human Perception and Performance*, 31, 210–20.

MacNeilage, P. F. (1970). Motor control of serial ordering of speech. *Psychological Review*, 77, 182–96.

Maeda, F., Chang, V. Y., Mazziotta, J. and Iacoboni, M. (2001). Experience-dependent modulation of motor corticospinal excitability during action observation. *Experimental Brain Research*, **140**, 241–4.

Mahon, B. Z. and Caramazza, A. (2005). The orchestration of the sensory-motor systems. Clues from neuropsychology. *Cognitive Neuropsychology*, **22**, 480–94.

Malouin, F., Richards, C. L., Desrosiers, J. and Doyon, J. (2004). Bilateral slowing of mentally simulated actions after stroke. *Neuroreport*, **15**, 1349–53.

Marshall, J. C., Halligan, P. W., Fink, G. R., Wade, D. T. and Frackowiak, R. S. J. (1997). The functional anatomy of a hysterical paralysis. *Cognition*, **64**, B1–8.

Marteniuk, R. G., MacKenzie, C. L., Jeannerod, M., Athenes, S. and Dugas, C. (1987). Constraints on human arm movement trajectories. *Canadian Journal of Psychology*, **41**, 365–78.

Martin, A., Haxby, J. V., Lalonde, F. M., Wiggs, C. L. and Ungerleider, L. G. (1995). Discrete cortical regions associated with knowledge of color and knowledge of action. *Science*, **270**, 102–5.

Martin, A., Wiggs, C. L., Ungerleider, L. G. and Haxby, J. V. (1996). Neural correlates of category-specific knowledge. *Nature*, **379**, 649–52.

Matelli, M., Luppino, G. and Rizzolatti, G. (1985). Patterns of cytochrome oxydase activity in the frontal agranular cortex of the macaque monkey. *Behavioral Brain Research*, **18**, 125–36.

Maxwell, J. C. (1868) On governors. *Proceedings of the Royal Society*, **16**, 270–83.

McCloskey, D. I., Ebeling, P. and Goodwin, G. M. (1974). Estimation of weights and tensions and apparent involvement of a 'sense of effort'. *Experimental Neurology*, **42**, 220–32.

McGuigan, F. J. (1966). Covert oral behavior and auditory hallucinations. *Psychophysiology*, **3**, 73–80.

McGuigan, F. J. (1978). *Cognitive psychology. Principles of covert behavior*. Prentice Hall, Englewood Cliffs, NJ.

McGuire, P. K., Silbersweig, D. A. and Frith, C. D. (1996a). Functional neuroanatomy of verbal self-monitoring. *Brain*, **119**, 907–17.

McGuire, P. K., Silbersweig, D. A., Murray, R. M., David, A. S., Frackowiak, R. S. J. and Frith, C. D. (1996b). Functional anatomy of inner speech and auditory verbal imagery. *Psychological Medicine*, **26**, 29–38.

McGurk, H. and MacDonald, J. (1976). Hearing lips and seeing voices. *Nature*, **264**, 746–8.

McNeill, D. (1992). *Hand and mind*. University of Chicago Press, Chicago.

Mehring, C., Rickert, J., Vaadia, E., Cardoso de Olivera, S., Aersten, A. and Rotter, S. (2003). Inference of hand movements from local field potentials in monkey motor cortex. *Nature Neuroscience*, **6**, 1253–4.

Meltzoff, A. N. (1995). Understanding intentions of others: reenactment of intended acts by 18 months-old children. *Developmental Psychology*, **31**, 838–50.

Meltzoff, A. N. and Moore, M. K. (1997). Explaining facial imitation. A theoretical model. *Early Development and Parenting*, **6**, 179–92.

Merians, A. S., Clark, M., Poizner, H., Macauley, B., Gonzalez-Rothi, L. J. and Heilman, K. (1997) Visual imitative dissociation apraxia. *Neuropsychologia*, **35**, 1483–90.

Michelon, P., Vettel, J. M. and Zacks, J. M. (2006). Somatotopy during imagined and prepared movements. *Journal of Neurophysiology*, **95**, 811–22.

Milner, A. D. and Goodale, M. A. (1993). Visual pathways to perception and action. In *Progress in Brain Research* (ed. T. P. Hicks, S. Molotchnikoff and T. Ono), pp. 317–37. Elsevier, Amsterdam.

Milner, A. D. and Goodale, M. A. (1995). *The Visual Brain in Action*. Oxford University Press, Oxford.

Mlakar, J., Jensterle, J. and Frith, C. D. (1994). Central monitoring deficiency and schizophrenic symptoms. *Psychological Medicine*, **24**, 557–64.

Morris, J. S., de Gelder, B., Weiskrantz, L and Dolan, R. J. (2001). Differential extrageniculostriate and amygdala responses to presentation of emotional faces in a cortically blind field. *Brain*, **124**, 1241–52.

Mott, F. W. and Sherrington, C. S. (1885). Experiments upon the influence of sensory nerves upon movement and nutrition of the limbs. *Proceedings of the Royal Society B: Biological Sciences*, **57**, 481–8.

Mountcastle, V. B. (2005). *The sensory hand. Neural mechanisms of somatic sernsation*. Harvard University Press, Cambridge, MA.

Mühlau, M., Hemsdörfer, J., Goldenberg, G., Wohlschläger, A. M., Castrop, F., Stahl, R., et al. (2005). Left inferior parietal dominance in gesture imitation: an fMRI study. *Neuropsychologia*, **43**, 1086–98.

Mulder, T., de Vries, S. and Zijlstra, S. (2005). Observation, imagination and execution of an effortful movement: more evidence for a central explanation of motor imagery. *Experimental Brain Research*, 344–351.

Muller-Preus, P. and Ploog, D. (1981). Inhibition of cortical neurons during phonation. *Brain Research*, **215**, 61–76.

Murata, A., Fadiga, L., Fogassi, L., Gallese, V., Raos, V. and Rizzolatti, G. (1997). Object representation in the ventral premotor cortex (area F5) of the monkey. *Journal of Neurophysiology*, **78**, 2226–30.

Murata, A., Gallese, V., Luppino, G., Kaseda, M. and Sakata, H. (2001). Selectivity for the shape, size and orientation of objects for grasping in neurons of monkey parietal area AIP. *Journal of Neurophysiology*, **83**, 2580–601.

Neisser, U. (1976). *Cognition and reality*. Freeman, San Francisco.

Neisser, U. (1993). The self perceived. In *The perceived self. Ecological and interpersonal sources of self-knowledge* (ed. U. Neisser), pp. 3–21. Cambridge University Press, Cambridge.

Nelson, C.A. (1987). The recognition of facial expression in the first two years of life. Mechanisms of development. *Child Development*, **58**, 889–909.

Ni, W., Constable, R. T., Mencl, W. E., Pugh, K. R., Fullbright, R. K., Shaywitz, B. A., Gore, J. C. and Shankweiler, D. (2000) An event-related neuroimaging study distinguishing form and content in sentence provesing. *Journal of Cognitive Neuroscience*, **12**, 120–133.

Nicolelis, M. A. L. (2001). Actions from thoughts. *Nature*, **409**, 403–7.

Nicolelis, M. A. L. (2002). The amazing adventures of robotreat. *Trends in Cognitive Science*, **6**, 449–50.

Nielsen, T. I. (1963). Volition: a new experimental approach. *Scandinavian Journal of Psychology* **4**, 225–30.

Nielsen, T. I. (1978). *Acts. Analyses and syntheses of human acting, concerning the subject and from the standpoint of the subject.* Dansk Psykologisc Forlag, Copenhagen.

Nielsen, T. I., Praetorius, N. and Kuschel, R. (1965). Volitional aspects of voice performance: an experimental approach. *Scandinavian Journal of Psychology*, **6**, 201–208.

Nisbett, R. and Wilson, T. (1977). Telling more than we can know: verbal reports on mental processes. *Psychological Review*, **84**, 231–59.

Nishitani, N. and Hari, R. (2002). Viewing lip forms: cortical dynamics. *Neuron*, **36**, 1211–20.

Nordstrom, M. A. and Butler, S. L. (2002). Reduced intracortical inhibition and facilitation of corticospinal neurons in musicians. *Experimental Brain Research*, **144**, 336–42.

Ochipa, C., Rapcsack, S. Z., Maher, L. M., Rothi, L. J. G., Bowers, D. and Heilman, K. M. (1997). Selective deficit of praxic imagery in ideomotor apraxia. *Neurology*, **49**, 474–80.

O'Craven, K. M. and Kanwisher, N. (2000). Mental imagery of faces and places activates corresponding stimulus-specific brain regions. *Journal of Cognitive Neuroscience*, **12**, 1013–23.

Paccalin, C. and Jeannerod, M. (2000). Changes in breathing during observation of effortful actions. *Brain Research*, **862**, 194–200.

Papaxanthis, C., Schieppati, M., Gdentili, R. and Pozzo, T. (2002). Imagined and actual arm movements have similar durations when performed under different conditions of direction and mass. *Experimental Brain Research*, **14**, 447–52.

Parsons, L. M. (1994). Temporal and kinematic properties of motor behavior reflected in mentally simulated action. *Journal of Experimental Psychology. Human Perception and Performance*, **20**, 709–30.

Parsons, L. M., Fox, P. T., Downs, J. H., Glass, T., Hirsch, T. B., Martin, C. C., *et al.* (1995). Use of implicit motor imagery for visual shape discrimination as revealed by PET. *Nature*, **375**, 54–8.

Pascual-Leone, A., Dang, N., Cohen, L. G., Brasil-Neto, J., Cammarota, A. and Hallett, M. (1995). Modulation of motor responses evoked by transcranial magnetic stimulation during the acquisition of new fine motor skills. *Journal of Neurophysiology*, **74**, 1037–45.

Patuzzo, S., Fiaschi, A. and Manganotti, P. (2003). Modulation of motor cortex excitability in the left hemisphere during action observation: a single- and paired-pulse transcranial magnetic stimulation study of self- and non-self-action observation. *Neuropsychologia*, **41**, 1272–8.

Paulesu, E., Goldacre, B., Scifo, P., Cappa, S. F., Gilardi, M. C., Castiglioni, I., *et al.* (1997). Functional heterogeneity of left inferior frontal cortex as revealed by fMRI. *Neuroreport*, **8**, 2011–6.

Paulignan, Y., MacKenzie, C., Marteniuk, R. and Jeannerod, M. (1991). Selective perturbation of visual input during prehension movements. I. The effects of changing object position. *Experimental Brain Research*, **83**, 502–12.

Pélisson, D., Prablanc, C., Goodale, M. A. and Jeannerod, M. (1986). Visual control of reaching movements without vision of the limb. II. Evidence of fast unconscious processes correcting the trajectory of the hand to the final position of a double-step stimulus. *Experimental Brain Research*, **62**, 303–11.

Penfield, W. (1947). Ferrier Lecture. Some observations on the cerebral cortex of man. *Proceedings of the Royal Society B: Biological Sciences*, 134, 329–47.

Penfield, W. and Boldrey, E. (1937). Somatic motor end sensory representation in the cerbral cortex of man as studied by electrical stimulation. *Brain*, **60**, 389–443.

Perani, D., Cappa, S., Bettinardi, V., Bressi, S., Gorno-Tempini, M., Matarrese, M., *et al.* (1995). Different neural systems for the recognition of animals and man-made tools. *Neuroreport*, **6**, 1637–41.

Perenin, M. T. and Rossetti, Y. (1996). Residual grasping in an hemianopic field. A further instance of dissociation between perception and action. *Neuroreport*, **7**, 793–97.

Perenin, M. T. and Vighetto, A. (1988). Optic ataxia: a specific disruption in visuomotor mechanisms. I. Different aspects of the deficit in reaching for objects. *Brain*, **111**, 643–74.

Perrett, D. I., Harris, M. H., Bevan, R., Thomas, S., Benson, P. J., Mistlin, A. J., *et al.* (1989). Framework of analysis for the neural representation of animate objects and actions. *Journal of Experimental Biology*, **146**, 87–113.

Petrides, M., Cadoret, G. and Mackey, S. (2005). Orofacial somatomotor responses in the macaque monkey homologue of Broca's area. *Nature*, **435**, 1235–8.

Piaget, J. (1936) *La naissance de l'intelligence chez l'enfant*. Delachaux et Niestlé, Neuchatel.

Pons, T. P., Garraghty, P. E., Ommaya, A. K., Kass, J. H., Taub, E. and Mishkin, M. (1991). Massive cortical reorganization after sensory deafferentation in adult macaques. *Science*, **252**, 1857–60.

Porro, C. A., Francescato, M. P., Cettolo, V., Diamond, M. E., Baraldi, P., Zuiani, C., *et al.* (1996). Primary motor and sensory cortex activation during motor performance and motor imagery: a functional magnetic resonance study. *Journal of Neuroscience*, **16**, 7688–698.

Posada, A. and Franck, N. (2002). Use of a rule in schizophrenia. *Psychiatry Research*, **109**, 289–96.

Posada, A., Franck, N., Georgieff, N. and Jeannerod, M. (2001). Anticipating incoming events. An impaired cognitive process in schizophrenia. *Cognition*, **81**, 209–25.

Posner, M. I., Walker, J. A., Friedrich, F. J. and Rafal, R. D. (1984). Effects of parietal lobe injury on covert orienting of visual attention. *Journal of Neuroscience*, **4**, 1863–74.

Preston, S. D. and de Waal, F. B. M. (2002). Empathy: its ultimate and proximate bases. *Behavioral and Brain Sciences*, **25**, 1672.

Pribram, K. H. and Gill, M. M. (1976) *Freud's "Project" reassessed*. New york: Basic Books.

Prinz, W. (1990). A common coding approach to action and perception. In *Relationships between perception and action* (ed. O. Neumann and W. Prinz), pp. 167–201. Springer, Berlin.

Prinz, W. (2003). How do we know about our own action? In *Voluntary action. Brains, minds ans society* (ed. S. Maasen, W. Prinz, and G. Roth), pp. 21–33. Oxford University Press, New York.,

Prut, Y. and Fetz, E. E. (1999). Primate spinal interneurons show premovement instructed delay activity. *Nature*, **401**, 590–4.

Pulvermüller, F. (2005). Brain mechanisms linking language and action. *Nature Reviews Neuroscience*, **6**, 576–82.

Pulvermuller, F., Hauk, O., Nikulin, V. V. and Ilmoniemi, R. J. (2005a). Functional links between language and motor systems. *European Journal of Neuroscience*, **21**, 793–7.

Pulvermuller, F., Shtyrov, Y. and Ilmoniemi, R. J. (2005b). Brain signatures of meaning access in action word recognition. *Journal of Cognitive Neuroscience*, **17**, 884–92.

Ramachandran, V. S. and Blakeslee, S. (1998). *Phantoms in the brain, human nature and the architecture of the mind*. Fourth Estate Limited, London.

Ramachandran, V. S. and Rogers-Ramachandran D. (1996). Synaesthesia in phantom limbs induced with mirrors. *Proceedings of the Royal Society B: Biological Sciences*, **263**, 377–86.

Ramnani, N. and Miall, R. C. (2004). A system in the human brain for predicting the actions of others. *Nature Neuroscience*, **7**, 85–90

Raos, V., Evangeliou, M. N. and Savaki, H. E. (2004). Observation of action: grasping with the mind's hand. *Neuroimage*, **23**, 193–201.

Requin, J., Brener, J. and Ring, C. (1991). Preparation for action. In *Handbook of cognitive psychophysiology. Central and autonomic nervous system approaches* (ed. J. R. Jennings, and M. G. H. Coles). John Wiley and Sons Ltd.

Ribot, T. (1894). *Les maladies de la volonté*. Alcan, Paris.

Richter, W., Somorjai, R., Summers, R., Jarmasz, M., Menon, R. S., Gati, J. S., *et al.* (2000). Motor area activity during mental rotation studied by time-resolved single-trial fMRI. *Journal of Cognitive Neuroscience*, **12**, 310–20.

Rizzolatti, G. and Arbib, M. A. (1998). Language within our grasp. *Trends in Neuroscience*, **31**, 188–94.

Rizzolatti, G. and Matelli, M. (2003). Two different streams for the dorsal visual system: anatomy and functions. *Experimental Brain Research*, **153**, 146–57.

Rizzolatti, G., Camarda, R., Fogassi, L., Gentilucci, M., Luppino, G. and Matelli, M. (1988). Functional organization of area 6 in the macaque monkey. II. Area F5 and the control of distal movements. *Experimental Brain Research*, **71**, 491–507.

Rizzolatti, G., Fadiga, L., Gallese, V. and Fogassi, L. (1996a). Premotor cortex and the recognition of motor actions. *Cognitive Brain Research*, **3**, 131–41.

Rizzolatti, G., Fadiga, L., Matelli, M., Bettinardi, V., Paulesu, E., Perani, D., *et al.* (1996b). Localization of grasp representations in humans by PET: 1. Observation versus execution. *Experimental Brain Research*, **111**, 246–52.

Roland, P. E., Skinhoj, E., Lassen, N. A. and Larsen, B. (1980). Different cortical areas in man in organization of voluntary movements in extrapersonal space. *Journal of Neurophysiology*, **43**, 137–150.

Rosenbaum, D. A., Marchak, F., Barnes, H. J., Vaughan, J., Slotta, J. D. and Jorgensen, M. J. (1990). Constraints for action selection. Overhand versus underhand grips. In *Motor representation and control. Attention and performance XIII* (ed. M. Jeannerod), pp. 321–42. Erlbaum, Hillsdale, NJ.

Rosenbaum, D. A., Meulenbroek, R. G. J. and Vaughan, J. (2004). What is the point of motor planning? *International Journal of Sport and Execise Psychology*, **2**, 439–469.

Rossetti, Y., Vighetto, A. and Pisella, L. (2003). Optic ataxia revisited. Immediate motor control versus visually guided action. *Experimental Brain Research*, **153**, 171–9.

Rossini, P. M., Rossi, S., Pasqualetti, P. and Tecchio, F. (1999). Corticospinal excitability modulation to hand muscles during movement imagery. *Cerebral Cortex*, 9, 161–7.

Roth, M., Decety, J., Raybaudi, M., Massarelli, R., Delon-Martin, C., Segebarth, C., *et al.* (1996). Possible involvement of primary-motor cortex in mentally simulated movement. A functional magnetic resonance imaging study. *Neuroreport*, 7, 1280–4.

Rothi, L. J. G., Heilman, K. M. and Watson, R. T. (1985). Pantomime comprehension and ideomotor apraxia. *Journal of Neurology, Neurosurgery and Psychiatry*, 48, 207–10.

Rothi, L. J. G., Ochipa, C. and Heilman, K. M. (1991). A cognitive neuropsychological model of limb apraxia. *Cognitive Neuropsychology*, 8, 443–58.

Rothwell, J. C., Traub, M. M., Day, B. L., Obeso, J. A., Thomas, P. K. and Marsden, C. O. (1982). Manual motor performance in a deafferented man. *Brain*, 105, 515–42.

Ruby, P. and Decéty, J. (2001). Effect of subjective perspective taking during simulation of action: a PET investigation of agency. *Nature Neurosciences*, 4, 546–50.

Rumiati, R. I., Weiss, P. H., Shallice, T., Ottoboni, G., Noth, J., Zilles, K., *et al.* (2004). Neural basis of pantomiming the use of visually presented objects. *Neuroimage*, 21, 1224–31.

Runeson, S. and Frykholm, G. (1983) Kinematic specification of dynamics as an informational basis for person and action perception: expectation, gender recognition, and deceptive invention. *Journal of Experimental Psychology. General*, 112, 585–615.

Rushworth, M. F., Walton, M. E., Kennerley, S. W. and Bannerman, D. M.(2004). Action sets and decisions in the medial frontal cortex. *Trends in Cognitive Science*, 8, 410–7.

Sabaté, M., Gonzalez, B. and Rodriguez, M. (2004) Brain lateralization of motor imagery: motor planning asymmetry as a cause of movement lateralization. *Neuropsychologia*, 42, 1041–49.

Sato, A. and Yasuda, A. (2005). Illusion of sense of self-agency: discrepancy between the predicted and actual sensory consequences of actions modulates the sense of self-agency, but not the sense of self-ownership. *Cognition*, 94, 241–255.

Saxe, R. (2005). Against simulation. The argument from error. *Trends in Cognitive Science*, 9, 175–9.

Saygin, A.P., Wilson, S.M., Dronkers, N.F. and Bates, E. (2005). Action comprehension in aphasia: linguistic and non-linguistic deficits and their lesion correlates. *Neuropsychologia*, 42, 1788–2004.

Schneider, K. (1955). *Klinische Psychopathologie*. Thieme Verlag, Stuttgart.

Schnitzler, A., Selenius, S., Salmelin, R., Jousmäki, V. and Hari, R. (1997). Involvement of primary motor cortex in motor imagery: a neuromagnetic study. *Neuroimage*, 6, 201–8.

Schott, N. and Munzert, J. (2002). Mental chronometry in the elderly. *Journal of Sport and Exercise Psychology*, 24, 109.

Schubotz, R. J. and von Cramon, Y. (2002). Predicting perceptual events activates corresponding motor schemes in lateral premotor cortex: an fMRI study. *Neuroimage*, 15, 787–96.

Schubotz, R. J. and von Cramon, Y. (2004). Sequences of abstract non-biological stimuli share ventral premotor cortex with action observation and imagery. *Journal of Neuroscience*, 24, 5467–74

Searle, J. R. (1983). *Intentionality. An essay in the philosophy of mind*. Cambridge University Press, Cambridge.

Sebanz, N., Knoblich, G. and Prinz, W. (2003). Representing other's actions: just like one's own? *Cognition*, **88**, B11–21.

Senghas, A., Kita, S. and Ozyürek, A. (2004). Children creating core properties of language. Evidence from an emerging sign language in Nicaragua. *Science*, **305**, 1779–82.

Sereno, S. C., Rayner, K. and Posner, M. I. (1998). Establishing a time line for word recognition: evidence from eye movements and event related potentials. *Neuroreport*, **13**, 2195–200.

Serruya, M. D., Hatsopoulos, N. G., Paninski, L., Fellows, M. R. and Donoghue, J. P. (2002). Instant neural control of a movement signal. *Nature*, **416**, 141–2.

Shallice, T. (1988). *From neuropsychology to mental structure*. Cambridge University Press, Cambridge.

Shallice, T., Burgess, P. W., Schon, F. and Baxter, D. M. (1989). The origins of utilization behavior. *Brain*, **112**, 1587–98.

Shepard, R.N. and Metzler, J. (1971). Mental rotation of three-dimensional objects. *Science*, **171**, 701–3.

Shiffrar, M. and Freyd, J. J. (1990). Apparent motion of the human body. *Psychological Science*, **1**, 257–264.

Shimada, S., Hiraki, K. and Oda, I. (2005). The parietal role in the sense of ownership with temporal discrepancy between visual and proprioceptive feedbacks. *Neuroimage*, **24**, 1225–32.

Shmuelof, L. and Zohary, E. (2005) Dissociation between ventral and dorsal fMRI activation during object and action recognition. *Neuron*, **47**, 457–70.

Sirigu, A. and Duhamel, J. R. (2001). Motor and visual imagery as two complementary but neurally dissociable mental processes. *Journal of Cognitive Neuroscience*, **13**, 910–9.

Sirigu, A., Cohen, L., Duhamel, J. R., Pillon, B., Dubois, B., Agid, Y., *et al.* (1995a). Congruent unilateral impairments for real and imagined hand movements. *Neuroreport*, **6**, 997–1001.

Sirigu, A., Cohen, L., Duhamel, J.R., Pillon, B., Dubois, B., and Agid, Y. (1995b). A selective impairment of hand posture for object utilization in apraxia. *Cortex*, **31**, 41–56.

Sirigu, A., Duhamel, J.-R., Cohen, L., Pillon, B., Dubois, B. and Agid, Y. (1996). The mental representation of hand movements after parietal cortex damage. *Science*, **273**, 1564–8.

Sirigu, A., Daprati, E., Pradat-Diehl, P., Franck, N. and Jeannerod, M. (1999). Perception of self-generated movement following left parietal lesion. *Brain*, **122**, 1867–74.

Sirigu, A., Daprati, E., Ciancia, S., Giraux, P., Nigoghossian, N., Posada, A. and Haggard, P. (2004) Motor awareness and intention to move after focal brain damage. *Nature Neuroscience*, **7**, 80–4.

Slachewsky, A., Pillon, B., Fourneret, P., Pradat-Diehl, Jeannerod, M. and Dubois, B. (2001). Preserved adjustment but impaired awareness in a sensory-motor conflict following prefrontal lesions. *Journal of Cognitive Neuroscience*, **13**, 332–40.

Slachewsky, A., Pillon, B., Fourneret, P., Renié, L., Levy, R., Jeannerod, M. and Dubois, B. (2003). The prefrontal cortex and conscious monitoring of action. An experimental study. *Neuropsychologia*, **41**, 655–65.

Spelke, E. S., Breinlinger, K., Macomber, J. and Jacobson, K. (1992). Origins of knowledge. *Psychological Reviews*, **99**, 605–32.

Spence, S. A. and Frith, C. D. (1999). Towards a functional anatomy of volition. *Journal of Consciousness Studies*, **6**, 11–29.

Spence, S. A., Brooks, D. J., Hirsch, S. R., Liddle, P. F., Meehan, J. and Grasby, P. M. (1997). A PET study of voluntary movement in schizophrenic patients experiencing passivity phenomena (delusions of alien control). *Brain*, **120**, 1997–2011.

Spence, S. A., Hirsch, S. R., Brooks, D. J. and Grasby, P. M. (1998). Prefrontal cortex activity in people with schizophrenia and control subjects. Evidence from positron emission tomography for remission of 'hypofrontality' with recovery from acute schizophrenia. *British Journal of Psychiatry*, **172**, 376–23.

Sperry, R. W. (1943). Effect of 180° rotation of the retinal field in visuomotor coordination. *Journal of Experimental Zoology*, **92**, 263–79.

Sperry, R. W. (1950). Neural basis of the spontaneous optokinetic response produced by visual inversion. *Journal of Comparative and Physiological Psychology*, **43**, 482–9.

Stelmach, G. E., Castiello, U. and Jeannerod, M. (1994). Orienting the finger opposition space during prehension movements. *Journal of Motor Behavior*, **26**, 178–86.

Stephan, K. M., Fink, G. R., Passingham, R. E., Silbersweig, D., Ceballos-Baumann, A. O., Frith, C. D., *et al.* (1995). Functional anatomy of the mental representation of upper extremity movements in healthy subjects. *Journal of Neurophysiology*, **73**, 373–86.

Stevens, H. (1965). Jumping Frenchmen of Maine. *Archives of Neurology*, **12**, 311–4.

Stevens, J. A.(2004). Interference effects demonstrate distinct roles for visual and motor imagery during the mental representation of human action. *Cognition*, **95**, 329–50.

Stevens, J. A., Fonlupt, P., Shiffrar, M. and Decety, J. (2000). New aspects of motion perception: selective neural encoding of apparent human movements. *Neuroreport*, **11**, 109–115.

Strafella, A. P.and Paus, T. (2000). Modulation of cortical excitability during action observation. A transcranial magnetic stimulation study. *Neuroreport*, **11**, 2289–92.

Stratton, G. M.(1899). The spatial harmony of touch and sight. *Mind*, **3**, 492–505.

Stürmer, B., Aschersleben, G. and Prinz, W. (2000). Correspondence effects with manual gestures and postures: a study of imitation. *Journal of Experimental Psychology. Human Perception and Performance*, **26**, 1746–59.

Tai, Y. F., Scherfler, C., Brooks, D. J., Sawamoto, N. and Castiello, U. (2004). The human premotor cortex is 'mirror' only for biological actions. *Current Biology*, **14**, 117–20.

Taira, M., Mine, S., Georgopoulos, A. P., Murata, A. and Sakata, H. (1990). Parietal cortex neurons of the monkey related to the visual guidance of hand movements. *Experimental Brain Research*, **83**, 29–36.

Tettamenti, M., Buccino, G., Saccuman, M. C., Gallese, V., Danna, M., Scifo, P., *et al.* (2005). Listening to action related sentences activates fronto-parietal motor circuits. *Journal of Cognitive Neuroscience*, **17**, 273–81.

Titchener, E. B.(1908). *Lectures on elementary psychology of feeling and attention*. McMillan, New York.

Tomasello, M. (2000). *The cultural origins of human cognition*. Harvard University Press, Cambridge, MA.

Tomasino, B., Rumiati, R. I.and Umilta, C.A. (2003). Selective deficit of motor imagery as tapped by a left-right decision of visually presented hands. *Brain and Cognition*, **53**, 376–80.

Tremblay, G., Robert, M., Pascual-Leone, A., Lepore, F., Nguyen, D. K., Carmant, L., *et al.* (2004). Action observation and execution: intracranial recordings in a human subject. *Neurology*, **63**, 937–938.

Trevarthen, C. (1993) The self born in intersubjectivity: The psychology of an infant communicating. In: *The perceived self. Ecological and interpersonal sources of self-knowledge*, U. Neisser (Ed), Cambridge: Cambridge University Press, pp 121–173.

Tsakiris, M. and Haggard, P. (2003). Awareness of somatic events following a voluntary action. *Experimental Brain Research* **149**, 439–46.

Tsakiris, M. and Haggard, P. (2005). The rubber hand illusion revisited: visuotactile integration and self-attribution. *Journal of Experimental Psychology. Human Perception and Performance*, **31**, 80–91.

Tucker, M. and Ellis, R. (1998). On the relations between seen objects and components of potential actions. *Journal of Experimental Psychology. Human Perception and Performance*, **24**, 830–46.

Umilta, M. A., Kohler, E., Gallese, V., Fogassi, L., Fadiga, L., Keysers, C. and Rizzolatti, G. (2001). I know what you are doing. A neurophysiological study. *Neuron*, **32**, 91–101.

Van den Bos, E. and Jeannerod, M. (2002). Sense of body and sense of action both contribute to self-recognition. *Cognition*, **85**, 177–87.

Van Schie, H. T., Mars, R. B., Coles, M. G. H. and Bekkering, H. (2004). Modulation of activity in medial frontal and motor cortices during error observation. *Nature Neuroscience*, **7**, 549–54.

Vignemeont, F. de, and Fourneret, P. (2004) The sense of agency: a philosophical and empirical review of the 'Who' system. *Consciousness and Cognition*, **13**, 1–19.

Viviani, P. (1990). Common factors in the control of free and constrained movements. In *Motor representation and control. Attention and performance XIII* (ed. M. Jeannerod), pp. 345–73. Erlbaum, Hillsdale, NJ.

Viviani, P. and Stucchi, N. (1992). Biological movements look uniform. Evidence of motor-perceptual interactions. *Journal of Experimental Psychology. Human Perception and Performance*, **18**, 603–23.

Vogeley, K. and Fink, G. R. (2003). Neural correlates of the first person perspective. *Trends in Cognitive Science*, **7**, 38–42.

Vogt, S. (1995). On relations between perceiving, imagining, and performing in the learning of cyclical movement sequences. *British Journal of Psychology*, **86**, 191–216.

Vogt, S., Taylor, P. and Hopkins, B. (2003). Visuomotor priming by pictures of hand postures: perspective matters. *Neuropsychologia*, **41**, 941–951.

Von Bonin, G. and Bailey, P. (1947). *The neocortex of Macaca mulatta*. University of Illinois Press, Urbana.

Von Holst, E. (1954). Relations between the central nervous system and the peripheral organs. *British Journal of Animal Behavior 2*, 89–94.

Von Holst, E. and Mittelstaedt, H. (1950). Das Reafferenzprinzip Wechselwirkungen zwischen Zentralnervensystem und Peripherie. *Naturwissenschaften*, **37**, 464–76.

Vuilleumier, P., Richardson, M. P., Armony, J. L., Driver, J. and Dolan, R. J.(2004). Distant influences of amygdala lesion on visual cortical activation during emotional processing. *Nature Neuroscience*, **11**, 1271–1278.

Wang, Y. and Morgan, W. P.(1992). The effects of imagery perspectives on the physiological responses to imagined exercise. *Behavioural Brain Research*, **52**, 167–74.

Watkins, K. E., Strafella, A. P. and Paus, T. (2003). Seeing and hearing speech excites the motor system involved in speech production. *Neuropsychologia*, 41, 989–94.

Wegner, D. (2002). *The illusion of conscious will*. MIT Press. Cambridge, MA.

Wehner, T., Vogt, S. and Stadler, M. (1984). Task-specific EMG characteristics during mental training. *Psychological Research*, **46**, 389–401.

Weinberger, D. R. and Berman, K. F.(1996). Prefrontal function in schizophrenia: confounds and controversies. *Philosophical Transactions of the Royal Society B: Biological Sciences*, **351**, 1495–503.

Weiskrantz, L. (1986) *Blindsight. A case study and implications*. Oxford University Press, Oxford.

Whalley, H. C., Simonotto, E., Flett, S., Marshall, I., Ebmeier, K. P., Owens, D. G.C. *et al.* (2004) fMRI correlates of state and trait effects in subjects at genetically enhanced risk of schizophrenia. *Brain*, **127**, 478–90.

Whiten, A. and Custance, D. (1996). Studies of imitation in chimpanzees and children. In *Social learning in animals: the roots of culture* (ed. M. C. Heyes and B. G. Galef), pp. 291–318. Academic Press, New York.

Williams, J. H.G. Whiten, A., Suddendorf, T. and Perrett, D. I. (2001). Imitation, mirror neurons and autism. *Neuroscience and Biobehavioral Reviews*, **25**, 287–95.

Wittgenstein, L. (1953). *Philosophical investigations*. Blackwell, Oxford.

Wohlschläger, A., Haggard, P., Gesierich, B. and Prinz, W. (2003). The perceived onset time of self- and other-generated actions. *Psychological Science*, **14**, 586–91.

Wolpert, D. M.and Flanagan, R.F. (2001). Motor prediction. *Current Biology*, **11**, R729–32.

Wolpert, D. and Ghahramani, Z. (2000). Computational principles of movement neuroscience. *Nature Neuroscience*, **3**, 1212–7.

Wolpert, D. M., Ghahramani, Z. and Jordan, M. I. (1995). An internal model for sensorimotor integration. *Science*, **269**, 1880–2.

Wolpert, D. M., Doya, K. and Kawato, M. (2003). A unifying computational framework for motor control and social interaction. *Proceedings of the Royal Society B: Biological Sciences*, **358**, 593–602.

Wuyam, B., Moosavi, S. H., Decety, J., Adams, L., Lansing, R. W. and Guz, A. (1995). Imagination of dynamic exercise produced ventilatory responses which were more apparent in competitive sportsmen. *Journal of Physiology*, **482**, 713–24.

Yue, G. and Cole, K. J. (1992). Strength increases from the motor program: comparison of training with maximal voluntary and imagined muscle contractions. *Journal of Neurophysiology*, **67**, 1114–23.

Zago, M. and Lacquaniti, F. (2005). Cognitive, perceptual and action-oriented representations of falling objects. *Neuropsychologia*, **43**, 178–88.

Zajonc, R. B. (1985). Emotion and facial efference: a theory reclaimed. *Science*, **228**, 15–21.

Zalla, T., Labruyère, N. and Georgieff, N. (2006). Goal-directed action representation in autism. *Journal of Autism and Developmental Disorders* (in press).

Author Index

Subject Index